Polls,
Television, and
the New Politics

CHANDLER PUBLICATIONS IN
POLITICAL SCIENCE
VICTOR JONES, EDITOR

Polls, Television, and the New Politics

Harold Mendelsohn
University of Denver

and

Irving Crespi
The Gallup Organization

CHANDLER PUBLISHING COMPANY
An Intext Publisher · Scranton, Pennsylvania 18515

The following material is based on data collected and compiled by The Gallup Organization, Inc. and is reprinted by permission of George Gallup, Chairman, American Institute of Public Opinion:
"Trend in Party Identification among Adults"
"Top Concerns of Public: Jan., 1963–Jan., 1969"
"Responses to the question, 'Should legislation be enacted requiring a police permit before a gun can be bought?' "
"Trend in Johnson-Romney 'Trial Heats,' September 1965-June 1967"
"Trend in the Proportion of 'All Voters' Who Prefer Lyndon B. Johnson or Robert Kennedy for Democratic Presidential Candidate in 1968"
"Trend in the Proportion Expressing Approval of Johnson's Performance as President"
"LBJ's Popularity: Intensity of Feeling"
"Preferences of Republicans for Presidential Nominee"
"Preferences of Republicans Nationally for the Presidential Nomination"
"Preferences among Democrats between Johnson and McCarthy for the 1968 Democratic Nomination"
"Trend in Preferences of Democrats for Humphrey, Kennedy, and McCarthy for 1968 Presidential Nomination"
"Trend in Preferences of Democrats for Kennedy and Stevenson for 1960 Presidential Nomination"
"Comparison of Goldwater's Strength with Nixon and Scranton in June 1964"
"Preferred as Republican Nominee in June 1964"
"Preferences of Republicans as to Who Should Be Their Presidential Candidate in 1968"
"Analysis of Presidential Vote by Demographic Characteristics, from 1952 to 1968"
"Variations in Measured Voter Preferences as Reported in the Final 1952 Gallup Preelection Reports"
"Comparison of Gallup Poll and Harris Poll 'Trial Heats' Reported in January, 1964"
"Preferences of Republicans for 1964 Candidate"
"Comparison of Trends in Nixon-Humphrey-Wallace 'Trial Heats' as Reported by Gallup Poll and Harris Survey"
"Preferences for President among All Adults of Voting Age and 'Likely Voters' "
"Comparison of Gallup Poll with Official Election Returns in the 1966 Gubernatorial Election"
"Comparison of Gallup, Crossley, and Harris 'Trial Heats' prior to 1968 Republican Convention"
"Gallup Poll 'Trial Heat' Trend prior to 1968 Republican Convention"
"Relation between Party Identification and Presidential Vote in Four Elections"

The following material is based on data collected and compiled by Louis Harris & Associates Inc. and is reprinted by permission of Louis Harris:
"Comparison of Gallup Poll and Harris Poll 'Trial Heats' Reported in January, 1964"
"Comparison of Trends in Nixon-Humphrey-Wallace 'Trial Heats' as Reported by Gallup Poll and Harris Survey"
"Preferences for President among All Adults of Voting Age and 'Likely Voters' "
"Comparison of Gallup, Crossley, and Harris 'Trial Heats' prior to 1968 Republican Convention"
"Harris Survey 'Trial Heat' Trend prior to 1968 Republican Convention"
"Trend in Harris Preprimary Surveys in California, 1964"

Portions of Chapter 5 were originally published in a different version as "Election Day Broadcasts and Terminal Voting Decisions," by Harold Mendelsohn, in *The Public Opinion Quarterly*, 30 (Summer 1966), 212-215. © 1966 by Princeton University Press. Reprinted by permission of the copyright holder.

Third Printing, October, 1972

Contents

Preface

This book challenges some widely held conceptions about how American politics has been affected both by public-opinion polls and by television. There can be no disputing that politics, especially Presidential politics, has been undergoing a fundamental transformation, and that polls and television have played prominent roles in this transformation. It is our thesis that the nature of their roles is both less direct and more crucial than is ordinarily thought to be the case.

At the risk of oversimplification, the popularly held view of polls, television, and the new politics can be described like this: There is a growing disenchantment with the political process in the United States, characterized as it is by a cynical attitude toward voters and by its irrelevance with regard to the urgency of a host of critical problems. Moreover, so the proponents of this view contend, polls and television have swung elections, sometimes through the deliberate manipulative efforts of politicians, and more often through their appeal to a "bandwagon psychology." That is, voters subjected to poll- and computer-generated forecasts of how elections might turn out march lemming-like to the election booths to cast their ballots, not in order to express their true feelings, but, rather, in an overriding, irrational desire to be on the winning side, no matter what. In revulsion against this mockery of democracy, and in opposition to the worn-out machinery of existing parties, a "new politics" is arising in the United States based on the participatory involvement of the electorate. The 1968 "youth crusade" for McCarthy, and the yippie demonstrations at the Chicago Democratic Convention that year are the harbingers of this new politics.

In opposition to this popular interpretation, our thesis is that polls and television are indeed working to transform the party structure of American politics, but that they are effecting changes through a process that can be identified and understood only by an empirical analysis of how they function in the hurly-burly of election campaigns. We reject the "bandwagon psychology" hypothesis on both empirical and theoretical grounds. After decades of concern and research, it appears that if bandwagon effects do occur, their magnitude is so small that they simply cannot have the far-reaching consequences imputed to them by would-be Cassandras. Moreover, the primitive theoretical underpinnings of the bandwagon hypothesis are unacceptable, assuming as they do a chemical-like response on the part of the electorate whenever a poll measurement or computer forecast is "injected," as through a hypodermic needle, into the public consciousness.

The real combined effects of polls and television have been to make obsolete the traditional style of American politics, and to substitute a "cool," corporate-executive style. This is "the new politics" as it actually is today—purposefully analytic, empirically opportunistic, and administratively manipulative. As Richard Scammon has said, "If there is to be a New Politics in America it'll be the New Politics of the grey flannel suit, of Nixon's pragmatic center. I don't think it'll be the New Politics of the beard and the sandal and the shades" (quoted by Winthrop Sargeant in *The New Yorker,* September 20, 1969, p. 65).

The decay of the established party organizations is real, but it is best understood as the product of the rise of a new institutional form in which parties are organized around "political personalities." These personalities, in turn, are serviced by paid professionals, whose loyalties are to the individual employing them rather than to "the party." It should also be recognized that any period of rapid institutional change is marked by disorder, which is a symptom of the change, not the creator of it. The dislocations and upheavals of the 1968 Presidential election are the symptoms of the transition from the increasingly ineffectual quality of traditional parties to the technocracy of the new politics.

In this light, the urgent issue created by polls and television is not whether or not their roles in politics should be circumscribed. Realistically, there is little reason to believe that any effort to accomplish this kind of control could succeed. Rather, and of crucial significance, the issue is whether the new, "cool" politics will prove adequate to meet the nation's needs in a manner that will strengthen and not subvert democratic processes. Since polls and television have played major roles in the rise of the new politics, there can be little doubt that how they are used and how they are controlled will strongly affect the way in which the new politics will function.

It is our hope that in clarifying the manner in which polls and television have been influencing political life in the United States, we will be contributing to the development of realistic and effective efforts to strengthen the democratic process in the new American politics. If our efforts succeed in merely turning attention, at least temporarily, away from the possibility of direct effects upon voting decisions and toward the broader issues of the over-all relevancies of public-opinion polling and television to our national political life—past, present, and future—our reward will be generous far beyond any expectations that we, as concerned citizens, can realistically entertain.

The preparation of the manuscript was divided as follows: Chapters 1, 2, and 3 on polls were written by Irving Crespi, and Chapters 4 and 5 on the broadcast media by Harold Mendelsohn.

We wish to acknowledge the encouragement, counsel, and aid of the many individuals and organizations that made this book a reality. Our special gratitude goes to the Columbia Broadcasting System, which supported the study of voters' reactions to Election Night broadcasts in 1964 through a grant to the Communication Arts Center of the University of Denver. We owe a particular debt of gratitude to Dr. Joseph T. Klapper, director of the CBS Office of Social Research, and his staff for their special help, guidance, and patience. We are further indebted to Dr. Ira Cisin, Director of the Social Research Project, George Washington University.

Interviews for the California voting study discussed in Chapter

4 were obtained through the services of the Field Research Corporation of San Francisco. The help of Mervin Field and Aaron Levy of that organization is gratefully acknowledged. Qualitative interviews for the California study were obtained with the aid of Dr. Charles Wright, Department of Sociology, University of California at Los Angeles, who provided us with highly qualified interviewers.

To Dr. George Gallup we express our gratitude for providing unrestricted access to all Gallup Poll archives, and for sharing with us his personal insight into the polling process. We also thank Paul K. Perry, President of The Gallup Organization, Inc. Without access to his files on the Gallup Poll election surveys since 1950, his critical reading of that part of the manuscript pertaining to election polls, and especially his mentorship during twelve years of close professional association, our analysis of pre-election surveys could not have been written.

The intelligence, dedication, and skills of our secretaries, Miss Suzanne Bryan, Mrs. Marcia Grad, and Mrs. Geraldine Lewis of the Communication Arts Center at the University of Denver, and Mrs. Joan Hurley and Mr. Laurence Stookey of The Gallup Organization, Inc. deserve special mention. Without the help of these individuals we would still be enmeshed in a jumble of random notes, unintelligible tables, and scattered jottings. We also acknowledge the understanding patience of our families. Such contributions as theirs to works of this nature can never be adequately articulated.

Finally, we wish to thank the thousands of "respondents" who participated in the surveys. Without their willingness to express their opinions freely, honestly, and publicly, this book could never even have been contemplated, let alone written. We also owe our deepest gratitude to the numerous interviewers, coders, computer programmers, field supervisors, research assistants, and other anonymous personnel whose substantive contributions to contemporary social research can never be overstated.

Harold Mendelsohn

Irving Crespi

March, 1970

Polls,
Television, and
the New Politics

Introduction

What's New about the New Politics?

Suddenly, in the election year 1968, Americans became aware that the fabric of their political experiences had taken on an unusual form, an unfamiliar texture, a novel coloration. Since then, much discussion of "the new politics" has ensued. Although this phrase has already become a household word, there is considerable confusion both about its meaning and about its significance. Such confusion usually occurs when a catch phrase first captures the imagination of journalists and writers, and then the hearts of the public. Phrases like "the new politics" are extremely imprecise in their meaning when they enter the bloodstream of the body politic. They are subject to much heated debate, and they generally shed very little real light on the phenomena they supposedly represent. Witness our frustrating experiences with similar phrases that have become integral parts of our language in our clumsy efforts to understand and cope with the tremendous upheavals and changes that have taken place in our political and social lives: What exactly is meant by "overkill," "domino theory," "escalation," "culture of poverty," "militancy," "participatory democracy"?

Undoubtedly there has been significant change in the ways in which the business of politics is being conducted in the United States. This change has been ascribed to various social and political causes: shifts in the demography of the nation (the influx of youth into the electorate); the urbanization-suburbanization of

1

our society (paradoxically, the Democratic party has pledged a much stronger effort to attract suburban voters while ever since 1964 the Republican party has been focusing its efforts on recruiting big-city inhabitants). There is considerable speculation about the roles that students and blacks are playing in shaping the politics of the future. Additionally, the new politics has been attributed to the instability of voter coalitions that emerged originally as a consequence of the Great Depression.

It appears that profound processes of social and political change that have been going on subtly for several generations have suddenly surfaced and have penetrated into our awareness in rather dramatic ways. National elections in the United States afford an opportunity for the many and varied forces that make up social change in our land to come together in a confluence that appears to be startlingly unfamiliar. The new conflux represents a blending of phenomena that by themselves could be considered by many to be of minor significance. However, when they begin to merge into an agglomerate under the impetus of a national election, these hitherto separated and seemingly trivial phenomena become indicative of profound events indeed. From this perspective, the new politics that we have been hearing so much about simply reflects an emergent collective recognition that American politics in the next several decades will be substantially different from what it has been in the past. By itself this conclusion can hardly be considered to be an astonishing observation. Why, then, all this concern with the new politics? Our fascination with the new politics takes on importance when we concern ourselves with the elements that appear to have produced it and attempt to anticipate the consequences that will flow from its emergence.

This book addresses itself to two major influences among the varied factors that induce widespread social and political changes: (1) new knowledge about social systems and human behavior made possible by the ever more systematic gathering of social and psychological information, and (2) technological advances, particularly in the means of disseminating information to large masses of people.

There is very little doubt that as the social sciences become increasingly sophisticated in their theorizing and methodologies they enhance our knowledge about the world, and that simultaneously this knowledge in itself becomes a force in creating social change. On this score, the observations of economist Kenneth Boulding are of particular interest:

> In the social sciences . . . advance seems to have depended in the past on a combination of new theoretical insights and points of view with new methods for the collection, sampling and processing of data.[1]*

> . . . we must recognize that knowledge about the social system is an essential part of it (the social system) and that by affecting our behavior, it affects the social system itself. This is true even at the level of quite inexact or superstitious knowledge. As we move toward more secure and exact knowledge of the social system the process of change is likely to accelerate. The rate of social invention is likely to increase, and in a relatively short time we may see profound transformations in social institutions and behavior as a result of cumulating knowledge about the system itself.[2]

In our own time we have witnessed a monumental growth in our knowledge about human behavior and social-political systems, mainly through the efforts of a veritable army of economists, sociologists, anthropologists, psychologists, and political scientists. Of particular importance in the array of instrumentalities that have been applied by modern social scientists in their work are social-survey techniques that are based upon advanced sampling procedures. With the application of newly developed sampling methods to the measurement of public attitudes, "the public-opinion poll," which came into being in the 1930's, has been steadily increasing in its reliability and validity. The public-opinion poll has developed to the point where its accuracy has become accepted as reflecting a degree of objective "political evidence" that goes considerably beyond the results of individual, subjective speculation. As the accuracy of public-opinion polling has increased, the recognition of its applicability to politics has multiplied. Currently, public-opinion polling has become an integral part of the political process. In achieving such a status, this systematic method of accumulating politically rele-

---

* Notes follow the chapters.

vant information has made profound impacts upon our political systems and, consequently, upon our society. Exactly what effects public-opinion polling has had on contemporary American politics is one major concern of this book. At this point it is sufficient to point out that no meaningful discussion of the new politics can be carried out without recognizing that public-opinion polling is a major ingredient in this mix.

By now the statement that "technological innovations in the means of communication induce revolutionary social and political changes" is almost a cliché. First the printing press, then the motion picture, radio, and, more recently, television have served, either singly or in combination, to alter in far-reaching ways the lives of men and the institutions under which they live. Worth noting in particular are the impacts that the introduction of the electronic means of communication have had on the political process. With Franklin D. Roosevelt's use of radio we witnessed the emergence of the office of the Presidency as an all-powerful aspect of government and, simultaneously, the beginning of a decline in the traditional powers of political parties. Dwight D. Eisenhower's initial major resort to television as a standard technique of campaigning initiated a process whereby high-powered "promotion" appears more and more to displace less passionate approaches to the selection and election of candidates. Besides considering the impact of polls, therefore, this book assesses some of the issues that emerged from the introduction of television into the political process.

It is important to note that 1968 represents a point in time when the efficiency of both political-attitude polling and the utilization of television in political campaigns appears to have reached a zenith even though the ultimate potential of both has yet to be realized. Indeed, polling and television are now considered to be so effective that television and the polls were themselves injected into the 1968 campaigns as significant issues. Current public concern over the influences that political public-opinion polls and television allegedly generate surfaced precisely at the time when the dialogue regarding the new politics began in earnest. Presumably something more than sheer coincidence was at work here.

For the most part, the concern regarding the roles of public-opinion polls and television in current politics is expressed in the notion that both television and voter surveys exert "undue direct influence" in election campaigns. The doctrine of undue direct influence suggests that both the polls and television produce effects immediately as well as directly upon the electorate—effects of such an order that voters are persuaded against their wills to vote not in accordance with their actual dispositions, but rather in accordance with the politically relevant polls or television fare they may be exposed to during a particular campaign. The assumption here is that by themselves political polls and politically relevant television broadcasts (many of which may be built around voter surveys) are so powerful that they are capable of influencing voters to cast ballots for candidates they normally would not have supported and would not have wanted to support. In contrast to preexisting accepted campaign techniques, polls and television are imputed with the power to produce effects that border on magic. The seemingly irrational basis for their alleged effects has resulted in a common belief that the use of polls and television in politics is inherently "immoral."

Underpinning the undue direct influence doctrine is the assumption that simple exposure to the results of political opinion surveys or to political broadcasts via television results in direct and immediate effects upon the political choices of those who are witness to such fare. In the vernacular that has grown up around these allegations the doctrine of undue direct influence is referred to as the "bandwagon effect." With this phrase it is argued that the electorate, always hungry to be identified with a winning candidate, will eagerly endorse the candidate or candidates who appear to be "winners," regardless of all other factors that may operate in the ordinary vote-decision-making process. For many observers of the political scene, one of the more pressing problems that is posed by the new politics relates to the control of the allegedly direct effects of polls and of political telecasts upon voters.

Interestingly, the concern that polls and television exert undue direct influence on vote decisions comes to a head at the point where both the polls and telecasting merge into one seemingly powerful onslaught upon the tenacity with which voters hold on to their previously proclaimed vote-decisions. This occurs on Election Night when voters living in the western portion of the United States may witness televised projections of winners or the actual tabulation of votes well before they have had an opportunity to cast their ballots. In passing, it is worth noting that telecasts of forecasts utilize sampling techniques whose principles are also used in polls. Furthermore, the results of polls taken during a particular campaign are related to actual election results from selected early-reporting precincts in order to project voting forecasts via Election Night telecasts.

So serious is this concern that the Subcommittee on Communications of the United States Senate Committee on Commerce held extensive hearings on the matter—*Projections-Predictions of Election Results and Political Broadcasting*—during the Ninetieth Congress (July 18–20, 1967). In his introductory statement to the hearings, Senator John O. Pastore, chairman of the subcommittee, summed up the allegations of concern in this manner:

It is contended that the western voter who intends to cast his vote late in the day may be discouraged from doing so if he learns that the candidate of his choice has already clearly won or lost the election on the basis of the actual counts of more easterly votes or the western voter may be swayed by predictions or projections based on eastern voting. (p. 2)

One of the principal objectives of this book is to examine the bandwagon allegations from the perspective of scientific empiricism rather than from the perspectives of either the layman or the politician. It may prove well at this point to indicate that the scientific evidence that has been examined by the authors offers very little of a substantive nature to back up the undue *direct* influence doctrine. Indeed, much of the present work is oriented to an intensive examination of the viability of the bandwagon assertion as a scientific hypothesis. The examination is made by presenting evidence from a wide range of scientific research and empirical observation and analysis.

The basic proposition of this book is that the issue before us is not the potentiality of polls and television for swaying votes directly, but rather that the polls and television have already induced massive *indirect* effects upon the political process *per se* in America and undoubtedly will continue to influence the political process in the future. Already television and the polls have altered the manner in which candidates are first selected; they have modified and reshaped our expectations of political candidates; they have changed the national selection conventions; they are making fundamental changes in the traditional national political party structures and function; they have introduced new techniques of mass persuasion into the political process; they have had serious impacts upon the conduct of political campaigns. In short, they have been instrumental in the emergence of a new politics on the American scene.

Before one can gain a better understanding of how polls and television may shape the future of politics in this country it is necessary to take a short step backward into the immediate past. Up until very recently both polling and television were seen as existing in rather isolated and separate phenomenal compartments. Both opinion polls and the utilization of television in national politics were noted and more or less tolerated by professional politicians, but their serious impact on the political scene was, for the most part, ignored with a certain degree of casual indifference until 1960. This was so because up until 1960 professional politicians shared the same misgivings that the public had learned to harbor as a result of the inordinate failures of some polls in 1936 and again in 1948. Television just began to come into its own in the 1950s, and it took some time for the emergence of a new group of advertizing-media experts—nonpoliticians—to discern that particular medium's true potential in politics.

The Kennedy-Nixon campaign of 1960 brought into focus the nature of the power that both polls and television could wield politically when they are used *in tandem.* By 1960, the sophistication of polling techniques was no longer open to substantive challenge, and both the electorate and the advertising-media-specialist fraternity had undergone a rather intensive experience with the new visual medium. What happened as a consequence was that political polling and television were removed from their separate and isolated compartments and were placed into a new symbiotic juxtaposition as viable instrumentalities in national politicking. The new symbiosis produced a synergism of political impact which emerged full-blown in 1968. To the authors of this book this synergism reflects the essence of the new politics. It also presents issues of a magnitude that transcends the rather mundane dialogue that customarily focuses on the undue-direct-influence doctrine.

This book examines the bandwagon argument in great detail in order to demonstrate its lack of fruitfulness as an interpretive tool in the understanding of the impacts that political polling and television generate upon voters directly. With regard to polls, this book reviews past research efforts relating to the problem. With regard to television, a major piece of research conducted by one of the authors is reviewed in detail. The latter material is put forth not so much to demonstrate that bandwagon is or is not produced as a direct consequence of television exposure, but rather to show the tremendous complexities involved in attempting to cope with the bandwagon hypothesis seriously and objectively.

Following the discussion of bandwagon, first as it pertains to polls and then as it pertains to television, is a discussion of the *indirect* influences that each form generates in the political arena, and the issues that are raised as consequences of these indirect impacts.

NOTES

1. Kenneth Boulding, *The Impact of the Social Sciences* (New Brunswick, New Jersey: Rutgers University Press, 1968), p. 22.
2. *Ibid.*, pp. 6–7.

The Role of Public-Opinion
Polls in the United States

Almost a century and a half ago, Alexis de Tocqueville predicted that in an egalitarian society such as the United States "it may be foreseen that faith in public opinion will become . . . a species of religion, and the majority its ministering Prophet."[1] As he describes such a society, the principle of authority, which he felt must always exist in any society, moves in its origin from the traditional hierarchical ordering characteristic of aristocratic periods to a belief in the common opinion of all men. Public opinion in a democratic society, he continues, has a singular power that derives from the ability of the majority not merely to persuade, but to impose its beliefs upon all. He warned of the danger that, in the very process of freeing men from the fetters of traditional authority, the substitution of the absolute power of a majority would impose an even greater despotism. In posing the twin potential of majority rule for liberation and for tyranny de Tocqueville identified the central political problem facing any democratic nation.

The workings of public opinion, as de Tocqueville described it in the United States during the 1830s, were not confined to politics, but permeated all judgments of taste, literature, and morality. It was only in the realm of politics, however, that elections provided a mechanism for the formal legitimation of majority opinion. Periodic elections make binding the decision of a majority to turn over power to a new group of men or to retain

9

the old for a new term of office. Between elections, however, the direct expression of public opinion is difficult. In these periods, normally, political life is the expression of organized society acting through vested interests and concentrations of power. This contrasts with the mass one-man-one-vote quality of elections, which function as the legitimizers of organized political life. Inevitably, discrepancies exist between the direct expression of public opinion in elections and the channeling of its expression between elections.

The possibility that processes might be at work that could result in unforeseen shifts in forthcoming elections was recognized early in the United States. Even before de Tocqueville visited these shores, "straw" polls were being conducted to gauge how the next election might turn out. In 1824, the *Raleigh Star* canvassed political sentiment at various meetings in order to assess "the sense of the people."[2] On July 24 of that same year, the *Harrisburg Pennsylvania* conducted a "straw vote taken without discrimination of parties" which reported Andrew Jackson to be the popular choice over John Quincy Adams.[3] Crude as these straw polls were, they served as an informal medium of communication for the expression of probable voting intentions. Newspaper-sponsored straw polls designed to forecast elections continued to be conducted throughout the nineteenth century and into the twentieth century, utilizing methods that were essentially the improvisations of journalists. Then, the Presidential election year of 1936 saw the emergence of a type of newspaper-sponsored poll, such as those conducted by George Gallup, Elmo Roper and Archibald Crossley, which employed newly developed sampling techniques. However, the interest of both the public and politicians continued to focus on whether the license to govern that public opinion had granted to one group of men was likely to be continued or withdrawn.

In the act of satisfying that interest, however, polls may act to perpetuate the mass basis of elections into the intervening years. They can function as "continuing quasi elections" in competition with institutionalized legislative and governing processes. The delegation of the authority of organized society, as manifested in the deliberations and acts of legislatures and executive officials, and encompassing representation from diverse minorities, is put into doubt whenever a poll suggests that public opinion, always unstable, is inclining toward a reversal at the next election. For this reason, even as polls create a medium of expression for what would otherwise be a latent ineffectual public opinion, they may act to disturb the orderly working of established authority. The dilemma of democratic societies that so concerned de Tocqueville—how to free men from entrenched authority without subjecting them to a more powerful public opinion—is particularly relevant to the analysis of the role of public-opinion polls in the United States today.

In this analysis, our focus will be on identifying the political significance of public-opinion polls, how they are actually used, and how this use has affected the political process. We will take it for granted that public-opinion polls share the potential of democracy for both liberation and tyranny. Therefore, our concern will not be to determine whether polls are good or bad, but rather to specify how they function in contemporary political processes.

In itself, a review of the criticism directed at the role of public-opinion polls and the defenses presented in their favor can only lead to an indecisive conclusion. If polls were used *only* as their defenders maintain—and there is little doubt that they can be used to further the public good—then only the most doctrinaire critics would continue to attack them. Conversely, if they were applied *only* as the critics claim they are—and again, there can be no doubt that undesirable applications are within the realm of reality—then only the most naive would continue to support them. The probability is that public-opinion polls have been utilized both in ways that would be acceptable to most people who favor democratic political processes and in ways that must be deplored by anyone who has faith in democracy. For this reason, it is rather futile to focus an analysis of the role of polls on the determination of whether their effects are "good" or "bad." It is not even satisfactory to ask whether their net effect is positive or negative, since it is not the average consequence, but their roles in specific situations that must be of concern.

These reservations do not mean that an assessment is impossible, but rather that the goal of any useful assessment should be to examine the actual role of public-opinion polls and to attempt to discover how they have come to play this role. By setting this as our goal, we can hope to achieve the following:

Avoidance of the polemical quality that characterizes so much of the discussion as to what effect polls are having on the quality of politics;

Development of a factually sound description of what polls are like and how they are being utilized;

Placement of the analysis of polls within the context of the on-going political process, rather than in isolation, thereby making it more relevant to the realities of political life.

If these objectives can be achieved, the ultimate implications of the rise of public-opinion polls should be more readily apparent. The visibility of these implications would, in turn, contribute to the development of a scientific political sociology rather than to the rhetoric of political controversy.

How Polls Are Used

Different segments of the population use the results of public-opinion polls in different ways, and the same individuals use them in divergent ways as situational contexts vary. More concretely, the political significance of public-opinion polls is a consequence of the interaction between the uses to which they are put and the expectations held for them by their users. This interaction, in turn, is determined first by the methodological capabilities and limitations of such polls, the users' understanding of these capabilities and limitations, and their feelings as to the proper place of the polls in the political process. Second and of equal import is the quality of the involvement of users of poll results, especially as it affects the decisions and actions they might make in light of their reading of poll results. A consequence of this interaction is, for example, that the criteria employed in evaluating the "success" of preelection polls—in fact, the criteria that define what "success" is—vary as a function not only of expectations and involvement, but also, more specifically, of the uses to which they are put.

One major use of public-opinion polls is *journalistic* in the sense of satisfying the public's curiosity about the world in which it lives. Journalism, in this sense, is not restricted to the creation and service of an informed public. It also caters to a wide-ranging curiosity about any unusual, startling, or otherwise salient event—a curiosity that seeks not enlightenment but involvement derived from what may be superficially grasped "facts." The human interest story is the archetype of this type of journalism. With respect to preelection polls, the public's curiosity tends to revolve around the question, "Who will win?" The ordinary newspaper reader is interested in these polls because he believes that such polls may be able to predict election outcomes. His criterion for success is not the poll's statistical precision but its ability to "call the winner." His interest in methodological considerations and in the political import of polls is either non-existent or peripheral. In sum, for much of the public preelection polls are little more than a journalistic stunt that makes reading about elections more exciting.

A second major use of public-opinion polls is *scientific*. For example, political scientists, sociologists, and psychologists utilize preelection polls as sources of data for analyses of the electoral process, for testing hypotheses about communications flow, and for investigating the dynamics of how choices are made.[4] They tend to be unconcerned with how well a poll "predicts" an election; they are more interested in whether the data available to them are of sufficient rigor and quality to be used analytically.

The statistical precision of preelection polls, in fact, may be denigrated by some as a methodological stunt with little significance for the scientific analysis of the dynamics of causation. In this sense, preelection polls have little more than curiosity value for many behavioral scientists. On another level, however, some behavioral scientists have expressed considerable concern about the possible harmful impact of preelection polls on the electoral process.[5] Interest in possible bandwagon effects—that is, a presumed tendency for voters to support whoever they think is going to win, regardless of actual preference—is illustrative of this type of concern.

These first two types of users have in common a disinterested orientation to public-opinion polls in that whatever impact the awareness of poll results might have upon one's political decisions, and whatever fears one may have about their influence, these factors are not the sources of their motivation to keep informed about poll results. The political sociologist's expressed interest is in making scientific decisions, not political ones, while the newspaper reader's overt decision is whether or not he can rely upon polls to satisfy his curiosity about the state of the political world.

In contrast are those uses of public-opinion polls that relate directly to political decisions. Users in this context include holders of or candidates for public office, political-party workers, public administrators, and members of special interest groups who seek to influence the former. There are two ways in which preelection polls are used by these "political-decision makers," and they contrast strongly with each other.

The first is *informational*—the poll is used as a guide in developing, implementing, and evaluating decisions such as who should run for office, what issues should be emphasized to whom, what types of appeals should be developed, and the like. For these purposes the overriding concern is with the ability of public-opinion polls to provide valid, reliable information. Politicians are necessarily vitally concerned that they be accurately informed as to the mood and thinking of their constituencies. Over the years, they have used many sources for keeping themselves informed including community and other formal leaders, news media, and party workers at all levels of organization. Surveys of public opinion are a new source of this kind of information, and the use of these surveys is justified essentially by their accepted accuracy. If there is doubt as to their accuracy, then there is no reason to give poll results any greater weight than those of any other type of field report. On a more amorphous level, the use of the survey method reflects a modern style of administration in which decisions must always be supported by research, regardless of how they may have been made initially.

This latter justification for using polls, which can best be described as a "legitimizing" function, shades over into another way in which public-opinion polls are used by political-decision makers. Because there is widespread belief that these polls are methodologically sound, they are susceptible to use in deliberate efforts to sway or *manipulate* political-decision makers. Results of privately sponsored polls may be released or withheld, depending upon their presumed manipulative utility. This manipulative use contrasts with the informational use of polls in that the intent is specifically to direct decisions in a way that will benefit the manipulator; little or no interest is taken in developing a correct understanding of the political situation. Potential contributors to campaign chests or possible political allies may be swayed by carefully timed releases of polls purporting to show the popular appeal of a candidate. Consequently, the manipulator, as distinct from the target, is not as concerned with methodological soundness or precision of measurement as he is with the faith of his target audience in the trustworthiness of the poll results. The manipulative use of polls can create situations in which methodological sloppiness, rigged research designs, and false reporting may proliferate.

The Effect of Polls on Political Leaders

There has been considerable controversy concerning the effects that surveys of public opinion, and more specifically preelection polls, have upon the responsiveness and the responsibility of political parties and decision makers. Defenders of polls tend to emphasize that polls act to make the electoral process more responsive to the needs and wishes of political constituencies. Critics, in contrast, are apt to stress that polls inhibit the responsible assumption of the duties of political leadership. Strong arguments backing both views can be, and have been, made.

On one hand, it can be pointed out that preelection polls, particularly those conducted before nominations are made, make it more difficult for parties to ignore their constituencies when selecting candidates. Similarly, candidates are provided with reliable bases for speaking out on the issues that are of greatest concern to the electorate. A perspicacious candidate might discover that the political power structure has ignored widespread needs of significant segments of his constituency, and even that the public's preferences on issues contrast with those of entrenched groups. This new awareness could lead to the satisfaction of unfulfilled needs of the electorate that might otherwise be neglected in peaceful political processes.

On the other hand, there is the ever-present danger that the aspirations of able men may be prematurely cut off because of an early weakness in polls. Support from party leaders and financial contributions which might have been theirs may never materialize. Furthermore, in the selection of issues and the determination of a position to take on them, candidates may be guided by a slavish adherence to transitory or uninformed public opinion. To the extent that this happens, the educational function of political leadership will atrophy to the detriment of democratic political processes.

The fact is that both types of arguments are correct, not because of the inherent qualities of preelection polls, but because the conflicting demands of responsiveness and responsibility are intrinsic to the democratic political process. Public-opinion polls may intensify these conflicting demands, but they do not create them. What is new, as a result of polls, is the context in which this conflict occurs.

One of the more significant political developments that can be ascribed specifically and directly to polling is the possibility of "continuing quasi elections" in contemporary society. Candidate preferences, the popularity of incumbents, and the relative standing of parties are measurable every month of every year, and they are being measured that frequently. In the past, political campaigning was a part-time affair, except for periods of intense activity during the formal campaign. Polls now make it possible, the day after a man has been newly elected as Mayor of a city or Governor of a state, for all to see if the public considers him "timber" for higher office. Moreover, the trend in the public's evaluation of the politically prominent is measured continually by published polls up to nominating time for the next election.

Thus, the politically-ambitious person must mature and develop under the pitiless glare of unending public assessment. He can never afford to let up in his campaigning if he aspires to an office, such as the Presidency, about which polls are regularly conducted. And the incumbents of such offices must take into account, as they seek to develop and marshal support for policies and legislation, that their prospects for reelection are continually being appraised in a way that is accepted by many as highly reliable. Newly elected Presidents, even before they assume office, are subject to public appraisal as to how great or poor a President they will make.[6] And trend measurements of the public's appraisal of their performance may start within days of their inauguration.[7] The effect of this constant measurement upon the electoral process is to make it an *endless event*, with elections as periodic climaxes.

What the ultimate effect of this development will be upon the functioning of our political institutions is a question that can best be answered by examining in detail precisely how polls have influenced the decisions made by political leaders and parties.

THE DIRECT EFFECTS OF POLLS ON VOTING BEHAVIOR

The hypothesis that publicizing the results of public-opinion polls has a direct effect on voting behavior has been widely held for many years. Various types of effects have been hypothesized, but most are classifiable into two general categories: (1) effects on candidate-preferences, and (2) effects on voter turnout. Each of these, in turn, is further divisible into effects that act to increase the lead of whoever is leading in poll reports, and those which act to decrease his lead.

The commonest type of claimed effect is that poll reports increase victory margins by inducing voters to cast their ballots for the leading candidate—the so-called "bandwagon effect." Less common are references to an "underdog effect," namely, the creation of sympathy for the presumed loser whose support is consequently increased. Interest in voter turnout has concentrated primarily on the possibility of a reduction in the proportion of eligible voters who actually vote on Election Day. For example, defeatism among supporters of the trailing candidate and over-confidence among the leader's adherents, purportedly generated by poll reports, could lead to a lowered turnout. On the other hand, if poll results indicate that an extremely close election is in the offing, it is conceivable that a larger turnout than normal might occur.

Despite the long-standing interest and concern over the possible existence of direct effects, especially bandwagon effects, of poll reports on voting behavior, there has been little systematic, empirical investigation of the issue. The little research that has been conducted has focused on the attempt to measure bandwagon effects. As a by-product of bandwagon research, some information about underdog effects has been gathered. However, virtually no research at all has been done with respect to turnout, the little that has been written on this topic being primarily speculative in nature.

Klapper has conducted an extensive review of the literature on bandwagon and other direct effects of poll reports upon voting behavior.[8] On the basis of this review, he concludes:

> . . . *there is no absolutely conclusive evidence that . . . the publication of poll results does or does not affect the subsequent votes.*
>
> . . . the existing literature provides considerable reason to believe that the publication of poll results *does not* produce any direct bandwagon or underdog effect of any significant magnitude among the electorate. The evidence, however, cannot be said to be wholly conclusive, since the possibility of small effects cannot be ruled out.
>
> . . . the publication of poll results in apparently runaway elections may create apathy both in the camp of the forecast victor and in the camp of the forecast loser. To what extent such effects occur, whether they affect the vote, and whether they cancel each other out, are all matters on which no reliable evidence is available.[9]

In light of the conviction of some critics that bandwagon effects are a major consequence of publicized poll results, the bases for Klapper's conclusion warrant careful scrutiny.

The data bearing upon the direct effect of published poll results that were reviewed by Klapper are of three types: (1) trends in voter preferences as measured by sequential polls, from which inferences about possible bandwagon effects can be drawn, (2) results of studies specifically designed to investigate whether such effects can be identified and their magnitude measured, (3) conclusions drawn from studies of how voters make up their minds.

SEQUENTIAL POLLS

Trends in voter preferences, as measured by sequential polls in numerous elections, are cited by polltakers, such as Gallup, as conclusive evidence that there is no bandwagon effect.[10] For example, both in 1936 when the then prestigious *Literary Digest* poll incorrectly forecasted a decisive Landon victory, and again in 1948 when the Gallup, Roper, and Crossley polls wrongly indicated that Dewey would defeat Truman, the leading candidate in the polls was defeated. In the 1952 Presidential election, the very popular Eisenhower actually lost some ground to Stevenson as the campaign progressed, the former's support dropping from 58 percent to 54 percent. Another instance cited by Klapper is the 1962 California gubernatorial election. The California Poll, which conducted nine widely publicized polls from March 1961 to November 1962, charted a trend in Richard Nixon's strength from 56 percent in March 1961 to 59 percent in June 1961, down to 48 percent in April 1962, and a further decline to 46 percent just before the election. Klapper comments, "Obviously no bandwagon effect occurred either in the course of the polls or between the final poll and election."[11]

Sequential polls do measure changes in voter preferences, but these can more reasonably be related to the effects of specific events rather than to the effects of polls. For example, in the 1956 Presidential election campaign, the Gallup Poll charted a steady 55 to 56 percent for Eisenhower from the beginning of the campaign up to the final two weeks. Neither a bandwagon nor an underdog effect was discernible. However, the final preelection survey, conducted immediately after the Suez and Hungarian crises, then showed an increase to 59.5 percent in Eisenhower's support. By Election Day, both crises had abated and Eisenhower received 57.8 percent of the major-party vote.

Klapper considers the evidence of sequential polls "extremely persuasive" but not "absolutely conclusive."[12] It is conceivable, he notes, that the magnitude of Roosevelt's plurality over Landon in 1936, or of Truman's over Dewey in 1948, was reduced by poll reports. Also, there may have been both bandwagon and under-dog effects which, in net, canceled each other out. Consequently, Klapper feels that some element of doubt, albeit small, remains, so that a more intensive analysis of data from sequential polls is necessary if those data are to be considered conclusive.

The indications are that such analyses would reinforce the tentative conclusions that can now be drawn from sequential poll data. Gallup Poll trend data show that, with the above noted exception of 1956, the pattern is for the margin between Presi-dential candidates to get smaller in the final weeks of the campaign. This trend was dramatically the case in 1968, when Humphrey all but wiped out an early 13 percentage point deficit by regaining strength among normally Democratic blue-collar workers. But, it also occurred in 1964, 1960, 1952, and 1948. This decreasing margin is in large part the result of the return to the fold of potentially defecting members of the trailing candidate's party. Thus, in 1968, Humphrey's resurgence was due to the fact that many Democrats who early in the campaign had favored Wallace switched back to their party's candidate in the final weeks.[13] In 1964, Gallup Poll data show that Goldwater picked up strength from September through Election Day. Among Re-publicans his share of the vote went up during this period from 77 percent to 80 percent, among Democrats from 8 percent to 13 percent, and among Independents from 42 percent to 44 per-cent.[14] The fact that Goldwater gained among adherents of both parties, and possibly among Independents, reduces the likelihood that a bandwagon effect was being masked by other trends.

INVESTIGATIONS OF BANDWAGON EFFECT

Klapper reports that he discovered very few soundly designed studies which test for the existence of a bandwagon effect.[15] While there have been many experiments which demonstrate the influence of group opinion upon individual opinion, the significant factor in these studies has been the direct exertion of group pressure in face-to-face situations. The pertinent question, as Klapper notes, is whether the communication of survey reports can sway opinion, not whether individuals tend to conform to the norms of groups to which they belong.

One relevant study reviewed by Klapper, the results of which are inconclusive, was conducted by Cook and Welch among University of Wisconsin students.[16] When students were asked to record their preference between Landon and Roosevelt before and then *immediately after* they were informed that the *Literary Digest* had reported Landon ahead, a statistically significant increase in the proportion favoring Landon occurred. When an interval of three to four weeks occurred before the retest, Cook and Welch discovered an increase that approached statistical significance for Landon among those who had *not* known the *Digest* results beforehand. Furthermore, being for Landon made for better recall of the *Digest* report than being for Roosevelt. That is, initial preference made for a selective memory of supporting poll results. Cook and Welch concluded that their data could be interpreted to mean *either* that they had measured a slight bandwagon effect *or* that causality might have worked in the other direction, with preexisting preferences leading to "greater attention to and better memory of the favorable results . . ."[17]

Another study cited by Klapper was conducted by Opinion Research Corporation immediately after the 1960 Presidential election.[18] For this study, persons who reported they had voted for Kennedy or for Nixon were asked, "Who did the opinion polls say would win the election?" Regardless of who the respondents thought had been ahead in opinion polls, they were equally likely to have voted for Kennedy or for Nixon. Also, the proportion who voted for each candidate was exactly the same among those who claimed to be aware of poll results and those who did not.

STUDIES OF VOTING BEHAVIOR

Studies of voting behavior conducted by the Bureau of Applied Social Research at Columbia and by the Survey Research

Center of the University of Michigan offer little support to the hypothesis that poll results induce changes in voting behavior. The Michigan studies have noted that there is a tendency *after* an election for more people to claim to have voted for the winning candidate than actually did, a tendency that also appears in Gallup Poll surveys.[19] But this tendency is different from the type of bandwagon effect under consideration here.

Two of the Columbia studies, one of the 1940 Roosevelt-Willkie election and the other of the 1948 Truman-Dewey election, contain assertions that bandwagon effects exist.[20] However, as Klapper points out, in these studies it is difficult to differentiate possible bandwagon effects from "projection" effects—that is, a tendency to assume that the majority vote will conform to one's own preference.[21] The data from the 1940 study, he concludes, indicate "that there is a high correlation between expectation of the vote outcome and vote intention, that vote intentions developed after expectations tend to accord with pre-campaign expectations, and that these phenomena hold true regardless of political predisposition. . . . The arguments advanced to support bandwagon effects are based on an extremely small number of cases, and, in any case, do not provide a demonstration of bandwagon effects . . ."[22] In a final footnote to their discussion on bandwagon, the authors of the 1940 study state that the high correlation between expectations as to who will win and voting intention may be the result of either bandwagon effects or projection.[23] In the 1948 study, it is asserted that "data from the 1940 and 1948 elections suggest that the bandwagon effect and the projection effect are approximately equal in strength."[24] Supporting data are not provided, however, and Klapper states that a reanalysis he conducted of the original data failed to uncover any supporting evidence.[25]

While the existence of any sizable bandwagon effect in the Columbia data is problematic, projective effects are well-documented. An intensive analysis was conducted of the relation between perceptions of the vote intentions of others like oneself and one's own vote intention. This investigation involved a cross-analysis of party identification with socioeconomic status, race, religion, and occupation. The analysis indicates that ". . . there

is an association between the respondent's vote and his percep-
tion of the predominant vote of his own minority group . . .
Republican Catholics see Catholics as voting more Republican
than do Democratic Catholics; and the same is true of Jews'
perceptions of the Jewish vote, Negroes' of the Negro vote, and
so on."[26]

DeGrazia, and Kitt and Gleicher have also independently
confirmed the existence of a projection effect.[27] This is not to say
that all presumed bandwagon effects are really the result of
projection. But it is evident that unless the two are differentiated,
it is impossible to make any conclusive statement about bandwagon effects. In any event, what data do exist in the Columbia
studies concerning bandwagon effects do not provide much
ground for believing they can be more than marginal in significance, while there are some grounds for believing that even
granting marginal significance may be an overstatement.

Klapper contrasts the tenuous nature of the data regarding
bandwagon with the documentation in both the Michigan and
Columbia studies of the extent to which voting behavior is
conditioned by one's group membership and the nature of one's
political involvement.[28] The political orientations of one's family,
friends, and other close associates are highly correlated with
one's voting behavior. Family political traditions as well as the
individual's own past voting behavior provide reliable bases for
predicting how he will vote. Similarly, position in the social
structure as identified by such characteristics as socioeconomic
status, religion, ethnic origin, race, educational achievement, and
the region of the country and the size of the community in which
one lives are all important correlates of voting behavior. Finally,
such factors as degree of political involvement, interest in an
election, and the extent to which one belongs to groups with
conflicting political identifications all strongly influence the possibility that an initial vote intention may change. The likelihood
that the combined net weight of all these influences may be
counteracted by the publication of a poll report would, on the
face of it, seem to be minimal.

Moreover, as Klapper points out, tendencies to conform to
majority opinion that do exist are more correctly to be under-

stood as conformity to the individual's "reference groups"—that is, those groups with which he identifies and whose approval is important to him.[29] This type of conformity was noted as early as 1940 by Gallup and Rae:

The urge to follow the majority, which the psychologists call the "impression of universality," must be interpreted to mean not opinion of the nation as a whole, but rather the small intimate group who make up the individual voter's circumscribed universe . . . The case studies to date which describe the movements of opinions on the issues of the day reveal absolutely no tendency for voters to herd together in order to be on the winning side.[30]

While the voting behavior of some individuals conceivably may be influenced by reports concerning the preferences of the majority of "the public," the norms of groups valued and accepted as points of reference are most likely to be decisive for the overwhelming majority of voters when they are deciding whom to vote for.

An attempt to investigate the possible role of reference groups in mediating any impact which poll reports might have on voter preferences was made by Atkin during the 1968 campaign. Conducted among a sample of 101 University of Wisconsin undergraduates, the study was designed to determine whether a poll report showing that the majority opinion among all college students is appreciably larger (or smaller) than one expected will influence one's own opinion.[31] Thus, in contrast with usual simplistic assumptions about bandwagon effects, this study posited that it is not merely who is reported to be leading in a poll but whether the lead differs appreciably from one's expectations that is of significance.

The study concluded that there would be "a very limited and directionally selective impact on aggregate voting behavior." That is to say, if a poll reports a split in opinion within one's reference group that differs appreciably from one's prior expectation, there is some tendency for one's opinions to shift in a direction that would reduce dissonance. Applying this observation to what might happen during an election campaign, we can make the following conclusion: Only if one were exposed to a poll report concerning one's own reference groups, and if that report conflicted appreciably with impressions one had garnered from other sources, would there be any likelihood that one's own preference would be affected to any degree. It is reasonable to conclude, therefore, that the aggregate effect of poll reports in real life situations is likely to be trivial.

If bandwagon, underdog, or other presumed effects of polls upon the electorate are minimal, as seems to be the case, the question arises as to why so much attention has been paid to the possibility that they are of major significance. A reasonable hypothesis is that polls have, in fact, had a major impact on politics, but that attention has been diverted from the real nature of this impact. Specifically, it is proposed that the true signifi-cance of polls lies in their direct influence not upon the elec-torate, but upon the behavior of politicians. Influences upon voting behavior, it would follow, are indirect consequences of how the behavior of politicians has been affected. To test this hypothesis, it is necessary to determine how politicians use polls and how this has affected their behavior.

Polls and the Formal Party Organizations

Politics has to do with the use of power to pursue conflicting interests, group or personal, in a way that is accepted as legiti-mate—that is, as moral. This use requires systems of communica-tion as well as negotiating procedures and formal organizations. Before the development of the mass media of communication, an intricate network of personal relations was the primary source through which a political party discovered the needs of citizens, persuaded them that it could satisfy them better than the opposi-tion, and evaluated how satisfied citizens were with its activities. In the United States, each party's network consists of a hierarchy of district clubs, county and state committees, and a national committee. Working within this framework are congeries of precinct workers, district captains, county chairmen, and the like.

The functioning of any institution is dependent upon and conditioned by the communications among those who act within its limits. For democratic political institutions, which have as central to their value systems the maximization of two-way communications between citizenry and government, the nature and adequacy of channels of communication is crucial. It is commonplace to note that in small-scale societies in which personal contact is maximal political communications can utilize community channels to good purpose. Within the context of a complex, urban environment, however, the effectiveness of such channels as media of communication can deteriorate rapidly. Counteracting the advantages of personal communications is the likelihood of distortion and inefficiency as messages pass through a series of "transmitters." As populations grow, community channels are accessible to fewer and fewer individuals so that the flow of information, including needs, sentiments, and preferences of constituents is subject to control by formal and other powerful authorities.

While the mass media enable parties and political figures to communicate to the electorate on a broad basis, the ability of the electorate to make its wishes known, except during elections, is severely restricted. Moreover, exactly what has been communicated in an election is often unclear since the effects of a variety of issues upon voter preferences are difficult to untangle. Thus, at the upper levels of party hierarchies there is considerable pressure to utilize new channels of communications, such as public-opinion polls, to keep informed about grass-roots sentiment.

It is for this reason that the increasing use of public-opinion polls to measure and analyze voter preferences has not resulted in the displacement or decay of the top echelons of formal party organizations. On the contrary, certain party leaders typically sponsor and utilize polls to aid them in the performance of their duties. These duties involve not only the selection of candidates, but also the development of over-all party strategies and policies. For example, in 1959, in the aftermath of their resounding defeat in the previous year's congressional elections, the Republicans prepared a "blueprint to rebuild party, win election in 1960," an integral part of which was the conducting of periodic surveys of public opinion. As reported in the *Wall Street Journal,* "President Eisenhower has just received—and GOP leaders are about to get—a sweeping set of proposals designed to remake the Republican party—its image and organization . . . A public opinion sampling service would provide Mr. [Mead] Alcorn with periodic reports on voter reaction to issues."[32]

Eight years later, in April 1967, both the Republican and Democratic National Committees utilized survey data in assessing their basic strengths and weaknesses as they developed strategies to build basic party strength for the 1968 Presidential election. Charles T. Weltner, head of an advisory group to the Democratic National Committee, took note of surveys that showed "only 35% of college students now regard themselves as Democrats" as indicative of an urgent need to attract the attention and loyalty of young voters.[33] In a parallel development, Ray C. Bliss, the Republican National Chairman, was quoted as saying, "Our own polls tell us we're the minority party with only about 29% of the American people identifying as Republicans. Naturally we're going to have to attract some people from the opposition."[34] The significance of both these comments can be evaluated by the twenty-seven-year trend in party identification among the nation's voters (Table 1). This trend shows a sharp decline in Republican identifiers and erratic fluctuations in the proportion who call themselves Democrats, the result being that

TABLE 1. Trend in Party Identification Among Adults

	Democratic	Republican	Independent
1940	42	38	20
1950	45	33	22
1960	47	30	23
1964	53	25	22
1966	48	27	25
1967 February	46	27	27
1967 September	42	27	31
1968 July	46	27	27

Sources: Gallup Political Index, no. 21, March 1967, p. 16; no. 38, August 1968, p. 2.

by 1967 more than one-fourth of the electorate did not align themselves with either party.

The extensive use of political polls during the 1968 Presidential election campaign was widely noted at the time. The April 29, 1968 issue of the *Congressional Quarterly* listed 42 public opinion firms that were conducting private polls and 24 published polls at that time, indicating that this was an incomplete list. Central to this development is the fact that both major party candidates used poll data for the specific purpose of developing their campaign strategies and for assessing their strengths and weaknesses. On August 10, 1968, within days of his nomination, Nixon was reported by *The New York Times* as concluding from poll data—reportedly showing 50 percent of Negroes as undecided and 10 percent supporting him—that he was already ahead of Goldwater's standing among Negroes in 1964 and that further advances could be expected. Similarly, Max Frankel, writing in *The New York Times* on September 3, 1968, as Humphrey's campaign was first beginning to get underway, observed:

Mr. Humphrey's private polls have shown that what voters of all persuasions want most is a sense of participation in the political process, a feeling that they can be heard and have their doubts addressed. For that reason, and because he thinks he is good at it, he plans to submit to questioning on campuses, in shopping centers, and broadcast studios, hoping that the answers will rebound around the community after he leaves . . . The private polls suggest that Mr. Humphrey still has traditional popularity as a liberal and as a fighter for civil rights among these groups, despite the flirtation of many middle class blue collar workers with the Wallace movement.

Instead of relying upon the subjectively perceived and evaluated reports that were the traditional products of precinct workers, leaders of both parties are placing their trust on presumably objective survey data, planned and evaluated by technicians who are in direct contact with upper party echelons.

Despite the fact that party organizations use polls extensively, within political circles there is considerable difference of opinion as to whether this should be done. The crux of the controversy is the effect that polls may have on the development and maintenance of an individual style and an individual position on issues.

In a mail survey of United States Senators on the role of public-opinion polls in American politics, conducted by Irving Crespi in August 1967, a Senator from the Mountain States replied:

I do not use polls and try very hard not to be guided by them. A senator's conviction should be the deciding factor.

A contrasting view is that of another Mountain State Senator who cited as "a realistic, practical significance of polls" their ability to

measure public's true feelings on issues, in contrast to the apparent temper reflected in the press, etc. . . . to assess public's reactions to programs and policies.

The first viewpoint is expressive of a style of politics which focuses on the question of what ought to be, while the second is concerned with identifiable reality. Political leaders of the second type seek to identify the influences that determine how voters exercise their franchise, believing that this information will contribute to their own effectiveness.[35]

The contrast between the two types of political leaders is in many ways parallel to the difference between the business entrepreneur and the corporate executive. The former relies on his seemingly intuitive grasp of a situation; the latter undertakes a systematized analysis of whatever pertinent data can be gathered. To the entrepreneur polls take the personal adventure out of politics and are thus superfluous.[36] To the executive polls provide a factual basis which he can use when formulating his plans and his evaluations of evolving situations. For example, one elected official, in personal conversation, expressed a concern with the results of surveys of public opinion not because they told him what decision to make, but because they enabled him to evaluate what would be the likely political consequences of whatever line of action he decided to follow.

Yet, there is a curious similarity between the political entrepreneur who says, "I have been talking personally to my constituents and I know what they are thinking" and the political executive who says, "I have just taken a poll of my constituents, and here is what they think." Thus, Representative Edna F. Kelly, a Brooklyn Democrat, was quoted in the April 2, 1967

issue of *The New York Times,* as giving this explanation for
thinking polls are not much help:

I stay so close to my constituents that I don't have to run a poll. Anyway, I've never liked questionnaires—yes, no, yes, no—How can you
find what people really think?

In contrast, Representative William F. Ryan, a Manhattan
Democrat, is described in the same article as writing to his
constituents, asking them to answer a questionnaire:

Although it may not be scientific, I think the questionnaire and your
answers give considerable insight into opinions on our West Side,
Washington Heights and Inwood.

Both types of politicians feel it essential to be in touch with grass
roots opinion and to convince others that their assessment of such
opinion is accurate. Inevitably, all politicians must be concerned
with finding out what the members of their constituency are
thinking, what is bothering them, what problems they feel must
be solved. The difference between these types is that the entrepreneurial politician's communications style is subjective, relying
on personal assessment, whereas the executive's style is objective
in that it utilizes a quantitative measurement of public opinion.

The New York mayoralty campaign of 1969, as described by
Richard Reeves in *The New York Times,* October 5, 1969, illustrates the contrast between the entrepreneurial and executive
politician:

The best polls being done here this year are being seen only by
people at Lindsay headquarters, but the Mayor himself rarely sees
them . . . But the surveys he personally ignores are often at the root
of the strategy laid out by Mr. Lindsay's most important advisors.
They live with detailed data supplied by pollsters, constantly checking voter attitudes on issues and candidates. . . .
On the other hand, Mr. Procaccino and Mr. Marchi are basically
working the way politicians did 50 years ago. "They're guessing," a
Lindsay man said, "and if they're lucky, they'll guess right."
It is not that Mr. Lindsay's opponents do not want polls. "The
Mayor's polls are the darling of the city," said a Procaccino advisor,
"but we don't have the money to pay for them and, face it, we don't
have the bright young guys who can work with that stuff."

Clearly, the use of polls in that election campaign was determined by which candidate's campaign was run by executive and which by entrepreneurial politicians.

No one politician is a complete embodiment of either type but, rather, encompasses qualities of both. Moreover, the demands of political rhetoric often conflict with a distinct need for information of the type provided by polls. As a consequence, such disparate political figures as Richard Nixon and Robert Kennedy, who have both on occasion spoken scornfully about polls, have nevertheless been assiduous users of them.

Sample surveys provide politicians with percentages which presumably indicate the size of each block of opinion in their constituencies. While an acute observer can achieve valid insights and can sense the general trend of opinion, surveys attempt to determine the *size* of a candidate's lead or the *magnitude* of a trend. Politicians look at poll results, initially at any rate, for "the figure" which shows who is ahead and by how much. As confidence in the trustworthiness of "the figures" increases, the scope of a politician's utilization of polls may expand to include an analysis of the role of issues, personalities, and party loyalties in the thinking of the electorate. Thus, while it is unlikely that the entrepreneurial politician will ever completely disappear from the scene, the need for effective media for communication from the public to the upper echelons of party organization in an urban society makes it likely that the use of public-opinion polls by executive politicians will continue to grow.

POLLS AND THE ENACTMENT OF LAW

The conflicting requirements of responsiveness to one's constituency and responsibility of leadership that face all politicians in democratic societies are intensified for the executive politician who utilizes public-opinion polls. Whereas for the entrepreneurial politician the conflict blurs in his subjective style of operation, for the executive politician it is sharpened because the results of any survey are external to his own convictions. Any discordance between measured opinion and personal conviction confronts the executive politician with the problem of how to serve his constituency's requirements while remaining true to himself.

A survey of public opinion has a plebiscite-like quality that contrasts with the complexities of the legislative process. Such surveys can measure the proportions of the general public that favor the principle underlying proposed legislation, such as medical care for the aged, gun control, and foreign aid. Therefore, since it is rare that election results give a clear-cut answer as to what the electorate's views are on specific issues, short of national referenda on issues, opinion polls provide the only practical means for measuring the public's wishes.[37] Nevertheless, poll measurements have not replaced the interchange of opinions that takes place in legislative committee hearings, presentations by special interest groups, staff research, and negotiations between opposing factions.[38]

To the legislator himself, the question is not whether to vote in accord with the dictates of a public-opinion poll or in response to the pressures of the legislative process. Rather, he must develop a stance that will resolve any conflicts between the two. Regardless of how informed or correct are the views of the public as measured by public-opinion polls, the legislator is concerned with reconciling his voting record with these views if he is to run successfully for reelection. To achieve this agreement, above all he needs to know what issues are of greatest concern to his constituency. If there is a groundswell of sentiment favoring action on some issue, it is essential for him to know this. It is also extremely valuable for him to know if there is a conflict between the type of solution he favors and that favored by his constituency. Of less significance is the determination of what specific type of legislation is favored.

The constituency-sounding function of polls is evident in the replies to the mail survey of United States Senators mentioned earlier. Questionnaires were mailed to all 100 Senators, twenty-nine of whom answered the questions. An additional four wrote explaining why they were not answering the questionnaire.

TABLE 2. Realistic Practical Significance of Public-Opinion Polls to United States Senators

Number of Senators	
26	To discover what issues are of most concern to your constituency
16	To determine if voter opinion agrees with or differs significantly from positions you have supported
15	To evaluate how voters are likely to vote on Election Day
11	To discover how well informed voters are of your position on current issues
11	To evaluate relative political strength in different segments of the population
9	To measure voters' opinions on legislation that may be introduced or that is under consideration
8	To discover what kind of legislation voters in your district favor
1	None of them
29	Number of Senators who answered question

As shown in Table 2, the primary use of polls for these Senators, cited by almost all of them, is to determine what problems their constituencies feel need action, while almost as important is the evaluation of their own electoral strength and possible sources of voter disaffection. Voter opinion on the detail of legislation is of significance to only one out of every three of the Senators who replied. Of these Senators, ten report they have a great deal of interest and fourteen a fair amount of interest in the results of opinion polls that are published in newspapers. Also, twenty-seven have had polls conducted for them—twenty-five prior to or during election campaigns, five prior to or during legislative sessions, and one after an election.

This pattern of response indicates that public-opinion polls are primarily used to select effective campaign issues rather than to determine what bills should be enacted. Illustrative of this are the following verbatim quotes of what have been "the most practical value" of polls to five Senators:

Extent of recognition among voters; determining what voters like least about positions or traits of mine. Discovering weak points politically in terms of voter attitude toward my over-all record.

Determination of issues and candidate's "image" with electorate are of most significance.

Indicating areas of relative strength on issues and by voter groups.

It is useful to discover which of the politician's traits and issues are most admired so that these points may be emphasized in campaign materials.

Graphic representation of issues and of opponents.

For these Senators "following the polls" does not mean accepting each poll result as a mandate as to how one should cast his vote in legislative sessions. Rather, this practice provides a signal as to whether he should take some kind of public position on the issue. The actual significance of polls in the legislative process is the fact that they can guide the development of campaign strategy and tactics, suggesting to the Senator what he should promise action on, what he should ignore, and what he should attack. The trend of response to such questions as "What is the most important problem facing this country today?" can be very instructive in the formulation of campaign strategy. (See Chart 1.) Indirectly, through their impact on campaign oratory and, thus, on much of the public discussion of issues, public-opinion polls may ultimately affect legislation.

In contrast, there appears to be little direct relationship between the views of the public on specific issues and the legislative record of Congress. For years the Gallup Poll has reported majorities in favor of a reform of the Electoral College so that its vote would be a direct reflection of the division of the popular vote. In 1967, when asked the question, "Would you approve or disapprove of an amendment to the Constitution which would do away with the Electoral College and base the election of a President on the total popular vote cast throughout the nation?" 58 percent voiced approval, 22 percent disapproval, and 20 percent had no opinion. Among those who had attended college, 68 percent said they approved.[39] Yet, presumably because the sentiment measured by the Gallup Poll has been inchoate in contrast with the entrenchment of those that favor the Electoral College, up until the 1968 Presidential election there had been no effective movement to enact any changes.

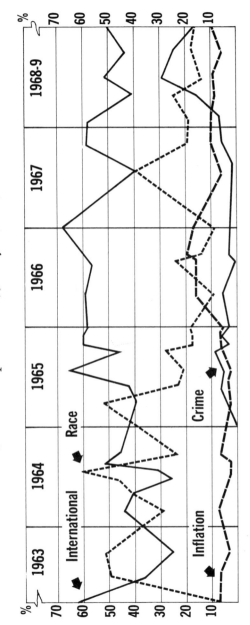

CHART 1. Top Concerns of Public: Jan. 1963–Jan. 1969
(Source: Gallup Poll Release, January 30, 1969)

The closeness of the 1968 election coupled with a widespread concern that in a three-way contest no one would win a majority of Electoral College votes strengthened the position of those who, like Senator Birch Bayh, had been attempting to generate Congressional support for a Constitutional amendment that would alter the existing procedure. One tangible effect of public debate on this issue was the increase in the size of the public majority in favor of abandoning the Electoral College, from 66 percent in September 1968 to 81 percent immediately after the election.[40] Moreover, the possibility that, if George Wallace ran again in 1972, he would prevent an Electoral College majority for any candidate continued to worry leaders of both the Democratic and Republican Parties. Legislative action and public opinion finally began to converge in September 1969 when the House of Representatives acted favorably on a Constitutional amendment to abolish the Electoral College in favor of direct election of the President.

Perhaps the most glaring recent example of how legislative action, or inaction, can be in direct opposition to measured public opinion is with respect to the regulation of firearms. Repeated surveys by the Gallup Poll have shown decided majorities in favor of "a law which would require a person to obtain a police permit before he or she could buy a gun" (Table 3). Senator Thomas J. Dodd has introduced, annually from 1963 through 1968, an act for stringent control of firearms, with a strong administration backing.[41] Nevertheless, during committee hear-

TABLE 3. Responses to the Question, "Should Legislation Be Enacted Requiring a Police Permit before a Gun Can Be Bought?"

		Favor	Opposed	No Opinion
		%	%	%
September	1966	68	29	3
February	1965	73	23	4
January	1964	78	17	5
	1959	75	21	4

Source: Gallup Political Index, no. 16, p. 19; no. 1 (unpaginated).

ings in the summer of 1967, Senator Joseph D. Tydings complained that the bill had "languished in Congress for two years (and) is hardly closer to passage now than on the day it was introduced."[42] Senator Robert Kennedy, strongly in favor of the proposed legislation, cited as proof of "a new surge of public support for gun control legislation" a 1967 poll which found 73 percent favoring a law that would require firearm registration and 75 percent in favor of the prohibition of all mail order sales.[43] Nevertheless, organized opposition, primarily from the National Rifle Association, was far more effective in influencing the legislative process than surveys of public opinion, so that two months later President Johnson issued an urgent appeal for passage of the bill which was then still blocked in committee.[44]

On June 6, 1968, two days after Senator Robert Kennedy was shot, and on the day he died, Congress enacted the Omnibus Crime Control and Safe Streets Act, which included some provision for gun control. In July 1968, the House of Representatives passed a bill specifically designed to regulate the sale of guns and ammunition, and the Senate completed action in September. The bill as enacted included a number of amendments which were considered by its proponents as weakening it seriously.

Central to an understanding of why public opinion has had so little influence upon enactment of gun control legislation is the fact that the issue has never been developed into an effective campaign issue. John M. Bailey, Democratic National Chairman, commenting in early 1967 on the difficulties that he anticipated in the 1968 elections, stated that he did not think gun control was a vote-getting issue.[45] If it were not for the rapid succession of two assassinations in the spring of 1968, it is problematical as to whether any legislation would have been enacted that year, regardless of what public-opinion polls were reporting.

When proposed legislation becomes a campaign issue, on the other hand, the likelihood that there will be congruence between measured public opinion and legislative action is increased. During the height of the 1964 Presidential election, 58 percent of a national sample said they approved of "a compulsory medical insurance program covering hospital and nursing home care for the elderly" which ". . . would be financed out of increased social security taxes." By January 1965, support for Medicare had increased further, with 63 percent approving. By way of background, in the January survey 48 percent said they thought they knew why the American Medical Association opposed the proposed legislation. The top two reasons imputed to the AMA were (1) Medicare would cut down the profits of doctors and (2) it would be a move toward socialized medicine.[46]

Medicare legislation had been considered by Congress a number of times since it was first introduced under the Truman administration. While its final passage in 1965 cannot be ascribed to a slavish following of the polls by Congress, neither should the publishing of these polls be considered irrelevant to enactment. After two decades of debate, not only was there a popular majority in favor of such legislation, but also the question had become an effective campaign issue. Thus, as more politicians use polls to discover such issues, the indirect influence of polls on legislation can be expected to increase. But there seems little reason to anticipate that the legislative record of future Congresses will be a mirror of what public-opinion polls report.

POLLS AND THE FORMULATION OF FOREIGN POLICY

The formulation of United States foreign policy has in recent administrations been dominated by the executive branch rather than by Congress. Since the executive branch focuses on one man, the President, the tension between responsible leadership and responsiveness to the will of the people in the formulation of foreign policy also focuses on him. For this reason, the question of what role polls may play in this area of government boils down essentially to how the President utilizes information gathered through public-opinion polls.

While the interest of Lyndon B. Johnson and John F. Kennedy in public-opinion polls has been widely noted, the fact is that, ever since the early 1940s, Presidents from Franklin D. Roosevelt to Richard M. Nixon have found polls of use to them in the area of foreign policy. Even during the Truman administration, a member of the State Department asserted that surveys of public opinion were ". . . helpful to those who are faced with the necessity of formulating particular elements of our foreign policy . . ."[47]

Hadley Cantril's depiction of the pioneering use Franklin D. Roosevelt made of polls is instructive. As Cantril describes it, Roosevelt utilized poll reports as political intelligence, a procedure analogous to a general's use of military intelligence in the planning of campaign strategy. Roosevelt did not alter his goals because uninformed public opinion reflected an antagonism toward them. Rather, he used such reports "to try to bring the public around more quickly or more effectively to the course of action he felt was best for the country."[48] For example, in 1941 he carefully paced the build-up of active support for Great Britain in a manner that retained public confidence in his leadership. Throughout the year, periodic surveys were conducted to determine whether the public felt he was going too far in sending aid to Britain:

The trend . . . indicates the uncanny way in which the President was able to balance public opinion around his policies. . . . In spite of the fact that United States aid to Britain constantly increased after May 1941, the proportion of people who thought the President had gone too far, about right, or not far enough remained fairly constant. This was precisely the situation he wanted to maintain during these critical months; hence his eagerness to learn the results of our periodic soundings.[49]

By way of contrast, Lyndon B. Johnson was not able to maintain public confidence in his handling of the Vietnam conflict. In the two and one-half years from July 1965 to March 1968, disapproval of his handling of Vietnam climbed from 28 percent to 63 percent.[50] Cantril also reports that Roosevelt "kept his eye on the trend . . . as to whether or not people approved the way he was handling his job"[51]—the same trend that, a quarter of a century later, the Gallup Poll still reports monthly, and a variant of which is now also charted by the Harris Survey.

As Cantril describes it, Roosevelt's "following the polls" did not mean abdicating his leadership role, but rather meant defining it.

For example, in 1944 poll data gave warning of undue public optimism as to the course of the war in Italy. Counteraction was taken that effectively reduced this optimism without creating an equally unrealistic pessimism. Similarly, prior to the bombing of railroad yards and airports in Rome, a survey was taken to determine whether this action would have a detrimental effect on Catholic morale and support of the war effort.[52] In the hands of a consummate politician like Roosevelt, who combined the qualities of entrepreneur and executive, polls served as tools in implementing policy rather than as determinants of policy.

A politician who uses polls in this way is subject to the charge of manipulating public opinion. For example, as of August 1943, the State Department officially sponsored surveys of public opinion to guide its public relations and information programs in overcoming public resistance to such policies as United States participation in an international peace-keeping organization. These surveys helped to "devise the right expression of policy at the right time or to decide the right moment to act."[53] Drawing the fine line of distinction between manipulation and leadership is inevitably conditioned by one's own policy preferences. While the correctness or wisdom of specific policies must be judged independently, the utility of poll data as political intelligence that can enhance the effectiveness of a leader is apparent.

If it is believed that the President is being influenced in his foreign-policy decisions by public-opinion polls, the polls themselves can become a matter of controversy. The validity or meaningfulness of reported measurements are always subject to question by critics dissatisfied with existing policy. Moreover, if the President is, in fact, being guided by polls in his formulation of policy, a possible way to induce change effectively would be to present him with poll data which show public thinking to be at variance with what had heretofore been reported to him.

On March 15, 1966 *The New York Times'* front page had a feature story on a public-opinion survey conducted by the National Opinion Research Center on behalf of a group of social scientists at Stanford University. The survey, paid for by social scientists at various San Francisco Bay area colleges, was concerned with the Vietnam conflict and focused on what course of action the American public favored regarding our involvement in that country. The import of the survey, as reported by the *Times*, was that public opinion was far more amenable to a conciliatory policy leading to negotiations than was generally thought to be the case. Moreover, a stated reason for conducting the survey was to provide a deeper understanding of the mood of the public than was provided by published public-opinion polls.

On an inside page of the same issue, Tom Wicker, a member of the Washington staff of the *Times*, in a signed commentary, offered a differing analysis based on his reading of the report. He concluded that rather than showing "dovelike" tendencies, the survey revealed a public that was disturbed and confused, and had contradictory leanings. Then, on March 30, there appeared in the *Times* "Letters to the Editor" an answer to Wicker's analysis signed by the sponsors of the study. They maintained that Wicker had missed the major point of the survey's results; namely, that while there were few consistent hawks or doves, the mood of the public was very close to that of such critics of the Johnson Administration as George Kennan. A week later, on April 6, another letter, this time from political scientist Herman Finer, came to Wicker's defense. Finer cited data from the report which he interpreted to support Wicker's conclusion of widespread public confusion, and ridiculed the contention that Kennan's position was similar to the dominant trend in public opinion.

The results of the Stanford-NORC survey were also reported in the *Washington Post*, the *Washington Star*, and the *Baltimore Sun*. The two Washington papers, according to Nelson Polsby, one of the social scientists involved in the project, "preserved the Stanford groups' emphasis upon what they regarded as their most newsworthy set of findings: Although 61 percent of those polled approved of President Johnson's handling of the Vietnam conflict, majorities also approved of a number of steps to de-escalate the war."[54]

Disregarding the question as to which interpretation of the survey data is more correct, one is struck by the political significance imputed to the survey. The fact that some of the nation's most eminent social scientists thought it important and worthwhile to conduct such a survey might be considered mere evidence of professional parochialism, but this could hardly account for the fact that a number of major newspapers felt that the survey was of front-page significance. Implicit in this interchange is the belief not only that opinion surveys can be trustworthy reflections of public opinion, but that the results of polls are given attention in the formulation of public policy. While it is impossible to decide with any certainty what role earlier poll reports (most notably by the Gallup Poll and the Harris Survey) had had in the development of the Johnson Vietnam policy, the sponsors apparently were convinced that the Stanford-NORC survey would be noticed, paid attention to, and perhaps even used as a justification for reversing the growing escalation of the conflict. Similarly, a number of leading newspapers apparently felt the survey was significant enough to give it extended coverage and editorial commentary. Nevertheless, the report had no discernible impact on United States policies regarding Vietnam. A year later, Polsby concluded that the one important aid that the survey had rendered was "the clarification of the premises upon which choices are being made." He asserts that "more compelling reasons of state than public support as measured by public opinion polls had now to (be) invoked to justify the policy that was being followed."[55]

In the area of foreign policy, the public tends, initially at least, to follow whatever leadership the President provides, in the hope that it will prove to be effective. Thus, in moments of crisis, even though responsibility could justifiably be charged to the President, confidence in the President as measured by the proportion who say they approve of how the President is handling his job characteristically increases.[56] It seems unlikely that under such circumstances a President would turn to polls for guidance as to what policy he should follow. Rather, as Lipset has observed, Johnson paid "so much attention to survey results . . . not . . . to convince himself that he is doing right, or that he is following the wishes of the people . . . [but] to be sure that his approach is reaching the American public in the way he wants them affected."[57]

Nevertheless, as public-opinion polls, as well as numerous demonstrations and protests, began to show that the American public was increasingly unresponsive to Johnson's leadership, the stage was set for his announcement, on March 31, 1968, of a contraction of the air war against North Vietnam and of the withdrawal of his candidacy for reelection. While there is little reason for believing that Johnson's decisions to deescalate the Vietnam war and to withdraw his candidacy were based on the reports of public-opinion polls, it would be surprising if the trend of these reports had not been taken into account by him when making his final decisions. If, for example, poll results had suggested that the rising clamor for a change in policy was restricted to a vocal minority, it is conceivable that Johnson would have followed a different course of action.

POLLS AS "CONTINUING ELECTIONS"

Whereas opinion polls on alternative courses of action have had little, if any, effect on the *formulation* of policy, trends in the public's confidence in President Johnson's handling of the Vietnam war had an observable impact on political currents. Early in 1967, *The New York Times,* commenting on the possibility that Robert Kennedy might attempt to seek the Democratic nomination in 1968, observed:

While President Johnson may not be the most popular figure in the country just now, polls show his Vietnam policy as widely supported, offering little encouragement for the thesis that there is a broad national peace movement waiting for Mr. Kennedy to lead it.[58]

Four months later, in the wake of measurements reported simultaneously by the Gallup Poll and the Harris Survey that public confidence in Johnson had dropped to its lowest point in his administration, the *Times* wondered whether the American electorate was turning against the Vietnam war. Both Gallup and Harris reported only 39 percent voiced over-all approval of Johnson, and Gallup measured 54 percent disapproval of his handling of Vietnam. The *Times* analysis concluded:

. . . some Washington observers think the President has demonstrated remarkable talent in keeping the war acceptable to the people as long as he has. Now, it may be, the reservoir of public tolerance is running dry.[59]

If it appears that the public's vote of confidence in a President's leadership is being withdrawn, the political impact is immediate. Hopes and fears as to the consequences at election time churn in partisan circles. It is in the charting of shifting prospects for election and reelection that public-opinion polls have a clearly identifiable effect on political processes. News columnist Alan L. Otten, writing in the aftermath of the June 1967 Israeli-Arab war, has described this process graphically:

. . . a feeling (exists in the White House) that the President has emerged from the Middle East crisis with prestige enhanced—that his diplomacy helped bring an early end to the war, without any commitment of U.S. military power. Even the possibility of an indefinite stretchout of the Vietnam war has lost some of its political horror for Administration strategists.
    . . . Mr. Johnson was (earlier) running poorly in the opinion polls. Both hawks and doves were banging away at his Vietnam policy. Bobby Kennedy was riding high in Democratic favor. Republican faces dominated the TV screens and front pages; Michigan Gov. George Romney loomed as a formidable foe.
    Now the mood in high Administration circles, whether justified or not, is far different. The President's comeback in the opinion polls has been a shot of adrenalin; his own sense of relief has infected his entourage . . . At the same time, Administration strategists are quite ready to write off the anti-Johnson showings of the earlier polls . . .
    The likely Republican candidates have, under closer public scrutiny, shown flaws of their own; Mr. Romney particularly has had trouble handling hot issues. Polls show the Bobby Kennedy balloon is now sagging badly. A third party race by Alabama's ex-Gov. George Wallace is counted on by most Administration strategists as more likely to help the Democrats than hurt them . . .
    Even allowing for reasonable accuracy in the current polls, the assessments for 1968, coming from such partisan sources, may smack strongly of wishful thinking. Yet they are made not only by White House staffers inclined to look for a silver lining but also by hardheaded Democratic politicians who must make dispassionate projections on which major campaign decisions can be based.[60]

Illustrative of the kind of poll results that were encouraging to the Johnson Administration in the summer of 1967 is the trend in

Gallup Poll "trial heats" between Johnson and George Romney. Periodically, a question was asked of national samples as to which man, Johnson or Romney, those being interviewed would like to see win if the Presidential election were being held "today." After eighteen months of steadily declining strength for Johnson, so that for a while Romney had the greater support, in the spring of 1967 there was a reversal in the trend (Chart 2).

CHART 2. Trend in Johnson-Romney Trial Heats, September 1965– June 1967 (Source: Gallup Poll Release, July 1, 1967)

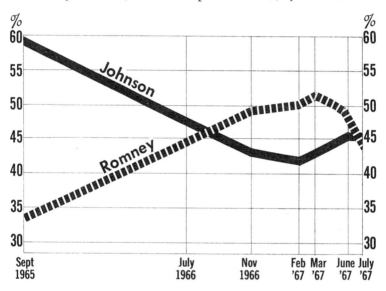

Johnson's resurgence proved transitory, however, so that by the end of the year he was once again vulnerable to challenge from members of his own party (Chart 3).

The trend in the public's confidence in the President, as reported most notably by the Gallup Poll and the Harris Survey, but also by the California Poll, the Iowa Poll, the Minnesota Poll, and the Texas Poll, produces a political "fever chart" that is closely watched by the White House and by the opposition party (Chart 4). The movement of the trend line when related to

CHART 3. Trend in the Proportion of "All Voters" Who Prefer Lyndon B. Johnson or Robert Kennedy for Democratic Presidential Candidate in 1968 (Source: Gallup Poll Release, September 30, 1967)

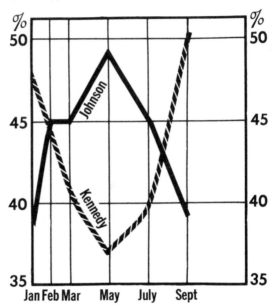

events reveals two things: (1) the public's satisfaction with the quality of leadership exhibited by the President, identified by the long-term trend, and (2) the public's response to specific acts of commission or omission.

By measuring the intensity of approval, a poll can chart the trend in the level of public confidence in a President with a heightened degree of sensitivity. For example, during the period March 1965–February 1967, not only was there a one-third decline in the proportion who voiced approval of Johnson—from 69 percent to 40 percent—but additionally the proportion who said they "strongly" approved was halved—from 32 percent to 16 percent (Chart 5). Indices such as this are carefully analyzed by leaders in both parties and by the people of the news media as these groups attempt to assess changing political currents.

CHART 4. Trend in the Proportion Expressing Approval of Johnson's Performance as President (Source: Gallup Poll Release, January 19, 1969)

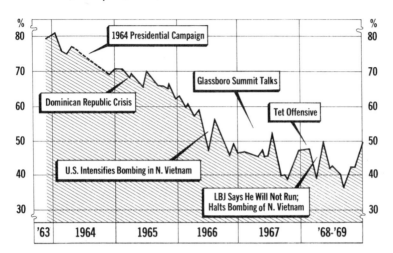

To the political analyst, the trend line measuring public approval of the President provides valuable insights as to the drift of the public's political allegiance, and into the reasons that explain that drift. On the other hand, attempting to analyze the drift in terms of opinion on specific issues, such as welfare legislation or foreign aid, often proves futile. This difference results from the often low correlation between the issue orientation of voters and their candidate preferences.[61] Voters often cast their ballots for men whose views they oppose on specific issues because those issues are not necessarily the determining ones. On the other hand, relating the trend in voter confidence to events can often identify the events which are the likely source of change in the electorate's preferences.

While the rating of the over-all confidence in the President has received most notice from the news media, other trend lines related to specific issues are also charted, though not with the same frequency. These trends, pegged as they are to specific issues, provide a basis for evaluating the impact of these issues to the over-all rating. For example, there was a close parallel

CHART 5. LBJ's Popularity: Intensity of Feeling (Source: Gallup Poll Release, February 18, 1967)

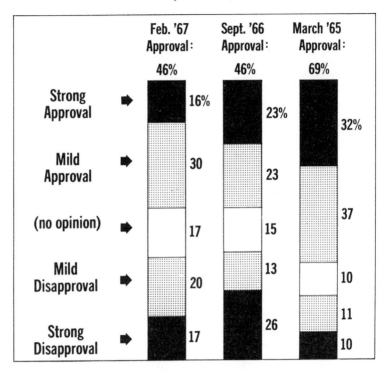

between the trend in the public's confidence as to how well Johnson handled Vietnam and his over-all rating.

Three other trend lines that have been charted by the Gallup Poll relate to confidence in the two major parties rather than in the President. They deal with opinion as to which party can do a better job of (1) handling the problem named by the persons interviewed as the most important one facing the nation, (2) keeping the nation out of another world war, and (3) keeping the country prosperous. The average of opinion, in recent elections, on the issues of peace and prosperity has approximated quite closely the actual division of the national vote as has the measurement of confidence in the ability of parties to handle the nation's "most important problem." In combination with the President's rating, these trends provide political parties with a continuing basis for evaluating their prospects for each upcoming election.

The issue-orientation of the electorate, at least as measured by opinion polls, becomes a matter of political import not in itself, but as an explanation of the trend in confidence in incumbent leaders. That is to say, responsiveness to the electorate's wishes as expressed in opinion surveys is not automatic, but is conditional upon the relevance to the vote-getting significance of those wishes. If, as is conceivable, a President retains public confidence despite the fact that the majority public-opinion favors a specific course of action to which he is opposed, it is likely that he can and will ignore with impunity the survey result. On the other hand, if his confidence rating starts dropping, dissident factions within his party as well as members of the opposition who sense a decline in his political strength may be emboldened to oppose his legislative program, and even his leadership, with greater vigor than they might otherwise have. It is the "continuing election" aspect of polls rather than their coverage of specific issues that results in their making government responsive to the public.

POLLS AND THE SELECTION OF CANDIDATES FOR OFFICE

The utilization of polls for evaluating trends in voter preferences inevitably has the effect of making the decision-making process within party hierarchies responsive to the mood of the electorate. Nevertheless, party organizations still remain powerful and exert a direct influence on political events that is distinct from and often more decisive than that of the polls. One of the salient features described by Theodore White in reporting on the 1960 and 1964 Presidential elections was the influence of party organizations and officials, plus that of wielders of economic power, in the selection of Presidential candidates.[62] In 1960, according to White, the candidacy of Stuart Symington, though unsuccessful, was wholly dependent upon the support of party and business leaders, while their counterparts in the Republican party vetoed Nelson Rockefeller's candidacy.[63] It is quite clear that if there were no specific channel for the electorate's views to become influential *before* the nominating conventions, the nominating process would be largely an expression of power and bargaining within the party hierarchies.

Two channels open to the electorate for communicating their views to the political parties are preferential primaries and preelection polls. The preferential primaries, imperfect as they are as soundings of national sentiment, do provide a setting in which potential candidates can demonstrate their ability to win votes. This opportunity is limited in that only a minority of states conduct preferential primaries. Moreover, with some exceptions such as California in 1964 and 1968, the primaries which are considered "important" in political circles often are in smaller states such as New Hampshire, West Virginia, and Oregon. For example, Tom Wicker reported in June, 1967 that looking ahead to 1968, Nixon was planning to campaign in the "major primaries," including New Hampshire and Oregon.[64] Similarly, a few months later, *Business Week* identified "three primaries as the ones to watch"—New Hampshire on March 12, Wisconsin on April 2, and Nebraska on May 14, with the May 28 Oregon primary as the possible "pay-off."[65] Thus a fraction of the total electorate can exert an influence upon the judgment of political leaders through preferential primaries far out of proportion to the number of voters involved.

Another limitation of primaries is that in many cases the choice presented to the electorate does not include the full slate of contenders. This was the case in California in 1964 when two of the leaders in nationwide surveys of rank-and-file Republicans, Nixon and Lodge, did not even appear on the ballot. Similarly, in 1968 Hubert Humphrey entered none of the Democratic primaries even though he was widely considered within the party to be the leading contender from the moment he announced his candidacy. For these reasons the true measure of public preferences becomes diffused and distorted through the primaries. But, since many delegates to the nominating conventions are committed by the results of these primaries, they do determine to some degree the distribution of actual delegate strength.

The practical significance of preferential primaries is also obvious in the reported decision of Johnson in September 1967 to organize support in New Hampshire and the immediate denial of the report.[66] As reported by Robert E. Semple, Jr., the decision was based on a concern that an unauthorized campaign to place Robert F. Kennedy on the primary ballot would threaten Johnson's reelection campaign by "touching off a major national movement behind the New York Senator." Regardless of how accurate the report may have been, the incident is illustrative of the role that preferential primaries play in the nominating process. In a comparable development, on September 28, 1967 *The New York Times* reported that Richard Nixon had declared that if he did not win both the New Hampshire and Wisconsin primaries, he would withdraw his candidacy for the Republican nomination.

The effect of public-opinion surveys contrasts sharply with that of the primaries. When carefully conducted and fully reported, surveys do provide a reliable channel of expression of the trend in the preferences of each party's rank and file. They also provide a measure of the ability of potential candidates to attract support from the opposition. Despite their measuring ability, survey results at most have respect, but not power. They cannot control delegate strength and they can be ignored in the nominating process without fear of immediate reprisal. The only sanction for ignoring public preferences as expressed in a poll, assuming that the poll is soundly conceived and validly executed, is the retribution that may take place on Election Day.

The interplay between the informational value of polls and the decisive effect of the primaries themselves has been documented by Theodore White. According to White, in 1959 John F. Kennedy concluded that "[t]he problem of the nomination hinged on the primaries; and the problem of the primaries focused on the first primary in New Hampshire to be held on March 8th, with filing required by January 28th."[67] Similarly, because of the need to demonstrate that he could win midwestern votes, Kennedy decided he had to enter the Wisconsin primary where Humphrey was expected to run strongly and where, in fact, surveys showed Kennedy trailing.[68] Additionally, the belief that he had to demonstrate an ability to win Protestant votes led to the decision to enter the West Virginia primary where early polls, conducted before the effect of the religious issue became apparent, had led Kennedy to believe he could win readily. As it turned out, later polls showed a startling reversal, so that a major, bitter effort was required to avert defeat in West Virginia.

Since effective party organizations must have adequate political intelligence, preelection polls can act to enhance the fruitfulness of campaign activities. Understanding polls as sources of political intelligence is different from assuming polls are, in themselves, political events. Illustrative of the value of the intelligence role of polls is the 1964 New Hampshire primary. White records that during the write-in campaign launched by Lodge's volunteer supporters in New Hampshire "[e]ach new effort would be measured by the public opinion analysts, who would, all through February, find a rising tide for Lodge." In contrast, Goldwater, relying upon local advisors inexperienced in Presidential politics, had expected to receive 40 percent of the vote in the New Hampshire primary.[69]

Tom Wicker, in an analysis of the difficulty Nixon was to face in his campaign for the 1968 Republican nomination, commented:

. . . Nixon's admitted weakness . . . is that he had lost two major elections in a row and has not won a campaign of his own since 1950. A recent Gallup Poll, nevertheless, showed Nixon as the choice of 43% of Republicans to only 28% for George Romney of Michigan; another poll gave him 1,212 Republican county chairmen to only 348 for Romney. To consolidate and keep that kind of support, however, Nixon has little choice but to enter the major primaries next year and prove that he can win against major opposition. . . .
A Reagan victory in Oregon could be profoundly important, in the west, where so many of Nixon's hopes are centered.[70]

Primary election results are, in contrast, decisive political events. This is why the primary elections in 1948 immediately made themselves felt in nationwide public-opinion polls on preferences as to who should be the Republican nominee that year.

TABLE 4. Preferences of Republicans for Presidential Nominee

	Dewey	Stassen
April, 1948	29	31
May, 1948	24	37
June, 1948	33	26

Source: Gallup Poll release, June 12, 1948.

The Gallup Poll in that year reported the trend in preference of Republicans as moving from Stassen to Dewey (Table 4).

In reporting this trend, the Gallup Poll noted that the survey data "reveal the shifts in voter preferences brought about by the Ohio and Oregon primaries and by the highly publicized Dewey —Stassen radio debate on Communism."

In 1964, after each of the three major primaries—New Hampshire, Oregon, and California—public-opinion polls detected shifts in voter preferences to the man who won that primary. The Gallup Poll's charting of the trend in that year shows how after each primary the victor registered gains nationally among rank and file Republicans (Table 5).

TABLE 5. Preferences of Republicans Nationally for the Presidential Nomination in 1964

	Before New Hampshire Primary, %	After New Hampshire, before Oregon, %	After Oregon, before California, %	After California Primary, %
Lodge	16	36	28	26
Nixon	34	27	29	25
Goldwater	17	15	16	21
Rockefeller	13	7	17	10
All others, no preference	20	15	10	18
	100	100	100	100

Source: Gallup Poll releases, June 21, 1964, and March 15, 1964.

In discussing the 1964 New Hampshire primary, White comments that after it

Lodge led every poll from coast to coast. From 19% in the polls in January he had become the leading choice of the Republican rank and file in April. In the aftermath of the New Hampshire victory, Oregon Republicans shifted as the nation's Republicans shifted . . . [Harris polls in Oregon showed] for Lodge 46%, for Nixon 17%, for Goldwater 14%, for Rockefeller 13%.[71]

Once Rockefeller started campaigning vigorously, however, the situation in Oregon changed so that, according to Harris, Lodge's strength faded from 40 percent to 35 percent. "Yet whether it was shifting from Lodge to Rockefeller or from Lodge to Nixon, no one could tell when the voting began."[72]

A similar relationship exists between the 1968 primary-election results and the trend that year in public preferences. In the period between Eugene McCarthy's entry into contention for the Democratic nomination and the New Hampshire primary, a period which encompassed the victory by North Vietnam and the Vietcong in their February "Tet offensive," McCarthy gained no measurable nationwide support among rank-and-file Democrats, as reported by the Gallup Poll. However, after his success in the New Hampshire primary, the result of an intensive campaign limited to that state, McCarthy's strength among Democrats nationally jumped from 18 percent to 29 percent (Table 6).

TABLE 6. Preferences Among Democrats Between Johnson and McCarthy for the 1968 Democratic Nomination

	Dec. 1967, %	Jan. 1968, %	Early March* 1968, %	Late March** 1968, %
Johnson	66	71	70	59
McCarthy	19	18	18	29
No opinion	15	11	12	12
	100	100	100	100

Source: Gallup Poll releases, February 4, 1968, and March 24, 1968.

* Before New Hampshire primary
** After New Hampshire primary

Subsequent to the New Hampshire primary, three national surveys conducted by the Gallup Poll in which the preferences of Democrats among Hubert Humphrey, Robert Kennedy, and Eugene McCarthy were measured also show how national sentiment responds to the fluctuating outcomes from primary to primary. The first survey was taken before the Indiana primary and prior to Humphrey's formal announcement of his candidacy; the second was taken after the Indiana primary but before the Nebraska primary; and the third, after Nebraska's primary but before the Oregon primary. Kennedy's assassination occurred before further surveys involving all three men could be conducted.

The trend of the three surveys (Table 7) shows that in the wake of Kennedy's entry into the race, he started as the strongest of the three. The strong showing of Branigin in Indiana, however, possibly reinforced by Humphrey's announcement, was followed by an increase in Democratic support for the latter's candidacy. Then, Kennedy's victory in Nebraska at McCarthy's expense, with Humphrey sitting it out, was followed by an increase in Kennedy's national standing among Democrats and a slight decline in McCarthy's.

Reports on public-opinion polls, on the other hand, are not followed by such shifts in voter preferences. Their impact, as information to parties and candidates planning and directing

TABLE 7. Trend in Preferences of Democrats for Humphrey, Kennedy, and McCarthy for 1968 Presidential Nomination

	April 6-11 1968	May 4-8 968	May 24-27 1968
	%	%	%
Kennedy	35	31	37
Humphrey	31	40	39
McCarthy	23	19	16
Undecided	11	10	8

Sources: *Gallup Opinion Index*, May 1968, no. 34, p. 9; and previously unpublished data from Gallup Poll Survey 762-K.

their strategies, has been indirect. In this advisory capacity opinion polls, either published or confidential, act as signals for caution or concerted attack. In this indirect and limited fashion they provide a countervailing machinery to the formal institutional processes that are otherwise dominated by entrenched powers. To be effective expressions of public preference, however, they must be soundly conducted and, most importantly, listened to and correctly interpreted.

By way of illustration, throughout 1959 John F. Kennedy and Adlai Stevenson ran neck and neck in the Gallup Poll measurements of rank-and-file Democrats (Table 8). No other candidate, including Humphrey and Johnson, really threatened either man in these national surveys. Stevenson apparently had the potential for amassing delegate strength in the preferential primaries if he wanted to use it, a potential that no contender besides John F.

TABLE 8. Trend in Preferences of Democrats for Kennedy and Stevenson for 1960 Presidential Nomination

	Named as first choice	
	Kennedy, %	Stevenson, %
January 1959	25	29
April	28	27
May	25	26
June	26	29
July	29	25
August	26	26
September	30	26
November	27	26
December	24	26
January 1960	32	28
February	35	23
March	34	23
April	39	21
May	41	21
June	42	24
July	41	25

Sources: Gallup Poll releases, February 26, 1960; April 20, 1960; July 10, 1960.

Kennedy possessed. His refusal to campaign actively surrendered the field to Kennedy, a contender with widespread appeal who also operated with effectiveness within the party organization.

In 1964, the Republican convention decisively and enthusiastically nominated a man, Barry Goldwater, that public-opinion polls had consistently indicated was the preference of a minority of the rank-and-file Republicans. Moreover, in "trial heats" against Johnson, Goldwater was one of the weakest of the Republican contenders for the nomination. A preconvention Gallup Poll, conducted in June, showed that while Johnson had a wide lead over all three leading contenders, Nixon and Scranton ran much stronger than did Goldwater (Table 9).

TABLE 9. Comparison of Goldwater's Strength with Nixon and Scranton in June 1964

	%		%		%
Nixon	27	Scranton	26	Goldwater	18
Johnson	70	Johnson	69	Johnson	77
Undecided	3	Undecided	5	Undecided	5
	100		100		100

Source: Gallup Poll release, June 30, 1964.

In a test of preference just before the nominating convention, assuming the choice for the Republican nomination were only between Scranton and Goldwater, the former emerged as the majority candidate among both Republicans and Independents (Table 10). But, as White comments,

. . . the Scranton leaders confused the applause of the press and the reading of polls with the will of the Republican party, [while] the Goldwater leadership confused the applause and praise of the San Francisco Convention with the will of the nation.[73]

The one preferential primary that Goldwater did win, against Rockefeller in California and by a narrow margin, was against the weakest of his three major contenders (Table 5 above).

The 1964 Republican nominating convention was able to ig-

TABLE 10. Preferred as Republican Nominee in June 1964

	Republicans, %	Independents, %
Scranton	60	61
Goldwater	34	26
Undecided	6	13
	100	100

Source: Gallup Poll release, July 11, 1964.

nore survey results, insofar as the nominating process was concerned, since within the structure of the party organization itself there was little recourse. It was only on Election Day, when each man's vote received equal weight, that the magnitude of the ignored opposition to Goldwater made itself felt.

One effect of Goldwater's resounding defeat has been to make leaders of both the Democratic and Republican parties increasingly sensitive to trends in public support of the incumbent President and aspiring contenders. A United Press International survey of Democratic leaders in all fifty states and the District of Columbia conducted in September 1967 "showed that in their opinion the President's margin of victory (if the 1968 election were being held then) might be as thin as 25 electoral votes, and a shift in one big state such as Illinois or Pennsylvania could turn the White House over to the GOP." The UPI analysis of this result noted that

[t]he poll results were particularly significant in view of the long standing custom of politicians to claim overwhelming victory before an election. They apparently reflected a sharp dip in the chief executive's popularity, as reported by the Louis Harris and Gallup polls last month.[74]

Simultaneously with the UPI survey, a Harris Survey reported a sharp drop in George Romney's strength in a "trial heat" against Johnson, conducted after the former's charge that he, Romney, had been "brainwashed" by the military and diplomatic corps in Vietnam in 1965. Reporting on the impact of this survey on Republican leaders, Warren Weaver, Jr. noted that Romney's "most important asset has been the fact that the polls showed him defeating President Johnson, always more decisively than any other Republican and sometimes the only Republican able to do so."[75] Weaver also commented on the effect that any decline in polls might have on Romney's financial backing:

If major contributors to the liberal Republican cause in the past should begin entertaining doubts that Mr. Romney is their best investment, it could have a paralyzing effect on his campaign, even if the public has largely forgotten his remark about brainwashing.

Coincidentally with the Harris measurement of Romney's weakening position, the Gallup Poll reported Nelson Rockefeller defeating Johnson 48 percent to 46 percent with 6 percent undecided in a "trial heat" that it had just conducted, despite the former's insistence that he was not a candidate.[76] Then, immediately prior to the New Hampshire primary, Romney announced his withdrawal because both his privately sponsored polls and the published Gallup and Harris polls were showing a continued weakness in his candidacy.

The prominent reporting of these Gallup and Harris surveys that charted Romney's declining strength and the concomitant increase in Rockefeller's strength led at least one political observer to speculate that the 1968 Presidential campaign might be "the one in which the polls replace the primary elections as the major influence in deciding which pair of a field of hopeful men will wind up running against each other for the honor of occupying the White House."[77] It is true that during 1967 the trend in voter preferences as measured by the Gallup Poll and the Harris Survey created a series of "boomlets" that significantly influenced the campaign strategies of the Republican hopefuls. It is possible that Romney's campaigning went into high gear earlier than he had planned, largely as a result of his strong standing against Johnson early in 1967 in Gallup and Harris "trial heats." Also, Rockefeller based his candidacy completely on his abortive hope that he would be able to outperform Nixon in poll measurements. Nixon, on the other hand, could anticipate that he would do well in the Republican primaries since polls consistently showed him to be far in the lead insofar as rank-and-file Republicans were concerned (Table 11).

Table 11. Preferences of Republicans as to Who
Should Be Their Presidential Candidate
in 1968

	March, 1968, %	July, 1968, %
Nixon	60	60
Rockefeller	25	23
Reagan	6	7
Lindsay	1	4
Percy	3	2
Hatfield	1	1
Stassen	1	1
No preference	3	2

Source: *Gallup Political Index,* no. 38, August 1968, p. 4.

Despite such consideration of poll information by these candidates, it seems premature to conclude that the significance of the preferential primaries as channels of communications from the electorate to party hierarchies has been eclipsed by opinion polls. Rather, politicians in 1968 used poll data in planning their strategies for the primaries and for the all-important nominating conventions. While it is clear that campaign decisions made by candidates within both parties were affected by the periodic publishing of Gallup Poll and Harris Survey measurements of voter opinion, it is also clear that the nominations were the decisions of the formal party organizations and not the parroting of what opinion polls were reporting.

In 1968 the formal Republican organization as represented at the nominating convention was reflective of its rank and file as surveyed by opinion polls. The situation in the Democratic convention, however, was comparable to that of the 1964 Republican convention in that the control of the convention was in the hands of a hierarchy that felt it could safely impose its will on the party. Most pertinent is the fact that of the three "insurgent" candidates in the two parties—Robert Kennedy, Eugene McCarthy, and Nelson Rockefeller—the man who relied exclusively on his performance in opinion polls to gain the nomination (Rockefeller) made absolutely no progress in winning support within his party. Although Humphrey easily achieved his nomination without entering a primary, Kennedy's assassination in effect abrogated much of the significance of the Democratic primaries. In any event, Humphrey's nomination was the direct consequence of his control of delegate strength, not his standing in opinion polls, and such control can be more easily influenced by the outcome of primaries than by opinion polls. While the "continuing elections" conducted by public-opinion polls did act in 1968, as in past elections, to condition the thinking and planning of those occupying positions of power in the Republican and Democratic parties, those "continuing elections" did not determine who would be nominated.

The Moderating Function of the Polls

As both the 1964 and 1968 Presidential elections show, if, when selecting candidates, party organizations ignore public-opinion polls on the electorate's preferences, they risk disaster on Election Day. Conversely, no matter how incisively public-opinion polls may report on the electorate's mood, their effect is contingent upon the willingness of political leaders to use them as reliable political intelligence.

The preelection poll has as its model Election Day, a time when each man votes once in a forced-choice situation. The differences between the preelection poll and Election Day are many, the most important being that the former is based on a sampling and the latter is institutionally binding. Nonetheless, insofar as a poll measures accurately what the result would be if an election were being held at a given point in time, it does provide a sound basis for evaluating the political wisdom of any act, regardless of whatever other justification for that act might exist. For this reason, office-holders as well as office-seekers increasingly pay attention to opinion polls, thereby giving them a quasi institutional power.

To the public, the results of preelection polls are not "events" but a possibly correct augury of what is going to occur. In contrast, to the politician public-opinion polls can be "events" if they care to see them as such. Increasingly, the trend is for politicians to react to such information as significant "events." Polls reporting changes in public sentiment assume importance in this context, not in terms of their possible influence upon the electorate, but in terms of their effect on organizational morale and the availability of support for contending candidates.

Perhaps the most significant consequence of measurements of public opinion in terms of the actual difference they have made in political life is the extent to which political leaders have come to rely upon them as trustworthy gauges of party and candidate strength. It is in this way that public-opinion polls have functioned to influence strongly the selection of each party's candidates. To the extent that they are valid and reliable measurements of overt preferences they can be expected to make parties more realistic in their selection of candidates and strategies that can win. Since this realism inevitably means the selection of candidates and strategies which will appeal to as many different segments of the electorate as possible so as to forge majority coalitions for each party, the result is likely to be a reinforcement of the tendency for elections to be fought and won on the middle ground. When, as in 1964, the middle ground is vacated by either of the two major parties, landslide elections can be anticipated. While a faction may be able to gain organizational control, such a situation is of little value on Election Day. Conversely, when, as in 1960, both candidates vie for mastery of the middle ground, extremely close elections are a likely outcome.

A long-term effect of the saliency given to the majority opinion by polls is likely to be the enhancement of the political appeal of candidates who manage effectively to compromise issues rather than to offer narrowly partisan or ideological choices. This situation in turn is likely to counteract any movements toward ideological party alignments and to strengthen the tendency for our two-party system to offer choices between candidates who differ only moderately from each other. In any event, the strategies of the competing candidates will be a direct consequence of how they interpret and use data obtained through opinion polling.

NOTES

1. Alexis de Tocqueville, *Democracy in America* (New York: Vintage Books, 1954) (paperback), vol. 2, p. 12.

2. John M. Fenton, *In Your Opinion* (Boston: Little, Brown & Co., 1960), p. 7.

3. *Ibid.,* p. 3.

4. See for example Paul F. Lazarsfeld, Bernard Berelson, and Hazel Gaudet, *The People's Choice* (New York: Duell, Sloan & Pearce, 1944); Bernard R. Berelson, Paul F. Lazarsfeld, and William N. McPhee, *Voting* (Chicago: University of Chicago Press, 1954); Angus Campbell, Gerald Gurin, and Warren E. Miller, *The Voter Decides* (Evanston: Row, Peterson and Company, 1954); Angus Campbell, Philip E. Converse, Warren E. Miller, and Donald E. Stokes, *The American Voter* (New York: John Wiley & Sons, Inc., 1960); Ithiel de Sola Pool, Robert P. Abelson, and Samuel L. Popkin, *Candidates, Issues, and Strategies* (Cambridge: The M.I.T. Press, 1964).

5. For example, Lindsay Rogers, *The Pollsters: Public Opinion, Politics, and Democratic Opinion* (New York: Alfred A. Knopf Co., 1949).

6. *Gallup Political Index,* no. 43 (January 1969), p. 6.

7. *The New York Times,* February 9, 1969.

8. Joseph T. Klapper, *Bandwagon: A Review of the Literature,* Office of Social Research, Columbia Broadcasting System, Inc., June 17, 1964 (mimeographed).

9. *Ibid.,* p. 55.

10. *Ibid.,* pp. 13–16 and Appendix A.

11. *Ibid.,* p. 15.

12. *Ibid.,* p. 16.

13. Gallup Poll release, November 4, 1968.

14. Gallup Poll releases, September 27, 1964 and December 13, 1964.

15. Six articles to which references are often made in the literature are discounted by Klapper as being topically irrelevant and/or methodologically deficient. They are: Floyd H. Allport, "Polls and the Science of Public Opinion," *Public Opinion Quarterly* (June 1940), pp. 249–257; Winston Allard, "A Test of Propaganda Values in Public Opinion Surveys," *Social Forces* (December 1941), pp. 206–213; Clare H. Marple, "The Comparative Susceptibility of Three Age Levels to the Suggestion of Group vs. Expert Opinion," *Journal of Social Psychology,* vol. 4 (1933), pp. 176–186; Daniel H. Kulp II, "Prestige as Measured by Single-Experience Changes and Their Permanency," *Journal of Education Research,* vol. 27, no. 9 (1934), pp. 663–672; David Wheeler, and H. Jordan, "Changes of Individual Opinion to Accord with Group Opinion," *Journal of Abnormal*

(*Social*) *Psychology*, vol. 24 (1929), pp. 203–206. A critique of these studies is to be found in Klapper, *op. cit.*, Appendix C.

16. Stuart W. Cook, and Alfred E. Welch, "Methods of Measuring the Practical Effect of Polls of Public Opinion," *Journal of Applied Psychology*, vol. 24 (1940), pp. 441–454.

17. *Ibid.*, p. 451.

18. Klapper, *op. cit.*, p. 18.

19. *Ibid.*, Appendix E.

20. Lazarsfeld, *et al.*, *op. cit.*; and Berelson, *et al.*, *op. cit.*

21. Klapper, *op. cit.*, pp. 31–38.

22. *Ibid.*, p. 35.

23. Lazarsfeld, *et al.*, *op. cit.*, p. 168.

24. Berelson, *et al.*, *op. cit.*, p. 289.

25. Klapper, *op. cit.*, footnote, p. 36.

26. Berelson, *et al.*, *op. cit.*, p. 85.

27. Alfred De Grazia, *The Western Public* (Stanford: Stanford University Press, 1954), p. 101 f; and Alice S. Kitt, and David B. Gleicher, "Determinants of Voting Behavior," *Public Opinion Quarterly* (Fall 1950), p. 410.

28. Lazarsfeld, *et al.*, *op. cit.*; Berelson, *et al.*, *op. cit.*; Campbell, *et al.*, *The Voter Decides*; Campbell, *et al.*, *The American Voter*.

29. Klapper, *op. cit.*, p. 23.

30. George Gallup, and Saul Forbes Rae, *The Pulse of Democracy* (New York: Simon & Schuster, Inc., 1940), p. 255.

31. Charles K. Atkin, "The Influence of Pre-Election Poll Information on Political Preferences." Paper presented to 24th Annual Conference of the American Association for Public Opinion Research, May 16, 1969, Lake George, New York (mimeographed).

32. *Wall Street Journal*, January 14, 1959.

33. Warren Weaver, Jr., *The New York Times*, April 26, 1967.

34. Warren Weaver, Jr., *The New York Times*, April 2, 1967.

35. See R. A. Butler as quoted in Mark Abrams, "Public Opinion Polls and Political Parties," *Public Opinion Quarterly* (Spring 1963), p. 12.

36. *Ibid.*, pp. 14–17 *passim*; also see Gideon Seymour in Norman C. Meier and Harold W. Saunders, eds., *The Polls and Public Opinion* (New York: Henry Holt and Company, 1949).

37. Gallup and Rae, *op. cit.*, p. 201.

38. James S. Bruner, *Mandate From the People* (New York: Duell, Sloan, and Pearce, 1944), pp. 4–5.

39. *Gallup Political Index*, no. 21 (March 1967), p. 17.

40. *The New York Times*, November 24, 1968.

41. "The Week in Review," *The New York Times*, July 9, 1967.

42. *The New York Times*, June 30, 1967.

43. *The New York Times*, July 11, 1967.

44. *The New York Times*, September 16, 1967.

45. *The New York Times,* March 11, 1967.

46. *Gallup Political Index,* no. 1 (June 1965), unpaginated.

47. Francis H. Russel in Meier and Saunders, *op. cit.,* p. 74.

48. Hadley Cantril, *The Human Dimension: Experiences in Policy Research* (New Brunswick: Rutgers University Press, 1967), pp. 41–42.

49. *Ibid.,* p. 44.

50. *Gallup Political Index,* no. 34 (April 1968), p. 3.

51. *Ibid.,* p. 51.

52. *Ibid.,* p. 54.

53. *Ibid.,* p. 81.

54. Nelson W. Polsby, "Hawks, Doves, and the Press," *Transaction* (April 1967), p. 34.

55. *Ibid.,* p. 41.

56. Fred E. Katz, and Fern V. Piret, "Circuitous Participation in Politics," *American Journal of Sociology* (January 1964), p. 369.

57. Seymour Martin Lipset, "The President, The Polls, and Vietnam," *Transaction* (September–October 1966), p. 24.

58. "The Week in Review," *The New York Times,* March 5, 1967.

59. "The Week in Review," *The New York Times,* August 13, 1967.

60. *Wall Street Journal,* June 12, 1967.

61. Berelson, *et al., op. cit.,* Chapter 10; Campbell, *et al.; The American Voter,* Chapter 10.

62. Theodore H. White, *The Making of the President 1960* (New York: Atheneum Publishers, 1961); and *The Making of the President 1964* (New York: Atheneum Publishers, 1965).

63. White, *op. cit.* (1961), pp. 73–74.

64. *The New York Times,* June 15, 1967.

65. "Washington Outlook," *Business Week* (September 9, 1967), pp. 55–56.

66. *The New York Times,* September 15 and 16, 1967.

67. White, *op. cit.* (1961), p. 74.

68. *Ibid.,* p. 83.

69. White, *op. cit.* (1965), pp. 110–111.

70. *The New York Times,* June 15, 1967.

71. White, *op. cit.* (1965), p. 112.

72. *Ibid.,* p. 115.

73. *Ibid.,* p. 198.

74. *Newark Evening News,* September 18, 1967.

75. *The New York Times,* September 18, 1967.

76. Gallup Poll release, September 16, 1967.

77. Warren Weaver, Jr., "The News in Review," *The New York Times,* October 1, 1967.

The Credibility of Voter-Preference Surveys

Preprimary and preconvention surveys of voter preferences have not changed the bases upon which candidates are selected, but have added a new dimension to the process of selection. Parties still seek men who are well known, or who are believed to have the ability to become well known rapidly. They still seek men who have a particular appeal, or who have an affinity to important interest groups such as the business community, ethnic groups, and organized labor. With rare exceptions, they still seek men whose positions on issues are sufficiently congruent with the dominant trend in the electorate so as not to lead to widespread public disaffection. Particularly when a major office is at stake, they still prefer men with that political "sex appeal" known as charisma. In sum, they still seek candidates who they think can win, or if victory is out of the question, candidates they think will run the strongest possible race.

These criteria for selection antedate preelection polls and have not been outdated by them. The contribution of the sample-survey method has been to provide a new source of information to use in evaluating the credentials of potential candidates. Two questions that arise with respect to preelection polls as a source of information are (1) How much credibility does this new source have? and (2) How subject are the polls to behind-the-scenes manipulation? This chapter is concerned with the first question; a discussion of the second is reserved for the following chapter.

The credibility of preelection polls has been defended primarily on the basis of the record of accuracy of published polls in elections. The published record of such polls for elections, national as well as local, dating back to 1936 is usually cited as incontrovertible evidence of the fact that the survey method has developed to the point where it is now capable of accurately measuring voter preferences within a small margin of error. In opposition, it has been maintained by some critical observers that a form of statistical legerdemain has been used to create an exaggerated record of reliability.

PERCENTAGE POINT VERSUS PERCENT ERROR

Specifically, some critics of public-opinion polls have attacked the practice of evaluating the accuracy of preelection polls in terms of *percentage points.* Survey organizations, when they point with pride to how close their polls come to the actual election results, characteristically use this method. Illustrative are the final Gallup and Harris surveys in 1968. Gallup's final report, after allocation of the undecided, measured Nixon's strength at 43 percent,[1] while Harris reported him as having 41 percent of the vote.[2] In the official returns Nixon received 43.5 percent, considering only the vote for the three major-party candidates. In percentage points, Gallup's error margin is 0.5 points, while Harris' is 2.5 points. Critics such as Lindsay Rogers[3] and Senator Albert Gore[4] have in the past contended that the use of percentage points for evaluating error is a subterfuge in that it understates the true error. They maintain that the proper criterion is the *percent* error—for example, the percent that 0.5 is of 43.5 percent, or that 2.5 is of 43.5 percent. In these terms, Gallup's error in 1968 was about 1 percent and Harris' about 6 percent. (Complicating the issue is the fact that all too frequently the niceties of statistical usage are ignored by the less rigorous and uninformed who calculate the percentage-point error but then proceed to call it the "percent" error.)

The critics' contention is that the use of percentage points is a deliberate attempt to make preelection polls appear more accurate than they really are. Thus the issue becomes not only the accuracy of these polls but also the integrity of the pollsters. Standard statistical practice and theory, however, indicate that the use of percentage points is proper and accurate. For example, consider the case in which a poll reports 80 percent for Candidate A and 20 percent for Candidate B, but the election returns are 90 percent to 10 percent. Using the *percent* criterion the error for Candidate A would be 11 percent, but for Candidate B it would be 100 percent. The *percentage-point* criterion, in contrast, shows an error of ten percentage points no matter which candidate is considered. Clearly, the latter method is less subject to misinterpretation and confusion.

Second, and even more to the point, every statistical textbook deals with sampling error in terms of percentage points. Standard tests of statistical significance are calculated in terms of percentage points because this is the criterion that conforms to the appropriate mathematical theory. Thus, when evaluating what allowance should be made for the fact that a sample rather than the entire population was interviewed, the prescribed procedure is to calculate how many percentage points, plus or minus, should be allowed for a given sample size. Whatever vulnerability pollsters may have with respect to claims they make as to the accuracy of preelection polls, there is no doubt that they are on solid statistical ground in using the percentage-point criterion.

WHAT DO "THE POLLS" SHOW?

A major difficulty in assessing the credibility of preelection surveys is the widespread practice of referring to "the polls" and to what "they" are showing. There are many different types of "polls," ranging from carefully designed sample surveys based upon personal interviews to such devices as counting how many people send away for free copies of photographs of contending candidates. Other frequently encountered methods are mail surveys to telephone or newspaper subscribers, invitations to clip coupons out of newspapers and mail them in, requests for listeners to send a postal card to their local radio or television station, and interviews with "quotas" of men and women at supermarkets, factories, and other heavy-traffic locations. To treat all such methods as comparable with personal interviews based on mathematically designed samples of the electorate can only becloud the issue. Unfortunately, as Elmo Roper has noted, "To too many members of the press, a poll is a poll is a poll."[5] Because of this "unwillingness to discriminate between the available polls," Roper continues, there is ". . . a general skepticism toward polls, which are often assumed to be as likely to miss as to hit election results on the nose."

In a pioneer effort to evaluate how well "the polls" did in 1960, Bernard C. and Erna R. Hennessy reviewed "26 separate measurements of electoral preference or voting intention. Of these, all except one were styled polls, straw votes, or opinion surveys."[6] The Hennessys used two criteria to measure the performance of these polls: (1) "error," that is, the percentage-point deviation from the election result; and (2) "accuracy," that is, whether the winner was predicted or not. In fourteen newspaper-conducted statewide polls, which used a conglomerate of methods ranging from postal cards mailed to subscribers to personal interviews with carefully drawn samples, thirteen correctly "predicted" the winner while one reported a 50–50 split. (The actual split in that case was 50.7–49.3.) In percentage points, one poll had an error of 16.8 points, four had errors between 3 and 6 points, four had errors between 2 and 3 points and five had errors of less than 2 points. Believing that "the critical question [is] who gets the most votes," the Hennessys maintain that the "errors were consistently errors which were irrelevant to picking the winner." They conclude that luck determines "accuracy," as they define it.[7]

They also reviewed "twelve" national polls, "three" of which were Gallup surveys. One of the Gallup surveys used, and the most accurate of all "twelve," was its final report of the 1960 election campaign. The other "two" Gallup surveys were results of a single national survey taken five weeks before the election and reported separately for the South and non-South. Since the *early* Gallup survey had "errors" of 1.8 points in the South and 2.7 points in the non-South, both in the wrong direction, they conclude that "luck again made Gallup a winner rather than a loser" in the *final* poll. The lesson the Hennessys draw from their analysis is that unsophisticated sampling such as loose quota samples and mail ballots may often be as satisfactory as rigorous adherence to the principles of scientific sampling, and that pollsters may, in close elections, have to rely to a considerable degree on hunch and luck.[8]

In a point-by-point critique of the Hennessys' analysis, Paul K. Perry made the following observations which are relevant to the issue of credibility:[9]

1. The Hennessys provide no specific information about sample sizes, without which it is impossible to compare the accuracy of any surveys. For example, all other things being equal, a sample of 5,000 interviews should be more accurate than one of 500 interviews. Reporting the size of "error" without relating this to sample size does not provide any basis for evaluating the accuracy of any survey.

2. The indiscriminate lumping of poll results regardless of proximity to Election Day, a practice which is reflective of the view that all results are equally "predictions," is not valid. The fact that a poll conducted more than a month before an election deviates from the election results more than another conducted a few days before is no proof that the former's methodology is inferior. Some voters always change their minds in the final weeks of a campaign, so that an early poll, even though accurate as of when it was conducted, may deviate significantly from the election results.

3. Without an elucidation of the methods used in each poll and the care with which they were administered it is impossible to assess the role that luck played. Since the sample method has built into it random or "chance" fluctuations, in any single election a poorly designed and administered poll, through luck, could be as close to the election results as one that was carefully planned and executed. A single "chance" congruence of results is little reason for preferring the less expensive and less soundly conceived poll.

Perry concludes:

. . . an evaluation of a poll or election survey result can be made only with reference to a number of factors. Some of the more important ones are: the length of time between the survey and the election, the sampling procedure, the method of obtaining a respondent's choice, the division of the vote, the method of selecting from among all the respondents those likely to vote, and the way in which the estimate is calculated.[10]

Unfortunately, since the Hennessys lacked detailed information about the methodology employed by the "polls" they reviewed, they had to proceed on the assumption that "a poll is a poll is a poll."

In addition, the Hennessys did not take into account a difficulty that arises in evaluating accuracy claims; namely, that even without a high degree of methodological sophistication the sample survey method has a basic validity in that a crude sampling can usually yield a rough approximation of the actual state of affairs. This makes it possible for many preelection "polls" which use crude methods to obtain measurements of voter preferences that often do not deviate excessively from actual election results. Thus, except in close elections, poorly designed polls may compile a seemingly impressive record of correctly "calling the winner" and consequently appear to be soundly conducted.

Illustrative of the inadequacy of the criterion of "calling the winner" is the case of the "*New York Daily News* Poll," acclaimed in the news media of 1966 as being "widely respected." In 1964, the *New York Daily News* had congratulated itself for its "bullseye accuracy" in correctly calling a landslide victory for Johnson in New York state.[11] Noted late in the story was their fairly large error of six percentage points. This was described as reflecting "one of the mysteries of polling . . . our concern has been with the people and how they want to vote, not with percentages, which are a statistical invention." An objective evaluation of the *News'* accuracy record and, therefore, its credibility, should be based on its percentage-point error. The actual performance of the *Daily News* Poll up through 1966 in terms of percentage-point error has been summarized by Roll:

The average deviation between the winner's election percentage and his final *News* figure (in 26 elections) is 5.9 points . . . There are, furthermore, some drastically wide discrepancies between forecast and fact. Five Straw Polls gave results between 5.3 and 9.2 points from the winner's actual total . . . and six others, more than 10 points . . .[12]

A lack of awareness on the part of politicians and the news media of the size of error in earlier *Daily News* Polls in all likelihood led to the unwarranted weight given to it when, in the New York gubernatorial election, it incorrectly forecast an O'Connor victory over Rockefeller. For example, *The New York Times* noted a few days before Election Day:

The News Poll in particular has made politicians cautious about predicting anything but an O'Connor victory. . . . It is the News Poll actually that is credited with producing much of the optimism that does exist in the O'Connor camp.[13]

Similarly, Rockefeller, despite his private polls which accurately measured his margin of victory, said after the election, "I didn't dare be optimistic in view of the *Daily News* Poll."[14]

If any methodological changes are made, however, as was done by the *Daily News* Poll for its 1968 operation, past performance may be a misleading guide. Changes in methodology undoubtedly account for the accuracy of the *Daily News* Poll in that year. Previously, the *News* had conducted its surveys as a single statewide operation based on 30,000 ballots accumulated over a 20-day period. In 1968, however, five statewide polls were conducted, each over a four-day period and each consisting of about 6,000 ballots. The *News* explained this methodological refinement in these terms:

By comparing the results of one sample with those of another, it was possible to gauge shifts in opinion. . . . Because (in past years) early straws were combined with late straws . . . last minute opinion shifts were difficult to detect.[15]

The final *Daily News* Poll showed 43.5 percent for Nixon, 46.8 percent for Humphrey, 6.8 percent for Wallace, and 2.9 percent undecided in New York state. Allowing for some ambiguity due to the unallocated undecided vote, this breakdown compares quite favorably with the actual vote of 44.3 percent for Nixon, 49.8 percent for Humphrey, 5.3 percent for Wallace, and 0.6 percent for other candidates.

METHODOLOGICAL PROGRESS IN PREELECTION POLLING

One objective, statistical criterion for evaluating preelection polls—those surveys conducted close to Election Day—is the degree to which they *consistently* report final survey results that, in percentage points, are close approximations of the actual split in the election. Using the percentage-point criterion, a poll which "predicted" the winner with a six percentage-point error did very poorly as compared with one with a two percentage-point error but with the loser ahead. Using this criterion, there has been appreciable progress in the precision of preelection poll methodology, at least as practiced by some survey organizations.

The record of the Gallup Poll, which is the only organization that has published preelection survey results in every national election since 1936, provides a basis for assessing the degree to which methodological advances have been made since the beginnings of modern polling in that year. In the nine elections between 1936 and 1950, the average error of the final preelection Gallup Poll survey, as published the day before election, was 3.7 percentage points. In the eight elections from 1954 through 1968, the average error was reduced to 1.4 percentage points. Moreover, during these last eight elections the *largest* deviation was 2.8 percentage points, which is less than the average error in the previous nine elections.[16]

The research methods employed by the Gallup Poll since 1950 for its preelection surveys, which account for this reduction in error, have been described in considerable detail by Paul K. Perry, president of The Gallup Organziation.[17] Perry, who has been in charge of preelection surveys since 1950, presents the most detailed description yet available of the actual methods employed by any public-opinion poll, which makes it possible to

relate the Gallup Poll's accuracy record specifically to its methodology. As he describes them, these methods derive from no
arcane techniques or subjectively derived insights, but rather
from the meticulous application of statistical and social-science
theory. The major features relate to the sample design, the
identification of likely voters, the obtaining of valid expressions
of voter preferences with a minimum "undecided" vote, and the
measurement of shifts in voter preferences during the campaign.

SAMPLE

A sample of election precincts is drawn for the entire nation
with probability of selection proportional to the size of the voting
population. Interviewers are provided with maps of these areas;
they follow a prescribed route and call at every $n'th$ household,
selecting those to be interviewed in accordance with a prescribed
selection procedure. No sex, age, or socioeconomic "quotas" are
used. Interviewing is conducted in the evening when both men
and women are to be found at home. While a tight schedule of
three days prevents calling back to interview people who are not
at home when the interviewer calls, a statistical substitute for call-
backs is employed.[18]

This sample procedure takes the selection of those to be interviewed completely out of the hands of the interviewer; without
this safeguard a sample bias could occur. While time schedules
make necessary some deviation from the rules of probability
sampling, this deviation is minimal. Thus, unlike hit-or-miss
street-corner interviews, mail surveys with low response rates, or
quota sampling, there is a reasonably sufficient mathematical
basis for calculating what allowance should be made for sampling error, and the dangers of sample bias resulting from some
kinds of people being systematically excluded from the sample is
at a minimum. (Moreover, using election precincts as the areal
sampling unit makes it possible to use the vote by precincts in a
previous election as supplementary data to reduce the sampling
variance [error] of the estimate of vote-preference formed from
the survey data.)

LIKELY VOTERS

A major source of error in election surveys, in addition to sampling error, is the fact that so many people do not vote. In 1968, about four out of every ten persons of voting age did not cast a ballot for any of the Presidential candidates. As Samuel Stouffer has pointed out, ". . . with the best of probability samples, if you get 85 percent of the people telling you whom they prefer, and only 50 percent are going to vote, you have a margin of error there that is positively staggering. . . ."[19]

Perry, beginning in 1950, developed for the Gallup Poll a method for identifying likely voters. First, to rank respondents by likelihood of voting the Gallup Poll in 1968 used a series of nine questions to construct a "turnout scale." (In earlier years, a shorter series was used.) This scale, first used in 1950 in its shorter form, has been validated in every election since then by checking registration books to find out *whether* respondents voted. The scoring system has been refined each year so that in 1966, of those identified as most likely to vote, 87 percent actually did so. Of those identified as least likely to vote, less than one percent voted.

Once respondents are ranked by likelihood of voting, it then becomes necessary to determine the "cutting point" on the scale; that is, the point that divides the sample into two groups—likely voters and unlikely voters. In 1956, a method was devised by Perry and Crespi using two of the items on the turnout scale to develop an index number which estimates the turnout in an election. In the four Presidential elections in which this method has been used, the estimated turnout ratio has been within less than two percentage points of the actual (Table 1). The reported Gallup Poll preelection survey results are based on the preferences of likely voters as identified by this method.

EXPRESSIONS OF VOTER PREFERENCE

A basic problem in obtaining valid expressions of voter preferences is the difficulty in minimizing the "undecided" vote and

TABLE 1. Voter Turnout in Four Presidential Elections
Compared with Gallup Poll Estimate

	Actual Voter Turnout[*]	Gallup Poll Estimate[**]
	%	%
1956	62.8	62.9
1960	66.5	68.3
1964	65.3	65.5
1968	64.0	64.7

[*] Percentage who voted of total civilian resident population of voting age, excluding aliens and inmates of correctional and mental institutions.
[**] Previously unpublished estimates based on interviewing conducted five weeks before Election Day.

possible evasive or misleading answers. Three techniques are used to solve this problem: (1) wording the question in terms of voting preference "if the election were being held today," rather than asking how respondents say they intend to vote in the future; (2) using a forced-choice question which asks those who are undecided or refuse to voice a preference in which political direction they "lean"; and (3) using a paper "secret ballot" on which respondents mark their choice and which they then place in a sealed box. (The specific method in which the secret ballot is used was developed by the late Sidney Goldish, who at the time had been director of the Minnesota Poll.)

The combination of these methods, when applied to "likely voters," typically reduces the undecided vote to about 3 to 5 percent, and the closeness of the final survey results to the actual returns is indicative of the validity with which the question is answered.

LAST-MINUTE SHIFTS

By asking for preferences as of "today," the Gallup Poll relates each measurement to a specific point in time. This makes it possible to measure trends in voter preference. The final preelection survey is taken during the week immediately preceding the election, and every effort is made to schedule the interviewing as close as possible to Election Day. In 1968 interviewing was conducted on Thursday and Friday evenings and Saturday morning through noon. Immediately upon completion of their assignments, interviewers wired their results to Gallup headquarters in Princeton where data processing and analysis were completed by Saturday midnight. On Sunday afternoon the results were wired to subscribing newspapers for Monday publication.

To make possible such a time schedule, two identically designed surveys are conducted, one about a month before the election and the other the week previous, as just described. In each survey in 1968, about 4,500 individuals of voting age were personally interviewed. The data from the first survey were fully analyzed to determine the division of voter preferences *as of that time*. Then, by calculating the difference between a gross measurement on each of the two surveys, and applying this difference to the refined estimate based on the first survey, the "final figure" was reached.

The use of this full method, Perry reports, has reduced the average deviation of the final survey from the election to a point "which conforms closely to the theoretical expectation for samples of the sizes used drawn as random samples."[20]

The value of timing the final survey as close as possible to Election Day is threefold. First, and of greatest relevance to the question of credibility, is the fact that the final survey establishes a meaningful basis whereby the public evaluates the accuracy of the sample-survey method. It is true that the final survey is not, as such, a prediction of what will happen on Election Day, since intervening events could lead to a significant shift in opinion over the final weekend. Strictly speaking, using the final survey as a prediction requires projecting the survey result into the future; and this projection involves making assumptions that are not always warranted. But, in the absence of any particularly startling or dramatic occurrence in the last few days before election, it is reasonable to expect that the final survey results should correspond closely to the actual vote cast. The record of these final surveys, consequently, is cited by the Gallup Poll as proof of the credibility of all its reports. Gallup has said:

> . . . I see no great social value in reporting twenty-four hours in advance of an election how the country is going to vote, or approximately how it is going to vote, but I do think that elections are valuable in providing an acid test for polling techniques.[21]

In the wake of the highly accurate 1968 results, Gallup made an even stronger claim as to the value of using preelection polls as a way of empirically validating the survey method:

> The Gallup Poll has developed a thoroughly scientific approach to election polling. Far more important than this, however, is that it has demonstrated that when a scientific method is used, instead of subjective judgment, human behavior in the aggregate can be predicted—the goal of social science. . . .
>
> Perhaps most important of all is the proof that reliable responses can be obtained from the public in sample surveys, and the employment of attitude measurements can be used to predict mass behavior with great accuracy.[22]

This function has been noted by the Social Science Research Council:

> Elections are useful for testing the adequacy of polling methods for estimating the percentages of the vote going to each candidate from various groups in the population. No better test is now known.[23]

Second, and of interest to politicians, political analysts, and social scientists, timing the final survey as close as possible to Election Day makes possible an analysis of the actual vote in terms of demographic and socioeconomic characteristics based on expressions of preferences voiced almost at the point in time when the votes are cast. Such analyses are regularly published after every election. Since actual votes are anonymous, they cannot be analyzed in terms of age, sex, income, or education, which makes the survey data extremely valuable to political analysts and scholars (Table 2).

The value of preelection polls to social scientists is also evident in Lazarsfeld's comment:

> I am very definitely in favor of political forecasts because only by trying and trying over again to make political forecasts will we finally learn to understand what really explains political behavior of people . . . forecasting and explaining are really the same. . . . If I under-

TABLE 2. Analysis of Presidential Vote by Demographic Characteristics, from 1952 to 1968

Dem.–D Rep.–R Wallace–W	1952 D %	1952 R %	1956 D %	1956 R %	1960 D %	1960 R %	1964 D %	1964 R %	1968 D %	1968 R %	1968 W %
NATIONAL	44.6	55.4	42.2	57.8	50.1	49.9	61.3	38.7	43.0	43.4	13.6
Men	47	53	45	55	52	48	60	40	41	43	16
Women	42	58	39	61	49	51	62	38	45	43	12
White	43	57	41	59	49	51	59	41	38	47	15
Non-white	79	21	61	39	68	32	94	6	85	12	3
College	34	66	31	69	39	61	52	48	42	54	9
High School	45	55	42	58	52	48	62	38	42	43	15
Grade School	52	48	50	50	55	45	66	34	52	33	15
Prof. & Bus.	36	64	32	68	42	58	54	46	34	56	10
White Collar	40	60	37	63	48	52	57	43	41	47	12
Manual	55	45	50	50	60	40	71	29	50	35	15
Farmers	33	67	46	54	48	52	53	47	29	51	20
Under 30	51	49	43	57	54	46	64	36	47	38	15
30–49 years	47	53	45	55	54	46	63	37	44	41	15
50 years & older	39	61	39	61	46	54	59	41	41	47	12
Protestant	37	63	37	63	38	62	55	45	35	49	16
Catholic	56	44	51	49	78	22	76	24	59	33	8
Republicans	8	92	4	96	5	95	20	80	9	86	5
Democrats	77	23	85	15	84	16	87	13	74	12	14
Independents	35	65	30	70	43	57	56	44	31	44	25

Source: Gallup Poll release, December 8, 1968.

stand something I can also predict what will happen, and if I cannot predict I cannot also understand . . . no one will seriously raise the question, "Should political behavior be understood?"[24]

Third, but of weight primarily to the financial security of the survey organization, is the preelection poll's journalistic value of being able to report a "final figure" the day before the election. If such a report were not available, it is likely that many newspapers would not support the published opinion polls. Gideon Seymour, Vice President and Executive Editor of *The Minneapolis Star and Tribune* which sponsors the Minneapolis Poll, in justifying the publication of preelection polls, has expressed the journalist's attitude in these terms:

. . . in many respects . . . the most important point . . . [is] that opinion studies are eminently newsworthy. . . . Public opinion surveying . . . reflects the impact of ideas and prejudices and events and propaganda upon the people themselves. It is simply news reporting in a new field, a field that has to be studied if a newspaper is to report fully the trend and patterns of the times and of the changing world.[25]

Gallup, in defending the publication of preelection polls, took essentially the same position when he said, ". . . as a matter of fact, I think the only justification for public opinion polls is to report the views of the people of this country on issues of the day."[26]

RECENT ACCURACY RECORD OF PUBLISHED POLLS

In the three most recent Presidential elections—1960, 1964, and 1968—as well as in the 1966 congressional elections, the final surveys of the leading published polls established the credibility of preelection polls for the general public, journalists, and politicians.

In 1960 all the major published polls indicated the closeness of the Kennedy-Nixon race. The two polls with the smallest deviations from the election results were those of Gallup and Roper. The final Gallup survey, published the day before election, reported a 51–49 lead for Kennedy, which was 0.9 percentage points from the actual vote. Roper's final survey, while it showed Nixon slightly ahead, was merely 1.1 percentage points off the mark.

In 1964 the final Gallup survey and the final Harris survey reported Johnson ahead in the popular vote by a 64–36 margin, which is quite close to the 61.7–38.3 percent split in the official returns. In the 1966 congressional elections the final Gallup Poll reported the Democrats ahead with a projected 52.5 percent of the total vote in all congressional races, indicative of a gain of 35 to 55 House seats for the Republicans. The final Harris Survey projected a 30–35 seat gain for the Republicans based upon a Democratic vote of 54 percent.[27] In the official tally of all votes, the Democrats received 51.9 percent of the vote and the Republicans gained 47 seats.

To evaluate the 1966 record fully, it should be noted that *The New York Times* had predicted that Republican gains were most likely to be limited to 29 seats.[28] In developing its forecast, *The Times* used the traditional journalistic method of having reporters interview leaders of both parties and other political "experts" in all states in order that an assessment of the outcome in each state's contests could be reached. Also reported by *The Times* was Richard Nixon's "optimistic," presumably partisan forecast of a Republican gain of about forty seats. The Gallup preelection report was given passing note, which would explain why on the day after election *The Times* headlined its report on the election results, "Republicans Stronger Than Expected In Off Year Vote." It is the increasing sophistication of the sample-survey method in accurately measuring trends in voter preferences, as compared with the methods of traditional journalism, that has made for the increasing credibility of preelection polls.

In 1968 the final Gallup Poll release reported 43 percent for Nixon, 42 percent for Humphrey, and 15 percent for Wallace, which results correctly presaged Nixon's narrow margin of victory over Humphrey—43.5 percent to 42.9 percent.[29] While the final Harris Survey had Humphrey in the lead, it was also very close to the actual election—Humphrey 45 percent, Nixon 41 percent, and Wallace 14 percent.[30]

VARIATIONS IN ACCURACY RESULTING FROM THE METHODS USED

To comprehend the significant improvements that have been made in sample surveys of voter preferences since 1936 and subsequent to 1948 it is necessary to recognize the extent to which different question-wordings and analytical procedures can produce varying results. The identification of how such factors affect survey results presents the pollster with the problem of determining which of the myriad methods that could be used will *consistently* produce accurate reflections of voter opinion.

For example, in 1952, before the efficacy of the Gallup Poll's new methodology had been validated, and in the wake of the 1948 experience, a very cautious way of reporting candidate strength was utilized. Two different questions were asked, one couched in terms of which *party* was preferred while the other measured the voter's preference of the *candidates themselves*. Also, in the analysis of the undecided vote, weight was given to such factors as past voting behavior, basic party loyalties, position on issues, and socioeconomic characteristics. No objective basis for weighting these factors was available, making possible plausible alternate methods of allocating the "undecideds." The consequence of this method was the reporting of a series of alternatives as measurements of the comparative strength of Eisenhower and Stevenson. The final Gallup Poll report before election consequently presented the array of measurements shown in Table 3; the report indicated a possible range from a decisive Eisenhower victory to a narrow margin for Stevenson. The actual election returns gave Eisenhower 55.4 percent of the popular vote.

The data in Table 3 show, first of all, that the "party" question produced a measurement that overstated Stevenson's strength. Apparently there were enough Democrats willing to say they preferred Eisenhower, the man, but who were reluctant to say that they preferred the Republican party's candidate. Second, since one of Eisenhower's strengths was his appeal to Democrats,

TABLE 3. Variations in Measured Voter Preferences as Reported in the Final 1952 Gallup Preelection Report

	As Measured by Candidate Preference Question		As Measured by Party Preference Question	
		%		%
Before allocating "undecided":				
	Eisenhower	47	Republican	45
	Stevenson	40	Democratic	44
	Undecided	13	Undecided	11
		100		100
Allocating "undecided" 2–1 to Stevenson:				
	Eisenhower	51	Republican	49
	Stevenson	49	Democratic	51
		100		100
Allocating "undecided" 3–1 to Stevenson:				
	Eisenhower	50	Republican	48
	Stevenson	50	Democratic	52
		100		100

Source: Gallup Poll release, November 2, 1952.

who tend to be of lower socioeconomic status than Republicans, assessing the undecided in terms of past preference and of socioeconomic characteristics also overstated Stevenson's position. A reanalysis of the same data, using only the candidate preference question and a "forced choice" follow-up to allocate the undecided vote, shows that if this method had been used, the final Gallup measurement of 1952 would have been within one percentage point of the actual vote.[31] This procedure for handling the "undecided," as already noted, is integral to the method now used by the Gallup Poll. This example demonstrates again the impossibility of evaluating the accuracy of polls as such. What must be assessed is the accuracy of a specific method, including sample design, interviewing procedures, and analytical techniques.

The importance and difficulty of fully and correctly assessing the reliability of preelection polls are further evidenced by the final Gallup and Harris reports in 1964. Both polls reported on the Monday before election a 64–36 margin for Johnson, after allocating the undecided votes. Their agreement, however, is not as complete as first reading might indicate. Throughout most of the campaign, the Gallup Poll measured Johnson's strength at a higher level than did the Harris Survey. Thus, in order for the two surveys to be in agreement at the end, they had to be in disagreement as to what the trend was in the final weeks of the campaign. Judging from the Gallup Poll, there was a slight movement toward Goldwater, accounted for primarily by the return to the fold of some defecting Republicans. In contrast, the Harris Survey trend indicated that Goldwater lost some strength in the final weeks of the campaign, though by a slight margin.[32]

By way of comparison, in a survey conducted in August 1964 for NBC, Roper reported 67 percent for Johnson, 28 percent for Goldwater, and 5 percent undecided.[33] At about that time, Gallup was reporting 65 percent for Johnson, 29 percent for Goldwater, and 6 percent undecided,[34] whereas the early August Harris Survey measurement was 59 percent for Johnson, 32 percent for Goldwater, and 9 percent undecided.[35]

Differences between the 1964 Harris and Gallup measurements may be the result of different methodologies rather than of sampling error. For example, early in the year, well before the conventions, Gallup and Harris issued reports that differed markedly as to how much stronger Johnson was than the three leading Republican contenders (Table 4). It is unlikely that sampling error could account for such a large divergence. In 1968 also, the somewhat divergent accuracy of the Gallup and Harris polls may have been the result of methodological differences as well as sampling error. The Gallup Poll had the smallest margin of error and indicated a Nixon victory by the narrowest of margins. While the Harris Survey indicated a Humphrey win, its error was within the "statistical margin of error of 3 to 4 points plus or

TABLE 4. Comparison of Gallup Poll and Harris Poll "Trial Heats" Reported in January, 1964

	Gallup %	Harris %
Johnson vs. Nixon		
Johnson	69	59
Nixon	24	41
Undecided	7	—
Johnson vs. Rockefeller		
Johnson	77	71
Rockefeller	16	29
Undecided	7	—
Johnson vs. Goldwater		
Johnson	75	67
Goldwater	18	33
Undecided	7	—

Source: *U.S. News & World Report*, February 10, 1964, p. 37.

minus" that Harris said should be allowed for his sample size.[36] This allowance for sampling error, Harris reported, made "the election too close to call in this highly volatile year."

In assessing the divergence of the Harris measurement, consideration must be given to the ways in which his methodology differs from that of the Gallup Poll. Harris has reported that three preference questions are asked in the course of an interview of one and one-half hours' duration—a direct question at the beginning of the interview, a secret question near the end, and another direct question at the end.[37] In contrast, the Gallup Poll asks one secret question relatively early in the interview. To measure last minute trends in 1968, the Harris Survey used a method very different from the Gallup Poll's. Surveys were conducted on the Friday, Saturday, and Sunday before the election, based on three independent, equal-sized samples, using a replicated sample design. In the Friday survey Nixon had a three-point lead over Humphrey, on Saturday Humphrey had achieved a one-point lead, and on Sunday Humphrey had a three-point lead. While a three-day average, Harris reports, would have shown Nixon and Humphrey in a dead heat, it was felt that the three surveys had measured a real trend, so the Sunday survey result was used by itself for the final Harris report.[38] This choice, apparently, is the basis for the last sentence in that report: "If the late trend continued, however, it would indicate a potential majority for Humphrey in the Electoral College."

A further differentiation between the two polls may lie in the area of identifying likely voters. The Gallup Poll samples all adults of voting age and then excludes likely nonvoters, as described earlier. The Harris Survey excludes from its sample persons who report they are not registered, and does not interview them at all. It then makes a further exclusion of likely nonvoters, but the specific manner in which this is done has not been published.

An incident in February, 1967 demonstrates the extent to which national political leaders who rely upon polls of voter preferences as they plan organization support for their candidates may be confused by methodological differences between surveys. On February 12, 1967, Warren Weaver reported in *The New York Times* that

[a] Gallup Poll that would have shown Richard M. Nixon surging past George Romney as the presidential candidate preferred by most Republicans was ordered withdrawn today hours before its scheduled publication.

A rough version of the poll figures, indicating an 11 point drop in Governor Romney's popularity in less than three months, had been circulating among politicians here for two days, causing consternation among supporters of the Governor and glee among his detractors.

Weaver also reported that it was "understood that the Harris poll will show Governor Romney with a lead of about 12 points over Mr. Nixon when all Republican candidates are considered," leading to speculation that political pressure had led to the suppression of the Gallup release.

The reason for the withdrawal of the release was given by the Gallup Poll in these terms:

The Gallup Poll originally scheduled for Sunday, February 12, was withdrawn two days before the publication date because the results were incorrectly dealt with in terms of a trend since the November survey. A difference in question wording between the two surveys makes such a comparison invalid. Today's release gives the full findings for the latest survey.[39]

The release referred to in the statement was published on February 14, reporting the latest standings of Romney and Nixon. The difficulty was that in the survey reported on February 14 the question asked referred to which man was rated the "best" candidate, whereas in November the question was worded in terms of which man was "preferred." Since such a difference in question-wording could in itself cause a shift in standings, the reporting of a trend on the basis of two different question-wordings, as was mistakenly done in the withdrawn release, would be misleading. To determine whether the question-wording would, in fact, alter standings, both wordings were used in two subsequent surveys, both of which used a split-sample design. The full question wordings were:

Best man: Which one of the men on this list do you think would make the best Presidential candidate for the Republican Party in 1968?

Like to See Nominated: Here is a list of men who have been mentioned as possible Presidential candidates for the Republican Party in 1968. Which one would you like to see nominated as the Republican candidate for President in 1968?

The results for these questions as reported by the Gallup Poll on February 13 and March 19 are shown in Table 5. Comparing the two March figures, while the question-wording did not change the proportion that named Nixon, Romney fared somewhat bet-

TABLE 5. Preferences of Republicans for 1964 Candidate

| | Best Man | | Like to See Nominated | |
	Feb. 1967	Mar. 1967	Mar. 1967	Nov. 1966
Nixon	39	39	39	31
Romney	28	34	30	39

Sources: Gallup Poll releases, February 13, 1967, and March 19, 1967.

ter as the "best man" than as the man Republicans would "like to see nominated." While the difference is not large, reporting a "trend" based on the November and February surveys would have been incorrect.

The Harris Survey in February reported that 41 percent of Republicans named Romney as their first choice, while 28 percent named Nixon. These figures deviate significantly from the February Gallup Poll. However, since the exact wording of the Harris question was not given, since variations in question-wordings demonstrably can affect measurements of preferences, and since interviewing dates for the two surveys seem not to have been concurrent, it is difficult to evaluate the meaning of this deviation. In any case, this incident illustrates that party organizations, in their use of surveys of voter preferences, in order to interpret correctly exactly what a reported result means, must be informed about the specific methodology that was employed.

In the heat of a campaign, however, partisan allegiances make it very difficult for an objective assessment to be made of the effects of differing survey methodologies. During the 1968 Presidential campaign there were consistent differences between Gallup Poll and Harris Survey results that for a time seemed likely to form a political issue almost as important as some of those raised by the candidates themselves. Both survey organizations reported a dramatic surge in Humphrey's strength in the last weeks of the campaign. Nevertheless, they differed in that (1) the Gallup Poll trend showed Humphrey coming from further behind than did the Harris Survey; (2) the final Harris Survey indicated the probability that Humphrey had managed to move ahead of Nixon, whereas the final Gallup Poll indicated that Nixon appeared to have managed to hold on to a tenuous lead; and (3) the Gallup Poll showed Nixon picking up strength in July, which he mostly managed to retain up through Election Day, whereas the Harris Survey showed Nixon making a smaller gain in August, which he then held on to with little subsequent change (Table 6).

The press focused on this systematic difference between the two polls, and reported considerable speculation—some of which was obviously colored by political loyalties—as to the methodo-

TABLE 6. Comparison of Trends in Nixon-Humphrey-Wallace "Trial Heats" as Reported by Gallup Poll and Harris Survey

Gallup Poll				
Interviewing dates	Nixon	Humphrey	Wallace	Undecided
Oct. 31–Nov. 2	43	42	15	—
Oct. 17–21	44	36	15	5
Oct. 3–12	43	31	20	6
Sept. 27–30	44	29	20	7
Sept. 20–22	43	28	21	8
Sept. 3–7	43	31	17	7
Aug. 8–11	45	29	18	8
July 19–21	40	38	16	6
June 29–July 3	35	40	16	9
June 15–16	37	42	14	7

Sources: Gallup Poll releases, July 31 and November 4, 1968.

Harris Survey				
Interviewing dates	Nixon	Humphrey	Wallace	Undecided
Nov. 4	41	45	13	—
Nov. 1–2	42	40	12	6
Oct. 27–28	40	37	16	7
Oct. 9–11	40	35	18	7
Sept. 11–13	39	31	21	9
Aug. 24	40	34	17	9
July 25–29	36	41	16	7
July 6–11	35	37	17	11
June 11–16	36	43	13	8

Sources: *New York Post*, November 4 and 5, 1968; *Philadelphia Inquirer*, November 1, 1968.

logical reasons for it. Illustrative of the latter is a statement from a campaign speech by Senator Joseph D. Tydings about the credibility of the Gallup Poll:

There is good reason to believe that the Gallup Poll is not properly weighted, is low on urban representation and minority group repre-

sentation and is based on 1960 Census tracts, which are somewhat outdated . . . I feel confident that the new Harris Poll . . . will show a
dramatic spurt and that the election will be, in Mr. Harris's words, "too
close to call" . . . Deficiencies [in Gallup's polling methods] . . . explain the discrepancy between the two polls.[40]

James M. Perry, writing in *The National Observer* a few days
subsequent to Tydings' statement, also attempted to explain the
difference between the reported results of the two polls in terms
of the sampling techniques used and methods for estimating
turnout:

It's not hard to determine where the problem lies. Both Mr. Gallup
and Mr. Harris are in general agreement about voting intentions in
the South, in the suburbs, in rural areas. But they are wildly at variance
in the cities with populations of 1,000,000 or more . . . Either Mr.
Gallup or Mr. Harris is doing something very wrong in measuring the
vote in these big cities . . . [Other] polltakers believe that Mr. Harris
tends to give more weight to the Negro vote than Mr. Gallup. Mr.
Harris, they believe, assumes that 50 percent of the big city Negro
electorate will actually go to the polls. Mr. Gallup, they believe, assumes a lower level of participation—perhaps on the order of 30 percent.[41]

Both of these attempts to account for the differences between
the Gallup Poll and the Harris Survey focus on the methodologies used, but fail to pinpoint the reasons for the differences
because the attempts are based on hearsay and speculation
rather than upon factual knowledge. For example, the Gallup
Poll's method of identifying likely voters is applied to the entire
sample and not to specific segments, such as Negroes. Rather
than allowing the analyst to "assume" what the turnout of any
ethnic group will be, the method makes it impossible to know the
measured turnout level for any segment of the sample until after
the analysis is completed. While it seems likely that differences in
methods for estimating turnout were involved—the Gallup Poll's
measurement for its entire sample including likely and unlikely
voters approximated the Harris Survey reports for likely voters
(Table 7)—the speculations reported by James Perry provide
little guidance for ascertaining with any precision how and why
these methods may have produced conflicting measurements.
Similarly, Senator Tydings' comments are the expressions of the

TABLE 7. Preferences for President among All Adults of Voting Age and "Likely Voters"

| | Gallup Poll | | Harris Survey |
	Likely · Voters, %	All Adults, %	Likely Voters, %
Nixon	44	41	40
Humphrey	36	35	37
Wallace	15	18	16
Undecided	5	6	7

Sources: Gallup Poll release, November 1, 1968, interviewing date October 17–21; The Harris Survey, *New York Post*, November 4, 1968, interviewing dates October 27–28.

needs of a political campaigner seeking to spur on his party's workers rather than the result of an empirical analysis of the sampling methods of the two polls in question. On the other hand, a major methodological characteristic of the Harris Survey—the use of a panel technique in which persons are reinterviewed, contrasting with the reliance of the Gallup Poll on independent surveys—was ignored by the press.

Complicating further any attempt to assess objectively conflicting survey results is the possibility that the press may be misled when seeking guidance from presumably qualified experts. Illustrative of this danger is a report by Steven V. Roberts that appeared the day Senator Tydings made his above comments:

A number of experts on public opinion polls agreed yesterday that the 7 point discrepancy between the current Harris and Gallup Polls on the Presidential race is too large to be caused by the normal imprecision of statistical surveys . . . For example, (the experts) said, an accurate survey has to screen out eligible voters who will not cast ballots. Although the pollsters have developed some techniques for eliminating stay-at-homes, the experts generally believe their methods are not foolproof.[42]

While it can be taken for granted that no sampling method is foolproof, it nevertheless appears that at least some of the experts who were contacted were unfamiliar with the power of the advanced techniques such as those described above.

In the light of the skeptical concern expressed and reported by the press about the conflicting Gallup Poll and Harris Survey results in 1968, it is noteworthy that after the election there appeared an uncritical feeling that "the polls" did well. William V. Shannon, after noting that the final Gallup Poll report "turned out to be almost exactly right," continued by observing that "[t]he Harris poll was equally accurate."[43] Similarly, *The New York Times* commented editorially:

Yet both the Gallup and Harris polls came extraordinarily close to mirroring the delicate balance of a final vote that gave both Richard M. Nixon and Hubert H. Humphrey almost exactly 43 per cent of the popular ballots as against 13 percent for George Wallace. The discrepancy between these figures and those forecast by the two major polling organizations in their concluding surveys is readily explained by undecided voters and the margin of error inherent in any sampling process.[44]

Once the heat of the campaign had abated, the fact that in the final reports there was a continuance of the systematic difference between the two polls—with Humphrey's strength still at a higher level in the Harris Survey than in the Gallup Poll—was overlooked. Yet it would be plausible to hypothesize that the persistence of such a systematic difference is the result of methodology, and not only of sampling variance. In any event, the credibility of poll results, although contingent upon the attainment of a reasonable degree of accuracy, is also clearly colored by the observer's political involvement in a campaign.

MEASURING THE DYNAMICS OF POLITICAL CAMPAIGNS

For polls to be helpful and accurate guidelines to political campaigns they must be capable of accurately measuring the trends in candidate strength during a campaign and detecting ups and downs as they occur. If such is the case candidates can act upon the reality of the movement of the campaign rather than upon their own subjective moods or those of their aides.

The 1960 Presidential election is illustrative of the polls' trend-measuring function. Throughout most of the campaign, Kennedy and Nixon were in a close duel, with the national popular vote hovering around the 50–50 mark. Then, as the campaign entered its final week, the Gallup Poll reported in the aftermath of the television debates a surge in Kennedy's strength, a movement that apparently had also been picked up by Harris in the private polls he conducted for Kennedy.[45] But in the final days of the campaign, with no additional television debates, the two candidates followed very different strategies. Nixon travelled wide and far, but mostly west of the Appalachians, and ended his campaign with an intensive television effort. Kennedy tended to concentrate in the northeast, with a triumphal tour of New England during the final weekend. The mood in the Kennedy camp was reportedly one of hopeful anticipation of a decisive victory, in contrast to the underdog atmosphere at Nixon Headquarters. The final Gallup Poll, published the day before election, reported a reversal in the trend, with Kennedy's lead a bare 51–49. Allowing for sampling error, even without assuming any further trend, this meant that Nixon had almost as good a chance as Kennedy to win a majority of the popular vote.

To evaluate the danger that campaign strategy will be unduly influenced by subjective interpretations of actual occurrences, compare these two comments by Theodore White concerning the 1960 campaign:

The candidate must feel the beat of the people he hopes to lead; their heart is his target. And no public opinion poll or analysis can tell him half so well whether he has reached that target as can the people themselves, giving him the best of their response.

What was wrong was that all the predictions of a Kennedy sweep based on crowd response ignored an enormous political truth that quiet people vote, too . . . No greater demonstration occurred than for Kennedy in Ohio, or for Nixon in Georgia, yet both of them lost these two roaring states stunningly.[46]

Nixon's private polls had, in contrast to Kennedy's, correctly indicated that the former was likely to carry Ohio by a safe margin, an outcome that was one of the most disappointing surprises to Kennedy.[47] All told, Nixon's private polls plus the final Gallup Poll measurement provided evidence to him that his final campaigning was making a dent in Kennedy's lead and gave him grounds for thinking that he might overcome it. In contrast, it is conceivable that a misconception of what had been happening during the last few days of the campaign may have caused Kennedy to neglect crucial states like Ohio and Illinois to a degree that almost cost him the election.

A careful reading of the trend of voter preferences during the 1968 campaign leads to an assessment of the dynamics of that election that differs considerably from the common assumption that Nixon "peaked" too soon and that his strength waned significantly in the closing days of the campaign. In fact, his support in both the Gallup Poll and the Harris Survey fluctuated within a narrow range of one or two percentage points from September to the end of the campaign (Table 6 above). The volatility of the electorate centered around the appeal of Wallace to traditionally Democratic voters. Beginning in June, Wallace began to make significant inroads outside the South among normally Democratic blue-collar workers. This impetus continued until early October, after which much of his non-South support shifted back to the Democratic fold. By Election Day, Wallace's strength had ebbed to about the level where it had been before the nominating conventions. Humphrey's resurgence was at Wallace's, not Nixon's, expense. Nixon successfully managed to retain the support he had. The crucial characteristic of the 1968 Presidential election, consequently, was that it was decided by the size and inclinations of a politically disaffected, and consequently volatile, segment of the "Democratic coalition." The political strategies of both Nixon and Humphrey reportedly were significantly influenced by an awareness of this characteristic. The efforts of Humphrey's labor supporters to woo back defectors to Wallace probably accounts for much of the improvement in his standings, while Nixon's campaigners were stressing the theme that a vote for Wallace would be a wasted one. It is also intriguing to note that Wallace's strength in the North started to climb sharply subsequent to Robert Kennedy's assassination, and that its decline followed the naming of Curtis LeMay as Wallace's running mate.

The value of preelection polls to politicians involves not only the accuracy of final measurements, but also, and of perhaps greater consequence, the accuracy of the polls' earlier measurements. Since there is no independent, objective criterion for evaluating the accuracy of early polls, the only realistic recourse open to politicians is to examine the credentials of a survey organization in terms of the accuracy of its final measurements. Then, if satisfied, they can require that the same methodology be utilized in polls conducted early in the campaign.

POLLS FOR IDENTIFYING PROSPECTIVE CANDIDATES

A criticism made by Senator Albert Gore, among others, is directed at the credibility of polls intended to discover which men are likely to become strong candidates. Senator Gore maintains that all such polls really do is measure the familiarity of a name.[48] If this criticism of one important way in which surveys of voter preferences are used is correct, there is no objective reason for party leaders to rely upon surveys as a guide when evaluating the popular appeal of potential candidates and in planning their campaign strategies.

Senator Gore's contention is that polls on prospective Presidential candidates are not a measure of popular support, but are largely a reflection of the familiarity of names. He cites as evidence a test by his staff among a sampling in Washington, D.C. in which, among Democrats, 25 percent selected from a list either "Franklin D. Roosevelt, Jr. or John D. Eisenhower as their preference for either first or second place" as Democratic candidate for the Presidency.[49] Other names which could have been selected by respondents in this survey were Allen Dulles, Hubert Humphrey, Lyndon Johnson, Thomas Jefferson Jones, John F. Kennedy, Adlai Stevenson, and Stuart Symington. The method used was avowedly patterned after the Gallup Poll's "open primary" question, so Gore's test is a direct challenge to the meaningfulness of a large body of poll data on surveys of voter preferences.

The views of Elmo Roper and George Gallup on this issue

contrast to some degree. A letter to both from Senator Gore asked, "Do you consider polls on Presidential candidates a measure of popular support? Or, in your opinion is it a reflection of familiarity with a name or names, or is it a favorable reaction to a name or names?" Roper replied, "It is certainly much more a reflection of familiarity with names than anything else . . . until after the campaign itself has started."[50] Behind Roper's comment is the concern, voiced by him on several occasions, that if too much weight is given to early measurements, holders of famous names, such as sons of eminent fathers, would be given undue consideration to the exclusion of worthy newcomers and to the detriment of the body politic. However, once the campaign proper is under way, Roper stated, he believes polls can validly measure voter preferences.

Gallup, answering the same question, wrote that he believes "the figures reported for each candidate constitute a good measure of the candidate's popular support" as of the time the survey is conducted.[51] His conviction is that "if there were a national primary held on a single day and with all candidates participating, then poll results should accurately reflect the outcome of such a primary."

The contrast between the replies of Roper and Gallup is, in the largest degree, a contrast in focus of concern. The former is concerned with the effects upon decision-making of what he would consider premature measurements. Roper does not doubt that polls can measure public preferences, but he questions the political meaning of polls taken before potential candidates have spoken out on the issues of the day. Gallup's answer, on the other hand, focused on whether poll results would be congruent with what voters would express in the election booth on the survey date, leaving aside a consideration of the quality of the reasons that might underlie their preferences. The issue, then, is twofold:

1. Do preelection polls, especially preconvention and preprimary polls, portray potential candidates with well-known names as having unrealistically high voter appeal because such names are selected if they are familiar and not because of any real voter preference?

2. To what extent can early poll results be treated as meaning-

ful approximations of what would result if an election were held at the time when the poll was conducted, rather than as essentially frivolous measurements of public reaction to men's names?

Considering the first question, there is every reason for believing that having a well-known name is a definite advantage in sample surveys. Thus, in Massachusetts a Saltonstall or a Lodge and, more recently, a Kennedy first starting out in politics would expect to fare well in a preprimary survey even though he had not as yet established a political identity or record of his own. The same would be true of a Roosevelt in New York or a Taft in Ohio. That measurement of such an early effect is politically unrealistic does not necessarily follow.

It is a political truism that the first order of business for a candidate is to make his name known. Part of the folklore of politics is that an inability of voters to identify the name of one's opponent is a sure sign of imminent victory. Illustrative of this is the following incident reported by political columnist Tom Wicker:

David F. Cargo, New Mexico's personable young Governor, was talking politics last night over a magnificent spread of Mexican food . . . when someone mentioned the name of his most likely Democratic opponent next year. Cargo, a Republican, summoned a Spanish-speaking waitress and asked her what she thought of the Democrat. "Who's he?" the girl said. Cargo smiled in satisfaction. "That's the reason he can't win," he said.[52]

Almost exactly the same attitude was expressed by Congressman Otis G. Pike, Democrat, running for reelection from New York's traditionally Republican First Congressional District. At a dinner dance held during the campaign, the following exchange took place:

[A] man came up, and pumped Pike's hand, grinning. "I understand you're up for election this year, Otis," he said. "I didn't realize that. Who are you running against?" Pike smiled and answered, "It's funny, Charlie, but I can never seem to remember his name." A moment later Pike said to me, "That's a good sign. It's surprising how many people don't know that members of the House are elected every two years. But it can be helpful. If they don't know there's an election, they haven't even heard his name by this time, he's in trouble."[53]

Pike, bucking a strong national Republican tide in 1966, won reelection by a comfortable margin.

With respect to Presidential politics, Theodore White reports that in 1960 James Rowe advised Humphrey that, above all, his major problem, if he was to get the Presidential nomination, was to become known to the electorate. White comments:

> To become known, to be identifiable to voters in terms of their own gut reactions, is perhaps the most expensive and necessary condition of American Presidential politics.[54]

Because of this acknowledged importance of public recognition, an important measure of a candidate's strength is the public's ability to identify him. For example, in the fall of 1966, in the wake of Ronald Reagan's election as Governor of California, the Gallup Poll reported that *one* asset he had on the national scene was his recognizability to the public.

Surveys taken by various polling organizations over many years have repeatedly shown that only a minority of the electorate is able to name its representatives in national and state legislatures.[55] If a candidate is to attract more than the loyal vote of his own party, which is necessary whenever there is a close contest or when the candidate's party is in the minority, he faces the task of making his name known to the electorate. Until that is achieved, he has little hope of winning converts. One advantage that any incumbent has is the opportunity that his office provides for making news, for making him a desirable speaker, and for providing service to his constituents in a way that helps publicize his name. The challenger, on the other hand, faces the ordinarily arduous task of making himself identifiable to the electorate.

In 1952, one of the major disadvantages that Adlai Stevenson faced in his campaign for the Presidency was that up to the last weeks before the Democratic Convention he was not well-known nationally. It was not until after he was nominated that he achieved any real exposure to the national electorate. Until then his reputation was confined to his home region and to a fairly small slice of the national population. Once he achieved public exposure, however, he established an identity that attracted many defecting Democrats back to their party.

On the eve of the 1952 convention, only 12 percent of rank-and-file Democrats selected Stevenson as their choice for their party's Presidential candidate even though he was preferred by 40 percent of Democratic county chairmen.[56] In contrast, Estes Kefauver, whose crime-commission hearings had made him a familiar figure on television and in newspaper headlines, was the choice of 45 percent of rank-and-file Democrats. Once the campaign started, an early Gallup Poll showed only 40 percent of the electorate preferring Stevenson,[57] but he gathered some additional strength to end up with 44.6 percent of the actual vote on Election Day. Other factors, such as confidence in the ability of Eisenhower, the hero of World War II, to bring an end to the fighting in Korea, were undoubtedly decisive in that election. Nevertheless, the lack of a public reputation was a contributing factor to Stevenson's defeat in 1952.

Franklin Roosevelt, Jr.'s bid for the governorship in New York in 1966 provides a basis for evaluating whether polls are capable of meaningfully measuring the political strength of a man with a well-known name. Early private polls showed him as the preferred candidate in opposition to the incumbent Nelson Rockefeller and the Democratic nominee Frank O'Connor of between 12 and 17 percent of the electorate. Much of his early strength, it seems reasonable to infer, stemmed from the glamour and fame of the Roosevelt name, rather than from his lack-luster political record. His campaign never got off the ground, however, as measured by subsequent preelection surveys. At no point during the campaign was there any evidence of a trend in his direction; rather, his level of support fluctuated at around 12 percent during most of the campaign and then collapsed during the final week.

Hitherto unpublished Gallup Poll data demonstrate that the survey method accurately measured this collapse. For methodological reasons, as part of the Gallup Poll's final nationwide survey of the congressional races, preferences for governor and senator were also obtained in those states which had such contests. An analysis of those interviews conducted in New York state showed a division of preferences for governor among likely voters that

TABLE 8. Comparison of Gallup Poll with Official Election Returns in the 1966 Gubernatorial Election

	Final Gallup Survey, %	Actual Results, %	Deviation, in percentage points
Rockefeller	43.2	44.8	−1.6
O'Connor	39.1	38.3	+0.8
Roosevelt, Jr.	8.8	8.4	+0.4
Adams	8.9	8.5	+0.4

Source: Unpublished Gallup Poll data.

was extremely close to the actual vote (Table 8). Thus, while it is probable that the fame of the Roosevelt name was a source of strength in early polls, the survey method demonstrated its capability for accurately measuring the trend in voter preferences away from a glamorous name as Election Day approached.

The attempted use of poll data to justify the selection of candidates generated considerable controversy during the 1968 Republican nominating convention. In this controversy, public attention centered not on whether such data are inherently meaningful, but on how to treat apparently contradictory survey results. Nelson Rockefeller, having stayed out of all the Republican preferential primaries, had stated that he was resting his candidacy upon the expectation that public-opinion polls would show him to be a much stronger Republican nominee than the favored Richard Nixon. He commissioned Archibald Crossley to conduct a nationwide survey immediately prior to the convention in which both he and Nixon would be tested against the leading Democratic contenders; the results were to be released when the delegates convened in Miami. Additionally, both the Gallup Poll and the Harris Survey could be expected to issue last-minute measurements based on their regularly scheduled national surveys.

The results of these three independently conducted surveys became available during the period of July 27–30—the Gallup Poll results first, published by the *Miami Herald* a day before the scheduled release date; the Crossley poll the following day; and the Harris Survey on July 30, also leaked by the press before its release date. The results of the Gallup Poll showed Nixon continuing to have a somewhat greater appeal to the electorate than Rockefeller, the Crossley survey indicated that Rockefeller's appeal was somewhat greater than Nixon's, and the Harris Survey showed Rockefeller to be considerably stronger than Nixon (Table 9). The interviewing dates, as reported to the press, also

TABLE 9. Comparison of "Trial Heat" Polls Prior to 1968 Republican Convention*

	July 20–21 Gallup, %	July 22–26 Crossley, %**	July 25–27 Harris, %
Nixon vs. Humphrey			
Nixon	40	39	36
Humphrey	38	36	41
Nixon vs. McCarthy			
Nixon	41	37	35
McCarthy	36	37	43
Rockefeller vs. Humphrey			
Rockefeller	36	37	40
Humphrey	36	31	34
Rockefeller vs. McCarthy			
Rockefeller	36	38	40
McCarthy	35	30	34

Source: *Washington Post*, August 1, 1968.

* These polls originally included data on Wallace.

** This poll was conducted by Political Surveys and Analyses, Inc., of which Archibald M. Crossley was then president. The term "Crossley" is used here for typographical convenience.

differed, the Gallup Poll having been conducted first and the Harris Survey last.

This rapid succession of conflicting poll reports generated a series of claims and counterclaims from Nixon and Rockefeller headquarters. Leonard W. Hall, Rockefeller's campaign strategist, dismissed the Gallup Poll measurement as a "freak" and "the

single exception to a clear national trend." Upon hearing of the
Harris Survey report, New York's Lieutenant Governor Malcolm
Wilson commented optimistically that the delegates were impressed by them. In contrast, Herbert G. Klein, Nixon's press
spokesman, who reportedly "trumpeted" the earlier Gallup Poll
figures, after Harris' findings were released asserted that "it was
time to end the numbers game."[58]

A joint statement issued on August 1 by Louis Harris and
George Gallup, Jr. for the avowed purpose of clarifying the
situation stated that the three surveys "are not as dissimilar as
they might appear to the public at first glance."[59] The statement
continued by proposing that if the Gallup, Crossley, and Harris
surveys were treated as if they had been conducted by the same
organization using the same methods, but at three different
points of time, then it could be concluded that a clear trend
would emerge showing Rockefeller moving ahead of Nixon.

This statement was widely interpreted as a public retraction by
the Gallup Poll, and the hypothesis that a shift in public opinion
had actually occurred was largely ignored. Moreover, the assumption in the statement concerning comparable methodology
was never seriously examined, despite the fact that one major
difference between the Gallup and Harris methods was reported
in the press. The Gallup Poll result was based on an independent
sample of registered voters, while 1,127 responses from the
Harris sample of 1,346 likely voters were reinterviews from a
June sampling.[60] Furthermore, a comparison of the trends in
voter preferences during the previous months as reported by the
Gallup Poll and by the Harris Survey (Tables 10 and 11) shows
that differences too large to be attributed to sampling error had
previously existed between the two, differences that, as discussed
above, are likely to result from differing methodologies.

The Gallup-Harris statement, regardless of what its intent may
have been, did not serve to clarify the situation. Instead, its
primary effect appears to have been the addition of a bizarre
twist to the normal last-minute scramble for delegates, possibly
without affecting the eventual outcome of the convention.
Nixon's majority of 692 out of a total of 1,333 votes is almost
identical with a forecast of 691 votes made by *Newsweek* in

May.[61] In any event, given the dramatic changes in voter sentiment that later occurred during the election campaign as measured by both the Gallup Poll and the Harris Survey, it is evident
that *none* of the preconvention surveys were reliable forecasts of
the eventual outcome of the election, since the split in voter
preferences changed considerably during the course of the campaign.

To the extent that early polls are accepted as predictions of
elections rather than as one means of assessing the "handicap
strength" of political candidates, they can lead to erroneous

TABLE 10. Gallup Poll "Trial Heat" Trend Prior to 1968 Republican
Convention

Interviewing dates	April 6–10 %	May 4–8 %	May 25–29 %	June 6–15 %	June 24– July 3 %	July 19–21 %
Nixon-Humphrey-Wallace						
Nixon	43	39	36	37	35	40
Humphrey	34	36	42	42	40	38
Wallace	9	14	14	14	16	16
Undecided	14	11	8	7	9	6
Nixon-McCarthy-Wallace						
Nixon	41	39	40	39	36	41
McCarthy	38	37	38	41	39	36
Wallace	10	14	13	14	18	16
Undecided	11	10	9	6	17	7
Rockefeller-Humphrey-Wallace						
Rockefeller	40	35	39	36	36	37
Humphrey	33	40	38	36	36	31
Wallace	16	17	17	21	21	22
Undecided	11	8	6	7	7	10
Rockefeller-McCarthy-Wallace						
Rockefeller	40	40	38	35	36	38
McCarthy	31	34	39	37	35	30
Wallace	17	17	16	20	20	22
Undecided	12	9	7	8	9	10

Source: *Washington Post*, August 1, 1968.

TABLE 11. Harris Survey "Trial Heat" Trend Prior to 1968 Republican
Convention

Interviewing dates	April 25– May 1 %	May 16–18 %	June 10–17 %	July 8–14 %	July 25–29 %
Nixon-Humphrey-Wallace					
Nixon	36	37	36	35	36
Humphrey	38	41	43	37	41
Wallace	13	14	13	17	16
Not sure	13	8	8	11	7
Nixon-McCarthy-Wallace					
Nixon	37	40	36	37	35
McCarthy	40	39	44	34	43
Wallace	13	14	12	19	15
Not sure	10	7	8	10	7
Rockefeller-Humphrey-Wallace					
Rockefeller	37	37	36	37	40
Humphrey	39	40	40	34	34
Wallace	16	17	15	10	20
Not sure	8	6	9	10	6
Rockefeller-McCarthy-Wallace					
Rockefeller	38	38	35	32	40
McCarthy	36	35	41	38	34
Wallace	15	19	15	20	19
Not sure	11	8	9	10	7

Source: *Washington Post,* August 1, 1968.

assumptions when nominations are being made. A sophisticated
use of early polls would include not only a measurement of
candidate strength at that time but also a detailed analysis of the
factors that *could lead to a change* as the campaign progressed.
Whether the use of polls in the selection of candidates will result
in the selection of superficially glamorous candidates to the
exclusion of better qualified but still obscure contenders will be
determined more by the sophistication of those who control the
parties than by the intrinsic character of the method of measurement. That polls can affect and have affected the selection of
candidates by those influential in the hierarchy of political parties

is not arguable. Whether this effect is beneficial or detrimental, aside from any controversy as to what really is good or bad, is determined not by the polls themselves but by the discrimination with which the nation's political leaders utilize survey data.

Charting Trends in Voter Preferences

While early polls can measure the initial strength of prospective candidates for office, the relevance of early assessments of candidates to the question of how likely they are to win is doubtful. (The criterion of ability, which admittedly should be uppermost, cannot realistically be divorced from that of winning. Highly qualified men who cannot generate voter appeal either become voices in the wilderness or must be utilized in appointive offices.) Survey data supply factual evidence that early strength can be dissipated and early weakness overcome.

The 1948 Truman-Dewey election is the most publicized instance of a "sure winner" going down to defeat. Stouffer and McRae, in their analysis of the evidence bearing upon this aspect of the performance of preelection polls in 1948, conclude that the data available indicate that there was a swing to Truman in the final weeks of the campaign.[62] (Also see Table 12.) Humphrey's resurgence in 1968 (Table 6 above), while not quite enough to gain victory, is equally impressive evidence that early polls may be bad barometers of what will happen on Election Day. Similarly, Louis Harris reports three elections in which late shifts proved decisive: the 1961 New York City mayoralty election, the

TABLE 12. Trend of Gallup Poll 1948 Trial Heats after Convention

	Aug. 1	Aug. 22	Sept. 8	Sept. 24	Oct. 17	Nov. 1
Dewey	48	48	48.5	46.5	46	49.5
Truman	37	37	36.5	39.0	40	44.5
Wallace	5	4	5	3.5	4	4
Thurmond	—	2	—	2	2	2
Undecided	10	9	10	9	8	—

1960 West Virginia primary contest between Kennedy and Humphrey, and the 1958 state elections in Ohio.[63]

The New York gubernatorial election in 1966 is a less publicized graphic demonstration of how an apparently hopeless candidate came from behind to a clear-cut victory. A series of polls conducted by Political Surveys and Analyses, Inc. for Nelson Rockefeller had been showing for some time that Rockefeller's past public appeal had been largely dissipated so that in the spring of 1966, he was clearly the underdog. Nevertheless, he decided to run for reelection as governor and did so successfully. His margin of victory was decisive, though greatly reduced from 1962.

Rockefeller's private polling effort, which provided a highly accurate final measurement, was used by him to assess his campaigning from summer through Election Day. A spring survey showed him far behind, with prospects that superficially looked as bleak as Goldwater's did at a comparable time in 1964. This survey also provided him with a picture of public discontent on a number of issues. Then followed a vigorous, statewide campaign effort, the effects of which were measured in a number of surveys which charted a slow but steady rise in Rockefeller's strength. By mid-October, according to these private polls, he and O'Connor were neck and neck, and in the final survey 43.9 percent of the likely voters expressed a preference for Rockefeller. The last measurement is very close to the 44.8 percent of the actual vote which he received and which provided a comfortable plurality in the four-candidate contest.

As quoted in the press on the day after election, Rockefeller's private polls were a source of confidence to him that his campaign strategy was correct and his efforts were paying off. If, instead of relying on the results of his private polls conducted by a survey organization which had demonstrated its accuracy to him in the 1964 primary battles, Rockefeller had accepted the results of the Daily News Poll which forecast an O'Connor victory, he might have mistakenly concluded that his campaigning was getting nowhere. This conclusion could easily have led to a change in tactics that might have reversed the favorable trend.

One aspect of Rockefeller's use of polls warrants emphasis—namely, his realistic acceptance of his initial weakness without a concomitant defeatism. The fact that a candidate is far behind in the summer does not necessarily mean that he cannot win in November. Weakness in early polls may be overcome if the sources of such weakness are correctly assessed and if the candidate's political orientation and style do not preclude his campaigning in a way that would overcome that weakness. The contrasts between Goldwater in the 1964 Presidential election, Rockefeller in the 1966 New York gubernatorial election, and Humphrey in the 1968 Presidential election are instructive in this regard. Whatever else may be said about the relative merits of Goldwater, Rockefeller, and Humphrey, and taking due account of the markedly different circumstances of the campaigns, the latter two demonstrated a remarkable ability to come from behind—one in winning by a reasonably comfortable margin and the other in almost closing the gap in the popular vote. On the other hand, it is conceivable that his ability to score rapid gains in the 1966 gubernatorial contest influenced Rockefeller to make his futile effort in 1968 to gain the Republican nomination by attempting to demonstrate an ability to surge ahead of Nixon in public-opinion polls. Despite a well-financed advertising campaign, Rockefeller failed in his efforts to obtain from public-opinion polls any evidence that he was the Republican aspirant with the best capability of winning the Presidency.

Rockefeller was not the only political leader in 1968 who displayed a proclivity to cite poll results as ammunition during the contests for the nominations by the Democratic and Republican parties. On the eve of the Democratic Convention, Warren Weaver, Jr. reported:

Senator Eugene J. McCarthy's Presidential strategists took heart today from the latest poll figures . . . To help bolster their case against Vice President Humphrey in the upcoming nomination contest, the McCarthy men called attention to the latest Gallup poll, which showed Mr. Humphrey 16 percentage points behind Richard M. Nixon and Senator McCarthy only 5 behind.

"It is now all too clear that the Vice President is not electable," Patrick B. Lucey of Wisconsin, one of the rotating team of McCarthy spokesmen, declared this morning. "It seems inconceivable to me that a convention victory could close a 16 point gap for a candidate who already has the visibility of an incumbent Vice President."[64]

Nevertheless, Humphrey eventually all but managed to close that gap.

It is clear that it can be self-defeating to treat public-opinion polls as crystal balls for foretelling the course of events months in advance rather than as political intelligence for use when evaluating possible candidates. Despite this danger there have been a number of instances in recent years in which the selection of candidates reportedly has been determined by standings in early polls. For example, the nomination of Henry Morgenthau, Jr. as the New York Democratic gubernatorial candidate in 1962 reportedly was influenced by private polls which allegedly showed him to be the strongest candidate the party had to offer then. Similarly, the selection of Arlen M. Specter as the Republican candidate in the 1967 Philadelphia mayoralty race was also influenced by early polls:

Mr. Specter was the unanimous choice of the Republican candidate selection committee, which acted on the basis of several polls conducted by the Republicans.[65]

The role of preelection polling has expanded considerably so that highly publicized polls conducted during Presidential campaigns may have become less significant than those taking place some months and even years before Election Day. It is in these early stages, when candidates are selected, that candidate-preference polls may have their most significant impact on the political process. For this reason, without questioning the accuracy or validity of early polls as measurements *at that point in time,* it is necessary to emphasize their lack of predictive power. Nevertheless, there appears to be a tendency, in the absence of contravening evidence, or when early poll results conform to the preferences of those in control of a political faction, to ignore the fact that preelection polls are never predictions but are measurements from which predictions must be extrapolated.

As a consequence of this tendency, potential candidates for offices important enough to be polled are under increasing pressure to do well in early polls. This circumstance, in turn, means that they can no longer wait until after they are nominated to begin running publicly for office. In order to hope to be nominated, they must start campaigning far in advance so that they can establish their credentials in early polls. The many different avenues for creating a political reputation—such as establishing a record in lesser offices, appearing on television, and conducting speaking tours—usually require sizeable financial support. The immediate consequence is that personal fortunes, the support of those with large funds, or access to party campaign chests becomes a *sine qua non* for those seeking any major office. This development is particularly evident with respect to the Presidency, with contenders for nominations of the losing party starting their campaigns almost as soon as an election is over. Comparable developments for other major offices, such as governor, senator, and mayor of large cities are also becoming evident.

Relying upon polls for developing campaign strategy and selecting candidates, it is clear, creates a host of new problems even as it assures some of the informational needs of parties. If survey data are not continuously up-dated, if the measuring techniques are imprecise, or if the analytical procedures are superficial, grievous errors can be made. The uncritical generalization that since some survey organizations have very accurate records, most any poll can be safely used is one that can be damaging to politicians who base their decisions on polls. It is of prime importance to remember that politics is a dynamic process (composed of individual actions within an institutional framework) which can never be captured completely in any one opinion survey. Only a series of surveys which chart trends and relate them to events can aspire to give evidence as to the nature of the political process.

The Accuracy of Preprimary Polls

The growing use of polls to help select prospective candidates for office, as differentiated from their use during the campaign proper, brings up the question as to whether preprimary polls can be treated as reliable measurements of voter preferences. The realities of the situation, as compared with preelection polls, are difficult to disentangle. It was not until 1964 that public attention focused upon the use of polls during primary campaigns. Expectations of accuracy were high as a result of the growing record of reliability in national elections that had been compiled by published national polls such as Gallup and Roper, as well as the record of published state polls such as the California, Minnesota, Iowa, and Texas polls. In 1960, despite the closeness of the election, all these polls published final survey results that, in percentage points, were very close to the actual vote cast. Additionally, the confidential, unpublished polls conducted by Louis Harris for John F. Kennedy in 1960 were prominently featured in Theodore White's *The Making of a President 1960*. The glamour and excitement of the Kennedy victory had a halo effect that encompassed all those who figured in his campaign. One result of this success and attention was that in many political circles, especially Democratic, Harris' role in conducting preprimary and preelection polls received almost as much attention as the elections themselves.

Among Republicans, too, the experience with preelection polls in 1960 was very encouraging. A panel study conducted by Opinion Research Corporation for Nixon is reported to have estimated the election result within 0.8 percentage points.[66] State surveys conducted by Public Opinion Surveys, Inc. for the late Dr. Claude Robinson, who was an advisor to Nixon, were also very accurate. During his post-election meeting with Kennedy in Florida, Nixon reports, he told Kennedy that these "polls in individual states were almost miraculously accurate."[67] Thus, among both Democrats and Republicans there seemed to be good reason for having high expectations of the accuracy of sample-surveys of voter preferences.

Largely ignored in these expectations were two crucial differences between primaries and elections, differences that came to plague those who ventured to publish preprimary poll results in 1964. As discussed earlier, it has long been recognized that one of the major potential sources of polling error in national elections is the large proportion of persons of voting age who do not exercise their franchise because of lack of interest and/or ability to meet eligibility requirements. If a survey organization does not have a reliable method of isolating nonvoters and excluding them, its poll results can deviate significantly from election returns even though in all other respects a valid and reliable measurement of voter preferences is obtained.

As difficult as this problem is in congressional and Presidential elections, in which 40 to 60 percent turnouts are typical, it becomes even more serious in primaries in which turnouts of 10 to 25 percent are common. Furthermore, methods for dealing with turnout which may have worked reasonably well in a Presidential election could prove to be inadequate in the different circumstances of a primary.

An additional difference is that there is a built-in advantage in preelection polls that does not pertain in preprimary polls—namely, the stability that party loyalties provide. The mere fact that a person considers himself a Republican or Democrat largely defines how he will vote in any interparty contest. Studies conducted by the Survey Research Center at the University of Michigan since 1952 have led to the conclusion that partisan preferences show great stability between elections, and that this, in turn, makes for a high correlation in vote decisions between elections.[68] It is to be expected, therefore, that elections are largely decided by how Independents split and any pattern of defection by adherents of the contending parties. Thus Gallup Poll data show that in 1952, 1956, 1960, 1964, and 1968 the rate of defection among Democrats and Republicans, plus how Independents split, identified who won and by what margin (Table 13).

In a primary, in contrast, party loyalties play virtually no role at all. The choice is not between the candidates of two parties but among a number of candidates all of whom have the same party identification. Changing one's mind does not imply disloyalty to one's party and all that this may involve, but rather means deciding that another man would better represent one's party. The impact of personalities, issues, and events under these circumstances can make for drastic swings in voter preferences. In short, the relative stability of preferences during election campaigns is a misleading guide to what happens during a

TABLE 13. Relation Between Party Identification and Presidential Vote in Four Elections

	Republicans, %	Democrats, %	Independents, %
1952:			
Voted for Eisenhower	92	23	65
Voted for Stevenson	8	77	35
1956:			
Voted for Eisenhower	96	15	70
Voted for Stevenson	4	85	30
1960:			
Voted for Kennedy	5	84	43
Voted for Nixon	95	16	57
1964:			
Voted for Johnson	20	87	56
Voted for Goldwater	80	13	44
1968:			
Voted for Nixon	86	12	44
Voted for Humphrey	9	74	31
Voted for Wallace	5	14	25

Source: Gallup Poll release, December 8, 1968.

primary campaign. While a poll taken a week before Election Day may normally be expected to approximate fairly closely what the actual outcome will be, a week-old survey may be a very poor guide as to what is likely to happen on Primary Day.

Another complicating factor is that private polls, such as those that Harris conducted for Kennedy in 1960, are intended primarily as guides to campaign strategy rather than as a basis for forecasting results. Harris writes, "If the private poll is to be put to use effectively, then, perforce, the ultimate standings should be different."[69] *Business Week,* in discussing the 1964 Presidential primaries, noted:

The Rockefeller people . . . used Crossley's [Political Surveys and Analysis, Inc.] polls more in terms of discovering what issues are good and what the candidate's image is. For example, Crossley found that Social Security was a good issue in New Hampshire; so Rockefeller hit it hard.[70]

Published polls, in contrast, are usually evaluated by the public not so much for their insight into the dynamics of a campaign as for their ability to presage the election. The pressures of journalistic requirements make this tendency inevitable. Consequently, the high expectations of published preprimary polls in 1964 were tested by their "accuracy" rather than by how useful they might have been to the candidates.

With these considerations in mind, it is not surprising that the actual performance of most published polls in the 1964 Republican primaries was disappointing to many. In all the major primaries that year—New Hampshire, Oregon, and California—the actual vote differed from what preprimary polls had led political observers to expect.

The Harris Survey was the only published poll that conducted surveys during all three primary campaigns; therefore public attention naturally focused on it. In each case, the volatility of voter preferences and the time required to process survey data made it virtually impossible for Harris to report last-minute shifts. In the aftermath of the California primary, critics claimed that "pollsters have to stand or fall by their last published figures." In reply, Mr. Harris and his associates said "the one big lesson they learned during the primaries this spring is that it is necessary to continue polling to the last possible moment because of pronounced voter shifts."[71] Similarly, Mervin D. Field, Director of the California Poll, which conducted its final survey a week before the California Primary, said in the bulletin reporting that survey's results, "a lot can happen in the closing days, if not the closing hours, of a campaign."[72]

Complicating the evaluation of the 1964 preprimary polls is the multiplicity of approaches used and the fact that not all contenders ran in each primary. Harris reported a variety of measurements based upon (1) volunteered responses, (2) an open question with a hand-out card, and (3) a "secret ballot." As was to be expected, each question yielded somewhat different measurements, creating the problem of deciding which one was the best indicator of the probable election outcome. In his final release before the New Hampshire primary, Harris reported three sets of figures. These figures as well as the actual outcome

TABLE 14. Final Harris Survey Measurements Prior to 1964 New Hampshire Preferential Primary

	First Choice	Selection from Five Listed Candidates Plus Write-Ins	Secret Written Ballot	Primary Election
Lodge (write-in)	31	23	16	35.4
Nixon (write-in)	24	20	15	16.3
Goldwater	18	19	29	21.6
Rockefeller	12	16	29	21.0
Smith	4	4	7	2.1
Stassen	1	3	3	1.5
Others	3	2	1	2.1
Not Sure	7	13	—	—
	100	100	100	100.0

Source: *Washington Post,* March 2, 1964.

are shown in Table 14. While on an *a priori* basis one might assume that a secret written ballot would most closely approximate how one would vote in the election booth, in this case it appears that asking for the respondent's first choice more accurately reflected the views of the electorate.

In Oregon Harris detected a trend away from Lodge in the closing days of the campaign with Lodge's share of the vote dropping from 40 percent to 35 percent, but his final release still showed Lodge leading (Table 15). In California Harris kept

TABLE 15. Comparison of 1964 Oregon Preferential Primary and Final Harris Survey

	Primary Election	Harris Survey
Lodge	27.7	35
Rockefeller	33.2	24
Goldwater	17.7	16
Nixon	16.9	21
Smith	2.9	2
Scranton	1.6	2

Source: Theodore H. White, *The Making of a President 1964,* p. 115.

polling even after his final newspaper report was released, so that his last report was on CBS Television on the night before the primary. His trend, after allocation of undecided voters, was summarized after the election by *The New York Times* as shown in Table 16.

TABLE 16. Trend in Harris Preprimary Surveys
in California, 1964

Poll Date	Rockefeller	Goldwater
May 10	45	55
May 18	57	43
May 23	55	45
May 20 (sic)	55	45
May 31	51	49
June 1	50	50

Source: *The New York Times,* June 4, 1964.

As the Harris experience in these three primaries demonstrates, surveys taken well before primary elections often bear little relation to the final outcome. This tendency does not necessarily deny the credibility of such surveys, but it does underline the necessity of properly evaluating them as early measurements. Valid interpretations of the meaning of early surveys, as Nick B. Williams, editor of the *Los Angeles Times* has noted, can be the foundation for electoral success:

. . . polls should be considered as trends and no more than that, which is fair enough. For instance, if the polls had not warned Goldwater's people that the trend (in California) after Oregon was sharply toward Rockefeller, they might well not have put on the tremendous drive they did—a tremendous drive that just barely managed to win victory. And while most of those who condemn the pollsters happen also to have been Goldwater supporters, they probably ought to be thanking the pollsters for giving them the warning in time to do something about it.[73]

The journalistic need to evaluate the preprimary poll as a prediction, in contrast to the politician's need for political intelligence, militates against such a balanced view. This makes for a proclivity for publicizing exaggerated claims of accuracy and of error in the news media. Sam Lubell, who relied on personal interviews of voters in selected districts rather than on scientific sample designs, reported on Primary Day that Lodge was the likely winner in Oregon, but that Rockefeller might run much stronger than expected:

The likely outcome remains: Henry Cabot Lodge in first place, with Gov. Nelson Rockefeller cutting in strongly on Lodge's lead to come in ahead of Sen. Barry Goldwater. . . . New York's Governor Rockefeller has been pushing from behind, and the extent of his gains are likely to be the big surprise of the primary vote.[74]

While Lubell's method did not permit him to estimate the outcome in percentage points, his assessment did catch the trend in voter preferences. Yet, it hardly merits the exuberant claim of columnist Harry Altshuler that Lubell "predicted Rockefeller's upset victory in the Oregon primary."[75]

Time, in its commentary on the accuracy of the preprimary polls, erred in the other direction by ascribing the reporting of changes in voter preferences to willful decisions on the part of the survey organization:

Pollster Lou Harris, who underrated Rockefeller in Oregon by 6%, was not about to underrate him again. In a poll taken shortly before Oregon, Harris called it Goldwater 55% to Rockefeller's 45%; in a post-Oregon poll he did a massive flip-flop, called it Rockefeller 57% to Goldwater's 43%.[76]

Following the California primary, *Time* commented in a similar vein:

Rarely have the pollsters shown to worse effect. Take the case of Lou Harris, who, after missing by a total of 13 percentage points in his prediction that Henry Cabot Lodge would beat Rockefeller in Oregon's May 15 primary, announced that Rocky led Goldwater by 57% to 43% in California. Then Harris began having anguished second thoughts. Twenty-four hours before last week's primary, he said that Rocky might get 55% or more. But on the morning of the election, he was less bullish about Rocky, declared, "Goldwater has seized the momentum in the last 24 hours. Dramatic changes now are taking place in California."[77]

By erroneously imputing changes that were taking place in the preferences of the electorate to "anguished second thoughts" of the poll-taker, *Time* missed the essential point of the drama that had taken place in California, and that the Harris Survey had measured. Riding on the momentum created by his Oregon victory, Rockefeller, who previously was the underdog, appeared to be on the way to smashing Goldwater's hopes for nomination. Then, on the final weekend, announcement of the birth of a son to his second marriage set the stage for an intensive, highly effective house-to-house canvass by the Goldwater organization. The result was Goldwater's narrow victory margin of 51.6 percent to Rockefeller's 48.4 percent.

Such misunderstanding of the logic of the survey method as evinced by *Time* in 1964 can lead to an unsubstantiated attack on the credibility of all preprimary polls. The temptation is either to generalize from such poorly founded criticisms and to conclude that "the polls" did very badly, or to overlook the difficulties that were encountered and to make exaggerated claims of accurate prediction. From what published evidence is available, it appears that in 1964 the preprimary polls did about as well as could be expected in charting trends, but that they provided an inadequate basis for projecting a prediction of what would actually happen on Primary Day.

Preprimary polls conducted in 1968 also became the target of considerable criticism, although some produced reasonable indications of the actual outcomes. The *Spivack Report* commented, subsequent to the disappointing performance of some polls in the New Hampshire primary, "The poll takers probably turned in their worst performance since they 'elected' Thomas E. Dewey in 1948."[78] Possibly as a reaction expressing dissatisfaction with the performance of preprimary polls in 1964 and the New Hampshire 1968 record, preprimary polls did not receive as much attention by the press in 1968 as might have been expected in light of the intense interest in the outcome of the Democratic primaries.

The 1968 preprimary polls conducted concerning the Democratic races, with one exception, exhibited a tendency for underestimating the proportionate share of the vote for Eugene McCarthy. Furthermore, there is no consistent record of a high degree of accuracy, considering only the polls conducted by such practitioners as Oliver Quayle, Louis Harris, Don Muchmore, and Burns Roper. In no case is an exact comparison with actual primary results possible, since sizable "undecided" votes were left unallocated, with no indication given as to how they might split. With anywhere from 8 percent to 18 percent undecided in California, the survey percentage for any one candidate could be appreciably altered by what undecided voters did—whether or not they abstained and how those who did vote split in their preferences. The only reasonable basis for an evaluation of the 1968 preprimary polls, consequently, is a comparison of the percentage-point spread in the survey reports and the actual spread between candidates. (The details of this comparison appear in Table 17.)

This evaluation shows that the Quayle and Harris polls in Indiana were quite close in indicating the size of Kennedy's lead over McCarthy, but underestimated his lead over Branigin. In Nebraska, Quayle overestimated somewhat Kennedy's lead over McCarthy and underestimated his lead over Humphrey. Similarly in California, Quayle's final survey overestimated somewhat Kennedy's lead over McCarthy and underestimated his lead over Lynch. Muchmore's preprimary poll in California underestimated to an even greater degree Kennedy's lead over Lynch, but was quite close in the Kennedy-McCarthy point spread. Quayle's Oregon survey was off the mark and incorrectly indicated a Kennedy lead over McCarthy, while the Roper, ABC, and CBS New Hampshire surveys (apparently conducted appreciably before Primary Day) were completely incorrect. Without knowing methodological details such as sample size, a valid assessment of how creditable these accuracy records are cannot be made. Nevertheless, it is apparent that while a repeat of the poor 1964 record was avoided, a level of accuracy comparable to what has been produced by some polls in general elections was not attained.

Given the intrinsic instability of primary elections and their highly variable turnouts, it seems unlikely that preprimary polls will ever be able to accrue an accuracy record comparable to that of preelection polls. By continuing to poll up through election

TABLE 17. Comparison of 1968 Democratic Primary Elections with Preprimary Polls

	%	%	%	%	%	%
New Hampshire	*Johnson*	*McCarthy*	*Kennedy*	*Others*	*Undecided*	
Election	49	42	1	8	—	
Roper (*Time*)	62	11	9	9	9	
CBS–TV	65	29	—	—	—	
ABC–TV	76	24	—	—	—	
Indiana	*Kennedy*	*McCarthy*	*Branigin*	*Undecided*		
Election	42	27	31	—		
Quayle (NBC)	37	24	30	9		
Harris	38	24	31	7		
Nebraska	*Kennedy*	*McCarthy*	*Humphrey*	*Johnson*	*Other*	*Undecided*
Election	52	31	8	6	3	—
Quayle (NBC)	47	22	9	7	7	8
Oregon	*Kennedy*	*McCarthy*	*Johnson*	*Humphrey*	*Other*	*Undecided*
Election	39	45	12	4	—	—
Quayle (NBC)	34	32	9	10	4	11
California	*Kennedy*	*McCarthy*	*Lynch*	*Undecided*		
Election	46	42	12	—		
Quayle (NBC)	39	30	13	18		
Muchmore	36	31	15	18		

Sources: *Philadelphia Inquirer*, March 14, 1968; *The New York Times*, May 7, May 8, May 14, May 28, and June 4, 1968.

eve, by reporting the final measurement on Primary Day, and by developing reliable methods of identifying the small proportion of the electorate that turns out to vote, preprimary polls may begin to approximate the accuracy of preelection polls. Taking into account all the added difficulties of conducting preprimary polls, their credibility is apt to remain lower than that of preelection polls. Nevertheless, they can be of great value to parties and prospective candidates in charting trends of voter preferences and determining what factors account for those shifts that do occur. Thus, while the general public and the news media may continue to voice skepticism of preprimary polls, parties and candidates can be expected to increase their use of these polls.

NOTES

1. *The New York Times,* November 4, 1968.

2. *Washington Post,* November 5, 1968.

3. Lindsay Rogers, *The Pollsters: Public Opinion, Politics, and Democratic Opinion* (New York: Alfred A. Knopf Co., 1949).

4. Senator Albert Gore, address to the Senate, February 11, 1960.

5. Elmo Roper, "Were the Polls Wrong?" *The Saturday Review* (December 10, 1966), p. 33.

6. Bernard C. Hennessy, and Erna R. Hennessy, "The Prediction of Close Elections: Comments on Some 1960 Polls," *Public Opinion Quarterly* (Fall 1961), pp. 405–411.

7. *Ibid.,* p. 410.

8. *Ibid.,* p. 411.

9. Paul K. Perry, Letter to the Editor, *Public Opinion Quarterly* (Spring 1962), pp. 133–135.

10. *Ibid.,* p. 135.

11. *New York Daily News,* November 5, 1964.

12. Charles W. Roll, Jr., "Straws in the Wind: The Record of the Daily News Poll," *Public Opinion Quarterly* (Summer 1968), p. 25.

13. *The New York Times,* November 4, 1966.

14. *The New York Times,* November 11, 1966.

15. *New York Daily News,* November 4, 1968.

16. *Gallup Opinion Index,* no. 42 (December 1968), inside back cover.

17. Paul K. Perry, "Election Survey Procedures for the Gallup Poll," *Public Opinion Quarterly* (Fall 1960), pp. 531–542; "Gallup Poll Election Survey Experience 1950–1960," *Public Opinion Quarterly* (Summer 1962), pp. 272–279; "Election Survey Methods," *Gallup Political Index,* no. 7 (December 1965), pp. i–xii.

18. Alfred Politz and W. R. Simmons, "An attempt to get the 'Not-at-Homes' into the sample without call-backs," *Journal of the American Statistical Association,* vol. 44, pp. 9–31.

19. Samuel A. Stouffer, "The S.S.R.C. Committee Report" in *The Polls and Public Opinion,* Norman C. Meier and Harold W. Saunders, eds. (New York: Henry Holt and Company, 1949), p. 210.

20. Paul K. Perry, *loc. cit., Public Opinion Quarterly* (1962), p. 279.

21. George Gallup, "Should Political Forecasts Be Made?" in Meier and Saunders, *op. cit.,* p. 286.

22. George Gallup, "Report on the 1968 Election" (mimeographed, undated).

23. Quoted by Gideon Seymour in Meier and Saunders, *op. cit.,* p. 272.

24. Paul F. Lazarsfeld in Meier and Saunders, *op. cit.,* p. 279.

25. Gideon Seymour in Meier and Saunders, *op. cit.,* p. 272.

26. George Gallup in Meier and Saunders, *op. cit.,* p. 286.

27. *Washington Post,* November 1, 1966.

28. Elmo Roper, *op. cit.,* p. 33.

29. *The New York Times,* November 4, 1968.

30. *Washington Post,* November 5, 1968.

31. Paul K. Perry, *op. cit.,* (1965), page v.

32. *Washington Post,* November 3, 1964.

33. *The New York Times,* August 25, 1964.

34. *Gallup Poll Report,* August 22, 1964.

35. *Washington Post,* October 12, 1964.

36. *Washington Post,* November 5, 1968.

37. Notes taken by Irving Crespi during talk given by Louis Harris on November 26, 1968, to the Princeton Chapter of the American Statistical Association.

38. *Ibid.*

39. *Gallup Poll Report,* February 9, 1967.

40. *Washington Post,* October 24, 1968.

41. *National Observer,* October 28, 1968.

42. *The New York Times,* October 23, 1968.

43. "The Week in Review," *The New York Times,* November 10, 1968.

44. *The New York Times,* November 8, 1968.

45. Theodore H. White, *The Making of the President 1960* (New York: Atheneum Publishers, 1961), p. 264.

46. *Ibid.,* p. 255 and p. 352.

47. *Ibid.,* p. 333; also Richard M. Nixon, *Six Crises* (Garden City: Doubleday & Company, Inc., 1962), p. 407.

48. Senator Albert Gore, *loc. cit.*

49. *Ibid.*

50. *Ibid.*

51. *Ibid.*

52. *The New York Times,* April 18, 1967.

53. Richard Harris, "How's It Look?" *The New Yorker* (April 8, 1967), p. 52.

54. Theodore H. White, *op. cit.* (1961), p. 33.

55. For example, see *Gallup Opinion Index,* no. 20 (February 1967), p. 17.

56. Gallup Poll release, July 12, 1952.

57. Gallup Poll release, September 20, 1952.

58. David Broder, *Washington Post,* August 2, 1968.

59. Chalmers M. Roberts, *Washington Post,* August 2, 1968.

60. *Washington Post,* August 1, 1968.

61. *Newsweek,* May 13, 1968, p. 29.

62. Samuel A. Stouffer, and Duncan McRae, Jr., "Evidence Pertaining to Last Minute Swing to Truman," in Frederick Mosteller, *et al., The Pre-Election Polls of 1948* (New York: Social Science Research Council, 1949), p. 251.

63. Louis Harris, "Of Polls and Politics in the United States," *Public Opinion Quarterly* (Spring 1964), p. 4.

64. Warren Weaver, *The New York Times,* August 22, 1968.

65. *The New York Times,* March 4, 1967.

66. Thomas W. Benham, "Polling for a Presidential Candidate: Some Observations on the 1964 Campaign," *Public Opinion Quarterly* (Summer 1965), p. 197.

67. Richard M. Nixon, *op. cit.,* p. 407.

68. Angus Campbell, Philip E. Converse, Warren E. Miller, and Ronald C. Stokes, *The American Voter* (New York: John Wiley & Sons, Inc., 1960), Chapter 6.

69. Louis Harris, *loc. cit.,* p. 4.

70. *Business Week,* June 6, 1964, p. 26.

71. Harold Faber, *The New York Times,* June 4, 1964.

72. *Ibid.*

73. *Los Angeles Times,* June 7, 1964.

74. *Philadelphia Evening Bulletin,* May 15, 1964.

75. *New York World Telegram & Sun,* June 1, 1964.

76. *Time,* May 29, 1964, p. 20.

77. *Time,* June 12, 1964, p. 31.

78. *The Spivack Report,* vol. II, no. 24 (undated, unpaginated).

3

Partisan and Manipulative Use of Polls

Whatever the merits of the claims and counterclaims as to the manipulative use of polls, and of the various proposals for controlling polls that might prevent such manipulation, there is no doubt regarding the intense interest and involvement politicians have in poll data. Interest and involvement exist on a number of different levels, but in all cases politicians are the ones who most actively use poll data. This use takes two forms—informational and manipulative. In the first instance, poll reports are carefully examined and analyzed for the political intelligence they contain. In the second, they are publicized, attacked, or buried for whatever partisan advantage may be anticipated.

The informational function of polls normally occurs at candidate and party headquarters. That is, private polls are commissioned by and reported to those persons in the highest positions within the party. Similarly, the systematic analyses of published poll reports are conducted by experts reporting to candidates and other leaders. Rank-and-file party workers participate little or not at all in these activities, while the involvement of the general electorate is indirect—it is the target of campaign decisions that have been influenced by poll data.

The locus of partisan and manipulative uses of poll data is also *within* the parties. Reports of privately commissioned polls and interpretations of published polls are communicated most purposefully to those who are in positions to offer financial backing and who control or influence nominations. Rank-and-file workers, whose morale may be seriously damaged by an adverse report or uplifted by a favorable one, also compose a prime audience. Although partisan claims based upon poll information are sometimes publicized in the mass media in the hope that some influence may also be exerted upon the general electorate, the dominant, immediate concern is with what happens within the party. In instance after instance—whether it be the attempts of a Rockefeller to convert convention delegates, the efforts of a Humphrey to find financial backers, the charges of a Wallace to revitalize the morale of his workers, or the exhortations of a Nixon to counteract overconfidence—the intense involvement of political leaders with polls has little to do with any direct influence upon the electorate. Rather, this involvement has to do with how the party organization, and consequently campaign effectiveness, will be affected. Only if it appears that a campaign issue can be developed out of charges regarding alleged unprofessional practice is there any likelihood that the general electorate will become the primary intended audience when polls are used manipulatively.

Within political circles the increased credibility of polls, based largely upon the accuracy of some of the major published polls, has created a generally receptive audience for all poll reports. As a consequence it is precisely within political circles that the potential for the manipulative use of polls is greatest. It is for this reason that those who are directly involved in making or influencing political decisions are subjected to the barrage of conflicting reports such as those which characterized the 1968 Presidential primaries and election. The significant long-term effects of public-opinion polls cannot be identified unless politicians' involvement with poll data is the focus of analysis.

The consistency with which many published preelection polls have come close to actual election results in recent years is impressive, and the increased use of privately sponsored polls is testimony to the extent to which political users have been impressed. For example, Harris estimated that in 1962 two-thirds of the senatorial candidates had private polls conducted for their guidance, as did three-fourths of the gubernatorial candidates.[1]

And, as noted earlier, 27 out of 29 Senators who responded to a mail survey in the summer of 1967 reported that they conduct polls. However, Harris estimated that, primarily because of financial limitations, only one out of every ten congressional candidates sponsor their own polls.

Yet there are still "polls" which reflect little awareness of the methodological requirements for precision of measurement which nevertheless receive respectful notice in the news media. The fact is that as the survey organizations which conduct published preelection polls refine their methodologies and produce highly accurate results, the reports of all poll results are legitimized. This situation can lead to the acceptance of poorly engineered polls and can facilitate the manipulative use of polls. For this reason, the manipulative use of polls can be expected to increase precisely as a result of methodological advances. Those persons concerned with how preelection polls serve the democratic process, therefore, increasingly feel that standards and controls over polls are required. As is the case with any invention or scientific advance, interest in using polls to further the common good focuses not only in the quality of the polls, but also on the development of appropriate institutional methods for controlling and directing their application.

THE PUBLICATION AND "LEAKING" OF PRIVATE POLLS

There have been various allegations as to the publication of privately sponsored polls for manipulative purposes. Since such allegations border on the libelous, it is difficult to document them even though within polling and political circles gossip is not uncommon. The type of manipulation that is most likely to come into public view is that of the "leaked" poll—that is, characteristically, a claim made by a candidate's spokesman that a recent poll shows his man in the lead. In some cases, the name of the organization that is supposed to have conducted the poll is named as a basis for establishing the credibility of the reported measurement.

One of the rare occasions for which we have a rather full picture of how a poll is leaked to the press took place in the fall of 1967. At that time many of the published polls, most notably Gallup and Harris, were reporting that President Lyndon Johnson's public support was weakening considerably. For example, in October the Gallup Poll reported Romney ahead of Johnson nationwide 48 percent to 45 percent, Rockefeller ahead 54 to 40, and Nixon ahead 49 to 45.[2] Then, on October 27 it was reported in the press that private polls were showing Johnson in the lead. Vice President Hubert Humphrey publicized the poll results at a Democratic dinner, and privately it was rumored that Johnson himself had informed news correspondents of the results. As interpreted by some columnists, these results cast doubt on the credibility of the Gallup and Harris measurement. Others, however, were skeptical of these private polls and the interpretation made of them, and insisted on obtaining further information.

The full story, as reported later by the press, emerges as follows:[3] In September, Arthur Krim, finance director of the Democratic National Committee, commissioned Archibald Crossley to conduct a number of polls measuring Johnson's strength vis-à-vis some of the leading Republican contenders. Surveys were taken in selected states (New York, California, Pennsylvania) and in Strafford County in New Hampshire, and one nationwide poll was conducted. Krim specified which Republican contenders were to be included in which surveys. For example, Nelson Rockefeller was not tested against Johnson in the former's home state, New York.

Crossley, as is his standard practice, included in the contract a statement to the effect that the survey results were confidential and not for publication, and that if any parts of a report were made public he would have the right to issue the entire report and make any corrective statement that might be indicated. This, in fact, was done by Crossley after the results were leaked. *The New York Times* quoted Crossley as saying that some things not circulated about the research were that "Strafford County is not typical of New Hampshire, that there were very few interviews there and that it is a Democratic county, running four to seven percentage points more Democratic than the state." He also pointed out to the press that the New Hampshire county, selected by Krim as a supposedly "bellwether" county, was actually 6.7 percentage points more Democratic than the rest of the country in the 1964 Presidential election. Crossley further noted that, as had been reported earlier by the Gallup Poll, the East was the one region of the country where Johnson was still doing well, and that when his New York and Pennsylvania results were compared with the Gallup reports for the entire East, they corresponded closely.

As for how the poll results came to be published, Crossley said, "I do not approve of the leaking of the reports and did not give sanction for them to be released. . . . It got released to Drew Pearson—how or why I do not know. Then it got leaked other places." He stated that the results he issued "had all sorts of cautions on their use that were not observed." Initially, he would not divulge his client's identity, declaring, "It was supposed to be a confidential relationship and I have kept my part of the confidence."

Reportedly "infuriated" by the deliberate leaking of selected local results to give the unwarranted impression that Gallup Poll and Harris Survey national results were wrong, Crossley cancelled further surveys for Krim, saying, "I just don't have any interest in polling for political promotion purposes." The distortion of poll results for such purposes, he added, "hurts the whole profession."

In this case, the attempt to leak polls to achieve a specific political purpose backfired for two reasons. First, a number of alert reporters refused to accept at face value the leaked results and the slanted way in which they were interpreted. Second, the pollster himself adhered to high professional standards and put the public interest ahead of personal profit. Unfortunately, it is difficult to estimate how many cases there have been in which questionable polls or interpretations of them have been leaked without the true picture becoming known to the public.

Claims and counterclaims as to who is leading in "the polls" are not infrequent, sometimes with the survey organization being incorrectly quoted unbeknownst to itself. Since newspapers do not always provide information that would enable a qualified person to evaluate the poll's results—such as sample size and the wording of questions—the credibility of these claims is usually not subject to objective appraisal. It is possible for an honest mistake to occur in a public interpretation of a poll's results, but there is always the possibility that a candidate's backers will use a deliberately fraudulent claim to attempt to garner support for him. Harris has reported that of the 514 political polls he conducted from 1955 through 1962, purported information "from our polls has been published only 11 times, while there were 20 cases of wholly made up results."[4] Many private pollsters, for the purpose of self-protection, follow Crossley's practice and inform their clients that if poll results are leaked or released out of context the entire report will be made public.

Manipulation can also take place without any awareness on the part of a survey organization, even without its having conducted a poll. For example, one private pollster discovered that he was being credited in political circles with being "right" in an election on which he had not conducted a single survey. Presumably, one of the candidates had felt it was to his advantage to circulate an unfounded rumor that "so-and-so" had conducted a poll which showed him to be in the lead.

Complicating the problem further is the fact that the persons involved occasionally find it difficult to keep separate the identity of the various organizations that conduct private polls. Thus *The New York Times* reported that Romney supporters were convinced of the accuracy of a private poll which had been conducted for him because "it was taken by Public Opinion Surveys, Inc. of Princeton, N.J." which ". . . after a series of polls paid for by Governor Rockefeller's re-election campaign organization in New York last fall, predicted the Governor's victory despite the contrary findings of several other polls."[5] This news report was in error on two accounts: (1) The polls conducted for Rockefeller had been the work of Political Surveys and Analyses, Inc. of Princeton, N.J., and (2) the Romney poll had been conducted by Market Opinion Research Corporation, a long-established Detroit-based organization which had worked for Romney often in past elections.

THE EFFECT OF POLLS ON PARTY MORALE AND FINANCING

The release of privately sponsored polls with full acknowledgment as to their identities has also become a characteristic of election campaigns. But even in such cases, controversy still arises as to the objectivity with which results are reported. For example, in the midst of the 1968 Presidential campaign the news media reported a barrage of private polls, each purporting to show that the sponsoring candidate was in the lead. The skepticism voiced by many news commentators about the credibility of these privately sponsored polls has in some cases been generalized to all polls, published and private.

It was reported in *The New York Times* on October 4, 1968, that a poll conducted by Oliver Quayle for the Nassau County (New York) Republicans showed Nixon leading in the county by 66 percent to 26 percent for Humphrey and 8 percent for Wallace, with 16 percent undecided. This poll, reportedly based on a survey of 306 registered voters, also indicated a marked trend from June, with Nixon gaining 14 points in that period, Wallace 5 points, and Humphrey losing 19 points.

Only a few days later, on October 8th, the *New York Post* reported that a Democratic-sponsored statewide poll showed Humphrey leading statewide 41 percent to 38 percent for Nixon, 8 percent for Wallace, and 13 percent undecided. While it is not surprising that suburban Nassau County should be more Republican than the entire state of New York (which is heavily weighted by normally Democratic New York City), the magnitude of the difference is striking.

Other Democratic-sponsored polls, also reported in the October 8 *Post* story, showed Humphrey stronger in some states than did independent published polls. For example, a mid-September Minnesota Poll reported Humphrey and Nixon in a virtual tie, 45 percent to 44 percent. The Democratic-sponsored poll, however, showed Humphrey ahead in Minnesota 44 percent to 33 percent.

The fact that the polls sponsored by the Democratic party (at least the ones that were released to the press) consistently favored the party's own candidates prompted speculation as to the reliability of these polls. Rowland Evans and Robert Novak, commenting on this speculation, said:

Since these state Polls show Humphrey considerably higher than other surveys, they are not taken seriously either in the polling fraternity or the Democratic National Committee's own research team.[6]

Evans and Novak also reported that a poll taken by Quayle showing Humphrey trailing Nixon by 17 percentage points in Illinois was withheld from public scrutiny by Democratic National Chairman Lawrence F. O'Brien. (It has been asserted that these state polls in fact were conducted as part of a deliberate effort "not merely to counteract Gallup but to discredit him," so that potential financial contributors would not be discouraged.[7])

Controversy in 1968 as to the objectivity of polls released by partisan sponsors was not restricted to the Presidential campaign. In that year's New York senatorial contest a bitter exchange was stimulated by a Republican report that one of their polls showed incumbent Jacob Javits leading Paul O'Dwyer 48 percent to 16 percent. O'Dwyer charged that this was a deliberate attempt to influence the *New York Daily News* Poll, which was scheduled to commence canvassing just after the Republican poll was released, "by attempting to create a bandwagon effect." He compared the Republican poll to one issued by Joseph Resnick during the Democratic primary campaign the previous June. The Resnick-sponsored poll had indicated that O'Dwyer was getting only 14 percent of the votes of Democrats in his fight for the nomination, whereas he actually received 38 percent, enough to win in a three-way contest.[8]

However justified or unjustified O'Dwyer's charges or the criticisms made by Evans and Novak may have been, the possibility that in some cases privately sponsored polls might be slanted in deliberate attempts to achieve partisan advantage inevitably creates suspicion about all such polls. To the extent that this suspiciousness becomes generalized, it can serve as the basis for attempting to create campaign issues by trying to discredit any poll which shows one's candidate trailing. Thus, during the 1968 Presidential campaign, George Wallace charged that "Eastern power money" was manipulating public-opinion polls as a way of winning the Presidential election for Richard Nixon. He asserted that a Republican strategy had been developed whereby Wallace would be shown gaining strength in September and then declining in October.[9] To substantiate his charge, Wallace claimed that Nixon headquarters had obtained an advance look at a Gallup Poll release:

I think the national polls are not showing my strength and to that extent they are rigged. . . . Mr. Nixon gave it away when he said up in Michigan yesterday (Tuesday) that the next poll would show I'm flaking off.[10]

However, a Wallace spokesman was quoted as saying later in the day that they too had managed to get an early look at the release in question. Since poll releases are sent to newspapers one or two days in advance of the publication date in order to make possible simultaneous nationwide publication, it is understandable that both Nixon and Wallace had been able to find out what the survey results were ahead of publication time.

Democratic campaign leaders also publicly questioned the reliability of published polls which showed Nixon leading Humphrey nationwide by margins of 8 to 12 percentage points as of the end of September. Only one day before the Wallace statement, it was reported in *The New York Times* that the Democratic party leadership was "searching desperately for ways to counteract what it considers to be misleading and injurious opinion polls and surveys."[11] Referring to the same polls that Evans and Novak were then criticizing, the *Times* story indicated that these polls provided the Democratic strategists with a basis for concluding that, even though Humphrey was behind nationally, his lead in a number of individual states with large blocs of electoral votes made the race close. The Democratic leaders were reported as feeling that

(t)he contradictory polls and surveys impede them at every turn . . . and are now feeding themselves by misleading the press, discouraging party workers around the country and putting off potential contributors of badly needed funds.

To place these comments in context, it should be noted that both the Harris and Gallup surveys for which interviewing had been conducted in early October and which were released, respectively, on October 18 and 22, showed a narrowing of Nixon's lead by about three percentage points, while a later Gallup survey, released on October 27, showed a further narrowing at the expense of Wallace.

In any event, it appears that the Democratic polls were commissioned not only to provide information that would give direction to campaign tactics but also in the hope that they would scare up badly needed funds. Without questioning the professional quality of these polls (which cannot be done properly on the basis of the limited disclosure of the methodology employed), there can be no doubt as to the partisan interest which was their *raison d'être*.

The possible effect of a poll upon the morale of party workers has long been a matter of utmost concern to candidates. Harris reports that in 1960 his state-by-state reports went to only two men, John F. Kennedy and Robert Kennedy.[12] Their concern on this matter was two-fold. If one's candidate is in the lead, there is the fear that campaign workers, if they find out, might slacken their efforts. Conversely, a poll showing a candidate trailing could easily discourage his workers. In contrast, however secretive a candidate might be with his private polls as concerns his own staff, the temptation to affect his opponent's staff might be hard to resist in a bitterly fought campaign.

The clash of polls conducted by organizations utilizing widely varying sampling, questioning, and analytical methods has occurred within the context of suspicions about the manipulative intent of those releasing poll results. These discrepancies have sharpened concern, extensively reported in the press during the 1968 Presidential campaign, about what might be done so that the public interest would not be subverted.

Even before the news media became fully aware of the problems involved, the polling profession had focused attention on them. In May 1967, a discussion titled "Polling and the Political Process," was conducted during the 22nd annual conference of the American Association for Public Opinion Research.[13] Mervin

Field, Director of the California Poll; Thomas A. Benham of Opinion Research Corporation (ORC); Oliver A. Quayle III, head of the firm bearing his name; and Frederick Currier of Market Opinion Research Corporation all asserted during their talks that they were concerned about the need to protect the public interest. For example, all stated that their firms inform political clients that if poll results are "leaked" or misinterpreted to the public, they will issue a corrective statement including release of the entire report.

This practice, however, offers only partial protection against the use of polls for the purpose of manipulating public opinion. For example, Benham referred to an incident during the 1964 Presidential campaign in which ORC conducted confidential polls for Goldwater. Misinterpreting an ORC survey measurement on voter beliefs as to how the election was developing, campaign manager Dean Burch declared that a private poll showed Goldwater getting 40 percent of the vote, which was considerably better than what the Gallup Poll was then reporting. In fact, Benham continued, the ORC survey corresponded almost exactly to the published Gallup Poll, which had reported Johnson leading Goldwater by a margin of better than 5 to 3. ORC immediately contacted Dean Burch and demanded a correction. This correction was made, but as is usually the case with corrections, it received little publicity.

During the discussion on this topic, Burns Roper, President of Roper Research Associates, commenting from the floor, reported that he had heard of a specific case which had occurred sometime during the seven preceding months, in which a private pollster released a survey measurement which he knew was wrong. Later, in private conversation, another type of abuse was mentioned by a member of the audience. He reported that immediately preceding a primary election, the candidate who was widely believed to be trailing (Candidate A) was allegedly shown a report, purportedly conducted on behalf of his opponent (Candidate B), which showed the former in the lead. Candidate A's consultant, however, discounted this "result," warning that it could well be a device to engender complacency. The primary outcome tended to support this interpretation since Candidate A did, in fact, lose by a sizable margin. The informant's conclusion was that either the winner's private poll was inaccurate or that there had been a deliberate effort to mislead. It is also possible that the poll had been a correct measurement at the time it was taken and that Candidate B, hoping to dislocate his opponent's campaign effort, had arranged to "leak" the poll. Whatever may have been the case, the temptation to attempt deceitful manipulation through leaking private polls can clearly be great in the heat of a campaign.

STANDARDS FOR REPORTING POLL RESULTS

Efforts to attain partisan advantage by the controlled reporting of private polls result not from the inherent characteristics of the survey method but from the partisan and occasionally unethical behavior of some politicians and some practitioners of the survey method. In reaction to such efforts, The American Association of Public Opinion Research (AAPOR), at its May, 1967 conference, approved the promulgation of a code titled "Standards for Reporting Public Opinion Polls."[13] A draft code that had been prepared by the Standards Committee was mailed to the entire membership for comment.[14] The revised code was adopted by the AAPOR Executive Council that winter and issued to the membership at the next conference held in Santa Barbara, on May 9–11, 1968.

The code is "a standard which news media can utilize when reporting poll results," thereby facilitating a differentiation "between surveys which are conducted with a proper concern for professional competence and those which reflect an ignorance of or willful unconcern with good research practice." Eight essential minima that were recommended for inclusion in all news reports are established by the code:

1. Identity of who sponsored the survey.
2. The exact wording of questions asked.
3. A definition of the population actually sampled.
4. Size of sample. For mail surveys, this should include both

the number of questionnaires mailed out and the number returned.

5. An indication of what allowance should be made for
sampling error.

6. Which results are based on parts of the sample, rather than
the total sample, for example, likely voters only, those aware of
an event, those who answered other questions in a certain way,
and the like.

7. Whether interviewing was done personally, by telephone,
by mail, or on street corners.

8. Timing of the interviewing in relation to relevant events.

The code continues:

*We strongly urge the news media to ask for and include ALL the
above information when preparing final copy for publication or broadcast.* This should apply not only to polls conducted for publication but
also to "private polls" whose results are publicized.

We strongly urge survey organizations that conduct polls for the
news media to prepare standard descriptions of their methods for
public distribution.

We recommend that survey organizations use professional journals
and meetings to inform their colleagues in detail of their activities and
methods.

We encourage the news media, and the professional staffs of political parties, to use these professional sources of information to become
aware of what is accepted research practice.

We wholeheartedly endorse the practice now adhered to by many
survey organizations of making their surveys available to scholars for
further analysis and recommend its extension to confidential polls
whenever possible.

The code also includes a detailed list of questions that might
be asked as needed whenever the credibility of a poll is in doubt.
These questions were formulated to illustrate that in order to
evaluate a poll professionally it is necessary to have considerable
information as to what methodology was used and how competently it was administered. Intrinsic to the code is the belief
that providing this information does not, in and of itself, establish
a poll's credentials, but does provide a basis for evaluating them.
Inferentially, to the extent that a survey organization is unwilling
to describe at least the general outlines of its methods, one might

reasonably assume that they would not stand up under professional scrutiny. It is also important to note that the code does *not* attempt to establish standards as to *how* a poll should be conducted but rather attempts to facilitate the professional evaluation of whatever methods were used. For example, there is no one way in which an acceptable sample must be selected, but there are criteria for evaluating the extent to which the method used conforms to good practice.

In September 1968, a copy of the code was sent to every United States Senator, Congressman, and Governor, as well as to over 200 newspaper editors.

A parallel, but independent, development was the formation, in June 1968, of the National Committee on Published Polls, a self-policing organization of survey organizations that conduct regularly published polls. Earlier, in 1967, Dr. George Gallup had contacted as many public and private pollsters as he could identify, soliciting their interest in forming a self-policing group. Sufficient interest was expressed so that by May 1967 a questionnaire was mailed to each asking for specific suggestions as to what this group might do. These suggestions were organized into a tentative code and by December sufficient progress had been made for the incipient formation of the group to be mentioned in the press.[15] In April 1968, Gallup invited some twenty-five pollsters to attend an organizational meeting to be held on May 8 in Santa Barbara, the day before the AAPOR meeting officially opened.

Twenty persons representing fourteen survey groups, the three television networks, and one news magazine attended the meeting. Under Gallup's chairmanship it was formally resolved that a self-policing group be organized, the purpose of which would be to fulfill the obligation of polling organizations to further the public good. Tentative agreement was reached on standards for reporting poll results to the press, and a Charter Committee was named to implement this decision. The committee consisted of Archibald Crossley (Chairman), Fred Currier, Mervin Field, Louis Harris, Glenn Roberts, George Gallup (ex officio), and Irving Crespi (Secretary pro tem).

The committee met in Philadelphia on June 18, 1968, and decided that an organization consisting only of published polls be formed to

publicize established standards for reporting poll results obtained by these state and national polling organizations;

aid in informing the public, and the news media, as to the proper interpretation of such findings;

work towards the maximum service to the public in polling operations.[16]

It was the decision of the charter committee that it would not include polling organizations which confine their efforts to the gathering of facts for candidates and parties and not for public consumption. Crossley is quoted as saying:

While we hope that such organizations will set up their own standards of operation, and while we would be glad to be of assistance informally, it is our feeling that in many respects the operating problems are different. But when a private poll, through leaks or otherwise, becomes public, we have common interests. It is proper then, we feel, to ask the media of communication and the client to cooperate with us by insisting that such results be accompanied by full disclosure of polling methods.

The polling organizations that formed the National Committee are The California Poll, the State Poll of California, The Gallup Poll, The Harris Survey, The Iowa Poll, Market-Opinion Research (*Detroit News*), The Minnesota Poll and the *Minneapolis Metro* Poll, Roper Research Associates, The Texas Poll, and The Pinellas (Florida) Poll. Archibald Crossley was named Executive Secretary of the National Committee.

Members of the National Committee on Published Polls agreed to public disclosure of the ways in which their results are obtained. Crossley explained:

Our aim is to give the public a better understanding and a better basis for interpreting poll results that have to do with elections and with issues of the day. To this end, members of this group agree to include the following basic information in, or accompanying, all public releases:

Identity of the polling organization.

A definition of the specific population sampled.

Size of the obtained sample.

How the survey was conducted (personal interview, telephone, mail, street corner, etc.).

The question wordings.

Timing of the field work, when wrong interpretation of the data might otherwise result.

In addition, members agree to make available to the Executive Secretary further information as to general procedures followed. This information would be used to deal with procedural problems that might be raised by news media or others.

The items included in the National Committee's code correspond very closely to those which comprise the AAPOR standards for reporting poll results. This correspondence reflects the considerable consensus that exists among survey researchers as to what are the essential bits of information that should accompany any news release about a public-opinion poll. Missing from the Committee code is a statement on what allowance should be made for sampling error, primarily because it was anticipated that newspaper editors would object that this would be too technical for the general newspaper reader. However, as editors become more sophisticated in this regard, we can expect that it will become standard practice to include some statement on sampling error when poll reports are issued. Thus, during the 1968 election campaign, Gallup, Harris, and Field, among others, periodically included such information in their releases.

To give greater weight to its self-policing efforts, the National Committee was reorganized on May 14, 1969 as a public corporation, the National Council on Public Polls. The incorporators were Archibald M. Crossley, Fred Currier (Market Opinion Research, Detroit), George Gallup (Gallup Poll), Louis Harris (Louis Harris Associates), and Burns Roper (Roper Research Associates). Richard M. Scammon of the Governmental Affairs Institute, and also Director of the Election Research Center, was named President of the Council. Scammon, in a mimeographed news release on May 15, 1969, announced the incorporation of the Council and described its purpose in these words:

A major part of its efforts will be to broaden public knowledge about published polls so as to give the media and the general public a better basis for interpreting polls and for protecting the public against misleading information.

The action taken by AAPOR and the formation of the National Council on Published Polls were intended to provide protection against certain types of abuse of poll results. Alerted to the standards that professional survey organizations can be expected to abide by, journalists and political leaders presumably will become better able to recognize incompetent or unprofessional research. Specifically, by providing an institutionalized framework for reporting poll results, these two developments should result in a better informed treatment of polls by the news media. Among other things, the inclination of many journalists to make blanket statements as to "what the polls are showing" hopefully will be reduced, and the reporting of *whose* poll using *which* methods shows *what* results will be encouraged. To the extent that this happens, the use of the news media to disseminate distorted information should decrease. Political leaders would then be protected against the danger of basing their decisions on false or faulty information.

The Role of the News Media

The importance of the news media in counteracting the manipulative or uninformed interpretation of poll results cannot be underestimated. One journalist who has specialized in the analysis of public-opinion polls has concluded that "the real policing will have to be done by the press."[17] For example, the reluctance of politicians to identify themselves as the sponsors of privately commissioned polls, which would reveal a possible source of bias, has in the past been reinforced by the news media, since reporters tend to feel bound by tradition to protect their sources. One reason for this tradition is that a source which is kept secret can provide more information—and with more exclusivity—than one whose identity is divulged. The onus is on journalists to develop a balance between preserving their news sources and protecting the public. This can be done if they learn to ask the right questions about a poll so that they can assess the credibility of a leaked result before reporting it. If they do not do so, they may make themselves tools, albeit unwilling, of those who attempt to use poll data for partisan purposes.

Meyer has described the results of misinformed reporting with respect to the Krim-sponsored polls discussed above:

> The reporters and columnists to whom the results were leaked, acted like patsies. *The Washington Post* called the New York poll "in sharp contrast" to the Gallup findings. Columnist Roscoe Drummond fretted that "it is a little unsettling" to find polls showing "opposite results." United Press International said the leaked polls were "in stark contrast" to what the public polls had been saying. The Washington *Evening Star* passed the word from "Democratic sources" that the Crossley polls were "more representative than the national polls because they contain a larger sampling." *The New York Times*, with a staggering ignorance of sampling error, said the Strafford County, New Hampshire, poll indicated that Nixon "could carry the state against President Johnson."
>
> The one-county poll indicated no such thing, of course. It didn't even indicate what Nixon could do in Strafford County, because his lead over Johnson was one percentage point, and the error allowance in the 241-person sample was close to eight percentage points.
>
> As the story churned along, the reporting did get better. The Washington *Star* noted the evident card-stacking in the omission of Rockefeller from the New York poll. *The Washington Post* eventually identified Krim as the sponsor and produced an interview with Crossley in which he lamented the twisting of his truths to make a trap for fools.[18]

A concern with the uninformed reporting of unscientific surveys led AAPOR, in October, 1966, to criticize the serious attention given by the mass media to opinion surveys not conducted by scientific standards. The AAPOR Executive Council resolved that

> many so-called "polls" are conducted in ways that cast considerable doubt as to how well their results can reflect public opinion. . . . *The prominent reporting of such polls as though they were true measurements of public opinion may be seriously misleading and so be a disservice to the public.*[19]

Two news stories, both published on the same day, one appearing in *The New York Times* and the other in the *Wall Street Journal*, highlight the significance of the AAPOR resolution. Warren Weaver, Jr., writing in the *Times*, reported that "national polls, which have been Governor Romney's strongest asset, have shown a decline in recent months."[20] He documents this statement by quoting the actual survey results, in percentages, that had been reported by the Gallup Poll and by the Harris Survey. In contrast, in a lead front-page story headlined "Mideast Outcome Gain in Polls Seen Brightening Johnson's 1968 Outlook," Alan L. Otten wrote in the *Wall Street Journal:*

The President's comeback in the opinion polls has been a shot of adrenalin; his own sense of relief has infected his entourage. . . . At the same time, administration strategists are quite ready to write off the anti-Johnson showings of the earlier polls.[20]

At no point in his story does Otten identify which polls were involved or mention the size of the increase in support that had taken place. The reader is left to guess whether the polls referred to were privately commissioned or published polls. Neither does the reader know whether the reported shift in opinion was of a magnitude that gave Johnson a marginal or a substantial lead over his rivals. Whereas Weaver's story gave the reader a factual basis for making an informed judgment as to the meaning and credibility of the apparent decline in Romney's support, Otten's story did not. In effect, Otten publicized the partisan conclusions of the Johnson administration. While this, in itself, is legitimate journalism, it is symptomatic of the type of news reporting that makes it easy for political leaders to use polls manipulatively.

There are indications that the AAPOR code and the code of the National Committee on Published Polls are beginning to influence the news media. During the 1968 election campaign, many news reports included information about sample size, question wordings, interviewing methods, and the like. Even when such information is included, however, the credibility of reported results may be subject to professional criticism. In a news story headlined, "Republican Poll Puts Nixon Ahead in State, but by a Slim Margin," Homer Bigart provided considerable information about the poll. He reported that the poll was conducted by the New York State Republican Campaign Committee, it involved 1,500 face-to-face interviews conducted over a two week period by seven full time interviewers, and respondents were "chosen at random and were questioned on the streets, in shopping centers and in restaurants." Bigart also noted that the text of the questionnaire was withheld.[22]

Missing from the Bigart story is the fact that no sampling statistician would accept the description of the sampling method as one that conforms to "scientific polling techniques." Rather, street corner and shopping center interviews are widely recognized as being subject to considerable bias, and it is difficult to conceive of how the selection of such interviews could even approach a mathematical definition of randomness. While Bigart's story provided information that would make a professional skeptical of the poll results, it would be highly unrealistic to assume that the average politician or the general newspaper reader is equally capable of making such an informed assessment.

MAIL SURVEYS OF CONSTITUENCIES

Congressmen often use "surveys" more as a method of campaigning than as a serious attempt to investigate what their constituency is thinking. For example, one Congressman mailed 180,000 questionnaires to voters in his district which included these two questions:

1. In 1958, I publicly proposed an extra tax credit for parents of college students. Are you in favor of such a tax credit exemption as presently gaining bi-partisan support in Congress?
2. Do you feel demonstrators who block U.S. troop trains, burn draft cards, send gifts and blood plasma to North Vietnam should be fined and imprisoned when such acts would be considered treasonous if we were in a declared state of war?[23]

Apart from the merits of the two issues, the question-wordings are clearly one-sided and violate the most elementary principles of questionnaire design. Moreover, only 12,134 replies were received, which was 7 percent of the total mailed out. Such a small return is inadequate by any standard of sampling if one is seeking an unbiased sample of the population being surveyed.

One Congressman who has regularly polled his constituency by mail is Frank Thompson, Jr., of New Jersey. His question-wordings generally meet professional standards of objectivity. However, from a sampling point of view, it is impossible to assess the meaningfulness of his reported results since he provides absolutely no information whatsoever as to how many questionnaires were mailed or how many were returned.[24] Neither does he report the background characteristics (e.g., sex, age, educational attainment, party affiliation, and the like) of those who returned their questionnaires. Without such information, one cannot judge whether—whatever the completion rate—the obtained sample is biased in any way.

Typically, the results of these mail surveys are placed in the Congressional Record and reprints are mailed to constituents. Illustrative of this procedure is the report on a mail survey conducted by Representative Charles Raper Jonas of North Carolina.[25] The reprint notes that questionnaires were returned by 13,379 persons, but does not say how many were mailed out. Question-wordings are quoted, and the objectivity of the tabulations is presumedly based on the fact that they were performed on data processing equipment by an independent firm. Nevertheless, the sampling procedure makes the results completely unacceptable as an unbiased (from a sampling viewpoint) measurement of public opinion.

Despite the methodological weaknesses of such mail surveys, their apparent newsworthiness on occasion results in a considerable degree of attention being given to them in the news media. *The New York Times* featured one such poll on the front page of its Sunday, August 28, 1966 issue with the headline "54% in Ohio Poll Assert U.S. Role in War Is Mistake." The reported poll had been conducted by Congressman Charles A. Mosher. He sent a questionnaire to every voter in his constituency, of whom about 4 percent filled out and returned it. In commercial market research mail surveys, by way of contrast, returns of about 20 percent are frequent and even then the survey results are treated with extreme caution. Not until about a 50 percent completion rate is achieved in mail surveys do experienced market researchers treat the findings as more than advisory. When important marketing decisions are to be made, every effort is made to obtain returns from 60 to 70 percent of the persons to whom the questionnaires are mailed, while in academic research even higher response rates are sought. If similar standards were to be adopted by the news media, mail polls conducted by many Congressmen would be given only minor, if any, attention.

On the other hand, unless and until political leaders become concerned with conducting polls and reporting results in conformity with professional standards, the news media are apt to be subject to pressure to report such polls. If they refuse to do so, charges of bias might well be made against them by offended politicians. Thus, for the AAPOR and National Committee on Published Polls fully to achieve their goals, political leaders as well as the news media will have to modify long-established practices. To the extent that such modifications are not made, efforts by professional pollsters to develop codes for reporting poll results in a manner that would serve the public interest can have limited effect on attempts to use polls for partisan purposes.

THE SUSCEPTIBILITY OF POLLS TO MANIPULATION

The promulgation of ethical standards, the establishment of self-policing procedures, and the development of a better-informed news media cannot protect against deliberate dishonesty. For this reason, it is germane to consider what aspects of polls are the most susceptible to unethical manipulation. First, there is the possibility of devising research designs that produce desired "findings." Second, but of possibly greater significance, is the nature of the relationship between the survey organization and the candidate or party.

POOR RESEARCH DESIGN

While the survey method is demonstrably capable of accurately measuring voter preferences, poor methodology can produce misleading results. A large part of the professional literature is devoted to the problem of avoiding such pitfalls as poor question-wording, procedures that result in unrepresentative samples, and inadequate analysis of data. Either through ignorance of sound survey methodology, or through deliberate intent to mislead, survey results can be developed that are distortions of the climate of public opinion. Moreover, even if the results are not in themselves distortions, their correct meaning can be lost.

For this reason it is essential to know more than what is expressed by the kind of statement frequently heard—namely, "polls show that Candidate X is ahead"—if a poll's credibility is to be adequately assessed. A comparison of two surveys of public opinion about the Johnson administration and Vietnam graphically illustrates this point. In May, 1967, the Harris Survey reported that 71 percent of the public approved of the Johnson administration's Vietnam policies.[26] Almost simultaneously, the Gallup Poll was reporting that only 43 percent approved of the way Johnson was handling the situation in Vietnam.[27] The apparent conflict between these two reports is, it seems almost certain, the result of a crucial difference in the questions asked in the two surveys. While the exact wording of the Harris question was not reported, it apparently asked about approval of "policies." In contrast, Gallup asked, "Do you approve or disapprove of the way President Johnson is handling the situation in Vietnam?" A reasonable conclusion is that while a large majority of the public supported in principle the policy of actively resisting Communism in Vietnam, less than half approved of the way in which that policy was being implemented. In fact, a later report of the Harris Survey which appeared in *Newsweek* drew such a conclusion.[28]

A key political question to ask is, Which measurement, approval of "policies" or approval of "handling the situation," is the better indicator of Johnson's political strength? This question can best be answered by further analysis of the relationship between voter preferences and how voters respond to the two questions. To conclude that neither measurement has meaning is to ignore the subtle but vital distinction between supporting goals and supporting the means selected to meet goals.

Obviously, it is possible for a private pollster, if he so desires, to fish around until a question-wording is developed that shows his candidate in a particularly favorable light, and to avoid using those question-wordings that reveal weaknesses. If a survey is so contrived the results can be reported as showing "our man's ahead." On the other hand, if politicians and journalists, when evaluating reports, have sufficient sophistication to take into account the specific meaning of the questions asked, assuming they have access to the question-wordings, the potential for manipulation is lessened.

Even if the specific question which tests candidate preference is objectively worded, answers can be significantly influenced by a judicious choice of the immediately preceding questions. A Democratic-sponsored poll conducted during the 1968 campaign reportedly asked a series of questions along the following lines:

1. The political party with which the respondent identifies. Independents were asked toward which party they lean.

2. The political party, rather than the man, the respondent would like to see win the Presidential election.

3. Strength of party identification.

4. Preference between Nixon and Rockefeller to have received the Republican nomination.

5. Preference between Humphrey and McCarthy to have received the Democratic nomination.

6. Opinion as to who would make the better President—Agnew or Muskie.[29]

Asking a series of questions like this—getting respondents to consider first their party identification and whom they would have preferred be nominated, then the relative merits of the Vice-Presidential candidate—might be an excellent way to obtain a considered judgment. On the other hand, one can easily imagine that a Republican-sponsored poll would have preferred that the series consist of "objectively" worded questions on some of the leading issues of the campaign—for example, "law and order," the conduct of the war in Vietnam, the high cost of living, and the like. The results of two polls conducted simultaneously and using identical sample designs, differing only in the questions asked before the candidate-preference question, could differ markedly, one can safely predict, if the preceding questions were in one case those used in the Democratic-sponsored poll while in the other case the "Republican" questions listed above were used.

When politicians, journalists, and the general public face the task of judging the acceptability of conflicting polls, they seldom have any information about the structure of the questionnaire that was utilized. If one of the polls had been conducted by a survey organization with a published history of accuracy, this record could provide some objective basis for evaluating results that it releases, even in the absence of such details. There are only a few media-sponsored polls, however, for which published accuracy records exist—for example, the Gallup Poll, the Harris Survey, the California Poll, the Iowa Poll, and the Minnesota Poll. In the greatest number of cases, private polling organizations, even those with well-established reputations, do not have any published accuracy record, nor have they made public any details of the methods they employ. As a consequence, while there is some meaningful basis for accepting or rejecting reports from the published polls, there is no such basis on which to evaluate private polls. In the latter case, the only practical criterion that has existed to date is faith in the professional competence and probity of the polling organization. (In 1968 one of the television networks assigned a reporter the task of finding out what the reputations were, within the profession, of the leading published and private polls, so that its news department would have some basis for deciding whose poll results to report.)

Poorly designed samples, or deliberately biased ones, are another potential source of significant distortion. A case in point is the mail survey in which tens of thousands of questionnaires are mailed and only a small proportion are returned. As already noted, survey practitioners have long since discovered that those persons who answer mail questionnaires typically differ in many ways from those who do not bother to do so. Using a mail survey with a low response rate as anything more than a clue to public sentiment is never justified. And even then, the likelihood of serious bias is always present. If only ten percent or less of those to whom the questionnaries are mailed bother to fill them out and return them, as is not infrequent in mail surveys conducted by Congressmen, there is a strong likelihood that these returns are from an atypical segment of the population and not at all reflective of the actual public mood. Moreover, the manipulative potential of a mail survey is quite high. In a preelection or preprimary poll, if conducted by mail in a single community, it would not be too difficult for the adherents of the candidate for whom the poll is conducted to canvass known supporters to return their questionnaires and so inflate his strength.

Properly conducted surveys use sample designs which have built-in protection against such distortion. The selection of those to be interviewed in a well-designed sample is not left to the judgment or whim of any individual, but is controlled by mathematically-based procedures. Furthermore, until the interviewer calls at a house, he does not know which specific person he will interview. The likelihood that the sample can be tampered with is virtually nil under such circumstances.

It is conceivable that someone who wants to affect a poll could attempt to do so by bribing interviewers, or by finding out which specific neighborhoods are included in a sample and then making a concerted campaign effort in those specific blocks. The likelihood that this could occur is minimal, both for reasons of practicality and because the standard checks that are made by professional surveyors would detect such an effort. A typical national Gallup survey, for example, involves about 150 to 300 interviewers living in all fifty states. Each interviewer is provided with a map of his assigned interviewing area which is prepared only a few days before the survey goes into the field. Furthermore, each interviewer's work is systematically checked to verify that it was done honestly and competently. As Paul K. Perry, president of The Gallup Organization commented, "Of course, you can do anything with money, I suppose. But anybody who's really an old hand at this business would begin to see something going wrong." Richard F. Link, chief statistician of Louis Harris and Associates made a similar observation: "Presumably, if you had the resources of the NKVD (Russian secret police), you could do it. But, I don't see how."[30]

Perhaps one of the more effective safeguards the public has against such tampering with samples is the fact that survey organizations must protect their reputations if they are to stay in business. Even unintentional errors hurt them, so they must concentrate their efforts on being as accurate as possible. Oliver Quayle, at the May, 1967 AAPOR Conference, answering a question from the floor as to whether clients may specify the research design or tailor the research to an obviously inadequate budget, said that he cannot allow this practice because he has to be accurate. "Being wrong" is a reputation that nobody in the survey research business can risk.

SURVEY ORGANIZATIONS AND POLITICAL CLIENTS

When the survey practitioner becomes an active member of a candidate's campaign staff, perhaps even its manager, there is a radical change in the pressures to which he is subject. Mervin Field, at the 1967 Lake George Conference, cited five conflict situations that the research-campaign manager role engenders:

1. *There is the basic conflict of knowledge for sake of general understanding vs. knowledge for specific action.* Political research is highly applied and there is little opportunity to investigate side issues or test methods. It leads to use of those basic techniques that the researcher feels "safe" with. If he is relatively unsophisticated about research, this means use of primitive sampling and questioning techniques.

2. *Another conflict situation has to do with the goals of the research.* There is the implicit pressure to use the research for other than purely objective fact-gathering. It is used to convince financial backers, to encourage party workers, to bolster the confidence of the candidate, to freeze out potential opponents, to support existing disposition and biases.

3. *A third conflict area is the dissemination of results.* Findings aren't kept to the central campaign staff for guidance only. Results are leaked. There is the problem of selective use of certain findings to create a misleading impression. There are leaks to newsmen for background, leaks to the opposition to lull them or to steer them in a direction which will help the sponsoring candidate. There is the tendency of newsmen to treat haphazard polls on the same basis as carefully

done studies. Reporters have shown the tendency of not being able to distinguish good from bad research.

4. *Finances.* Money is always in short supply for campaigns. Researchers have to fight to get adequate budgets. When money is tight and the need for data is great, there is the awful pressure to short cut techniques, cut sample sizes, to save money.

5. *Time.* There is never enough time in a campaign to follow a predetermined research plan. The pressure to do quick measurements increases during the campaign. If these are planned for, they can be effectively done, but all too frequently, they are hastily and poorly done. There is no time to test questions, for complex analysis, for reflection on significant findings. This puts a severe test on researcher's skills, judgment and integrity.

Field concludes that

for all these reasons it seems unlikely that the professional researcher can be a good campaign manager, or that a good campaign manager can be a good researcher.[31]

A typical conflict situation develops when the independent survey organization is requested not only to report its findings to a political candidate but also to interpret them and to develop recommendations. Normally, this is what might be expected in any research report. The problem arises as to what may happen to the researcher's objectivity once he gives advice as to how to conduct a political campaign. Some people have questioned whether, under those circumstances, the survey practitioner must have a personal commitment to the candidate and his success. Another question that has been raised is, Since any subsequent poll is, in effect, a test of the advice a pollster gave, may not this fact influence him as he develops his research design? The private pollster must maintain his objectivity despite his own political convictions and despite the temptation to seek out those facts that will prove his advice was correct. As Field commented, it is unrealistic to expect that a private pollster will not give advice, but for this very reason it is necessary to emphasize the nature of the conflict and to recognize it as a serious problem.

Observations made by two private pollsters during the 1967 AAPOR Conference indicate why the private pollsters will normally feel constrained to give advice. Quayle reported that he normally is asked to present his research report at campaign strategy meetings. In one campaign, when it was reported that the candidate was faring badly among union families even though he was a Democrat, Quayle was asked, "What do we do?" Quayle's claim that he was a fact-finder and not a strategist was countered by the candidate's question as to whether or not he had learned anything from past elections in which he had conducted polls. Under this type of pressure, Quayle said, he felt he had to offer some advice. He did, presenting it as his personal judgment based upon his interpretation of the data. Quayle's final comment on the issue was that providing such an interpretation is part of his role and that his clients are entitled to it.

Fred Currier then cited a different type of situation that can arise. In 1966 his firm conducted a survey in California for a candidate who had also retained a special campaign consultant. The consultant's specific role was, of course, to give advice. However, the advice the consultant gave conflicted with the conclusions that followed from the poll's findings. Currier commented that at that point he felt it was incumbent upon him to press his interpretation in opposition to the consultant's.

Louis Harris had written elsewhere on this same topic:

The pollster who is knowledgeable about politics will inevitably be invited to sit in on strategy meetings, mostly as a resource but also as a man of balanced judgment. The pollster will more and more be in the position of recommending when and how many polls should be conducted for his client, rather than simply waiting for the political powers-that-be to call him and set the time table.[32]

Describing Harris' role in the 1960 Presidential election, White reports that Harris was one of nine men who met on October 28, 1959 to plan Kennedy's candidacy:

Upon his reports, upon his description of the profile of the country's thinking and prejudices as he found them, were to turn many of John F. Kennedy's major decisions.[33]

The concern voiced by Field, as recorded above, is not that it is undemocratic or manipulative for a survey research specialist to provide reliable information to a candidate. Rather, like many others in the profession, he feels that unless a line is drawn to distinguish the specialist from the campaign manager, there is the ever-present danger that surveys will be perverted in their use. The difficulty in drawing that line is illustrated by this excerpt from a letter written by one private pollster to a political client:

It is the function of a private poll to show those who are engaged in political campaigns what the public is thinking, so that they may determine what they believe to be the best solutions of problems. Such polls therefore are a valuable aid to campaign planners. But their function does not include promotional use of the data to induce a change in the considered opinion held by a candidate, a delegate or a voter. It is the earnest hope of many of us in this profession that our results will be used only in full context for research purposes. It is for this reason, and for mutual protection, that our clients agree with us that neither we nor they will disseminate results generally except in a manner specifically agreed upon. This agreement is established first in a letter of understanding and later in a paragraph in the report.

It is obvious, of course, that the client's staff and those working on the campaign should have access to the full report, which contains the names of suppliers and statements of interpretation, methodology and any limitations of significance. But when selective material from the report is presented to others than those engaged in campaign planning, the use extends beyond the research stage into the very different stage of promotion, and the opportunity for misinterpretation, or even distortion by someone, increases. You probably know that the reputation of one polltaker was damaged on this particular account. My organization does not want to be in the position of seeming officially to imply support of the promotion of any candidate or any party.[34]

The ambiguity of the private pollster's role as he becomes a political advisor as well as a research specialist cannot help but create conflict. Obligations to the client deriving from a commitment to professional ethics clash with those deriving from a desire to help him get elected. Most private pollsters appear to have achieved a resolution, no matter how tenuous, by saying, in Max Weber's words, "this far and no farther." Some distance from the seat of decision is necessary, but how great the distance should be is a matter each must determine for himself. Short of denying to candidates the right to conduct private polls, which is hardly likely, the private pollster's role conflict seems to be an inescapable facet of the political scene.

The Use of Polls by Campaign Consultants

Distinct from but related to the problem of the research-campaign manager is the development in the past few years of a new campaign type, the "campaign consultant," who uses opinion polls as part of a total package designed to elect candidates. The backgrounds of these consultants are diverse, and some have had little or no prior experience with the survey method. They sometimes promote themselves as being able to get a candidate elected despite his lack of previous political experience or qualifications.

Notable among the growing numbers of campaign consultants is the Spencer-Roberts firm of Los Angeles which managed Ronald Reagan's gubernatorial campaign, and Tinker & Partners of New York which has worked for Nelson Rockefeller. Another very successful firm is Campaign Consultants, which worked for Senator Edward W. Brooke and then Governor Spiro T. Agnew. While unsuccessful in the races of Richard A. Snelling of Vermont and E. Clayton Gengras of Connecticut, Campaign Consultants nonetheless was retained early in 1967 to direct George Romney's campaign in the 1968 New Hampshire primary.[35]

During the 1968 Presidential campaign, Joseph Napolitan achieved public prominence as a campaign consultant to Humphrey. A former public relations partner of Lawrence O'Brien, who in turn played a key role in the 1960, 1964, and 1968 Democratic campaigns, Napolitan reportedly was a central figure in Humphrey's planning group. Claiming fifteen "victories" in the seventeen contests in which he had served as a consultant to Democrats, Napolitan was involved in the selection of Humphrey's advertising agency, the determination of which media to use and how, and the planning of what Humphrey "image" to package and project. Napolitan also conducted a series of statewide polls. The extent to which Napolitan has relied on polls as a campaign tool is indicated by the fact that he has achieved public recognition as a private pollster as distinct from his role as a campaign consultant.[36]

The discussion by Oliver Quayle at the 1967 AAPOR Conference touched on the conflicting perspectives of such consultants and the conventional private pollster. He voiced concern as to what the former's role in the political process will be. He reported that one of these consultants has made such advertising claims as having "elected" 24 out of 25 clients, while another claimed to have "elected" 84 out of 84 clients. The validity of these more extravagant claims may be open to serious question. For example, Quayle noted that in the 1967 Kentucky gubernatorial primary, one candidate, David Tratt, retained a well-known campaign consultant. Although Tratt had no prior political experience, he was young, handsome, wealthy, from a prominent Kentucky family, and the political climate was reputedly ripe for a change. In this case, the regular organization candidate ran so handily that *The New York Times* did not even report how many votes the also-rans, including Tratt, gained.[37]

Campaign consultants are of relevance since they conduct polls as part of their services, as an aid to developing campaign strategies and tactics. However, their major goal is not to provide information, but to get their candidate elected. The criterion for measuring their own success is not the accuracy of their polls but whether or not their candidate wins. The self-interest of the independent survey practitioner in maintaining his record of accuracy is not operative in the consultant's case. As a campaign develops, the pressures to win at any cost mount, and the temptation to use polls manipulatively might be expected to increase accordingly. If such a development does take place, the problems of maintaining professional standards may prove to be even more complex for the campaign consultant than they are for the private pollster.

THE REGULATION OF POLLS, PUBLIC AND PRIVATE

Published polls, because of their visibility in contrast to private polls, are the most vulnerable to criticism and to charges of bias. In 1966, Market Opinion Research Company, which conducted preelection polls for the *Detroit News,* was sued by supporters of Zolton Ferency, the Democratic candidate in Michigan's gubernatorial election. The Democrats "charged that the polls had created the impression that Mr. Romney was virtually unbeatable and that Ferency is a hopeless candidate and that, by implication, votes for him would be wasted."[38] They demanded access to the poll data that had been used and, barring that, asked that Market Opinion Research, Inc. be prevented from "making or permitting its public opinion polls to be published or used by any person in connection with the gubernatorial election." The nature of the suit leads to the inference that the plaintiffs may have thought that the reports were being biased and that they were exerting a so-called bandwagon effect upon voters. While the suit was lost, it is noteworthy that it was instituted at a time when the survey organization was in the crucial stages of its final survey when it could ill afford to have the attention of its key personnel diverted, even for a few days.

There have been some attempts to enact legislation to control alleged abuses in the publication of preelection polls, though to date none have become law. On March 7, 1963, a bill designed to control rigorously the publication of any preelection poll was introduced in the Texas State Senate [SB. No. 369]. Passed by both houses of the legislature, the bill was vetoed by Governor Connally. The bill established requirements for filing with state or county officials details of the survey design and procedures of any published preelection poll. Elements of a research design such as the question-wordings are facts that would normally be included in any professional research report. More significantly, the description of the act stated that it would provide "a cause of action for any person if a polling organization maliciously publishes or submits for publication any erroneous statement or set of figures with the intent to diminish such person's chances or expectations for election to political office. . . ." Punitive damages were provided for, even if no actual damages were proven ". . . if any polling organization knowingly publishes, or causes publication, or aids in publication, or submits for publication, any erroneous statement or set of figures or percentages, that tends to diminish or destroy any person's chances or expectations for election to any political office or for nomination as a candidate for any political office. . . ."

In evaluating the provisions of the above bill, note must be taken of the fact that all survey samples are subject to sample error. Thus, by definition, any preelection poll result can be considered erroneous. Moreover, it is always conceivable, even if unlikely, that publication of a preelection survey will diminish to some degree the trailing candidate's chance to be nominated or elected. Consequently, the effect of the bill, if it had become law, would have made it impossible for any survey organization to release its data for publication. On the other hand, private polls and unsystematic reporting by journalists would have been relatively immune from regulation. Pollsters have also contended that such legislation would infringe upon the freedom of the press.

A more recent effort to protect the public against misleading and manipulative polls is the "Truth-in-Polling" bill introduced into the House of Representatives on May 28, 1968, by Lucien N. Nedzi, Democratic Congressman from Michigan, and cosponsored by forty-eight other Congressmen. This bill would require that information be filed with the Librarian of the Library of Congress about any poll ". . . relating to any election for public office or to any political issue the results of which are intended to be and are disseminated to the public. . . ." The information to be filed covers eight facets of such polls: (1) the name of the sponsor, (2) sampling procedures, (3) sample size, (4) interviewing dates, (5) questions asked, (6) how the polling was done, (7) completion and refusal rates, and (8) poll results.

In explaining why he felt such a bill is desirable, Nedzi said that polls were being accepted by the public and by politicians on faith alone, without any real assurance as to their accuracy. He expressed concern as to bandwagon effects on voters and the possible influence of polls upon legislators' votes on pending bills.[39]

The provisions of the Nedzi bill parallel to a considerable degree the codes developed by AAPOR and by the National Committee on Published Polls described earlier. A major difference is that included in the Nedzi bill but in neither of these codes is a requirement for information about completion and refusal rates. Such information would indeed be useful, perhaps necessary, for a complete professional analysis. However, other information not included in the Nedzi bill is requisite for such an analysis—for example, sample composition, sample variance (necessary to calculate what allowance should be made for sampling error), veracity checks, and the like. In general, it would appear that the primary effect of the Nedzi bill, if it is enacted, would be to put government sanction on reporting standards that have already been developed and promulgated by the leading practitioners in the field. Additionally, requiring those responsible for published polls to file with the Library of Congress detailed information about each survey they conduct might prove to be of value if the news media and political leaders were actually to refer to these files when evaluating published poll results. If they do not, however, the prospects are that such a law would prove to be of limited value in fostering a more intelligent utilization of poll data either by politicians or the public.

One key provision of the bill, which casts doubt as to how effective the bill could be in protecting politicians and the public against the manipulative use of polls, is the exclusion of private polls. "Confidentially" circulated and "leaked" polls apparently would be immune from the bill's provisions. But, as has been discussed above, it is precisely in this area that the manipulative use of polls is most likely to occur. The thrust of the Nedzi bill, consequently, is similar to that of the 1963 Texas legislation in that it would impose regulations upon the one segment of the polling profession that has been making some effort to establish professional standards and at the same time exempt that segment which may include flagrant abusers of the public interest.

Support for such restrictive legislation has not been confined to the United States. In Great Britain, a Parliamentary Committee recommended that publication of preelection poll results be prohibited for 72 hours before any election.[40] The primary reason for this recommendation was fear of possible bandwagon effects. Opposition to the proposal was immediate, the major arguments being that there is no evidence of a bandwagon effect, that such a prohibition was impractical, an infringement upon the freedom of the press, and that the cure would be worse than the suspected disease.

In the wake of public controversy over the role of polls in the selection of the 1968 Presidential nominees, two resolutions were introduced into the California legislature by Assemblymen Moretti and Unruh which proposed that the Assembly Committee on Rules conduct an investigation on polls.[41] Both resolutions expressed concern about possible bandwagon effects and deliberate manipulation to achieve such effects. The Moretti resolution instructed that

. . . the study include, but not be limited to, the necessity for requiring that certain information be made available to the people of the state in regard to the conducting of every published or broadcast public opinion survey. . . .

The Unruh resolution was similar in tone. It proposed that the committee

. . . study the subject of political polling in California, its honesty and objectivity, and the effects which it has upon actual voting patterns, with a view to the development of legislation to safeguard the public interest from fraudulent polling practices. . . .

The wording of these resolutions suggests that they are addressing themselves to private polls as well as to published ones. To the extent that they are so concerned, any resultant legislative action may avoid the limitations of the Nedzi bill. However, while hearings were held on this matter, no regulations concerning polls were enacted during the 1969 session of the California legislature.

There are a number of major difficulties that face any legislation that seeks to control effectively against the manipulative use of polls, difficulties that appear to have been ignored. With respect to private polls, not only are they commissioned by parties and candidates, but their results, as has been seen, are often shown "confidentially" to potential financial contributors and news reporters. Regulating polls intended for publication would have absolutely no effect on these practices. In fact, any legislation that would effectively regulate the publication of "leaked" polls is likely to infringe upon the freedom of the press. For example, some "leaks" are the results of pressure from enterprising reporters upon campaign managers. Reporters, assuming that any responsible manager has had some polls conducted, will work hard to get results, even when the manager would just as soon not have them known.

Also of relevance are the mail surveys conducted by many Congressmen and other political leaders. As already noted, from a sampling point of view these surveys are virtually worthless, while in some cases highly biased question-wordings are used. One may hazard the guess that the likelihood that any legislation would regulate these polls is very small.

Similarly, it has long been the practice of the news media to conduct surveys of delegates to nominating conventions and of political observers during campaigns in order to predict who will be nominated and who will win. On May 13, 1968, *Newsweek* reported the prospective Republican delegate count as 238 for Nixon and 453 leaning to him, for a total of 691, more than enough to be nominated. (He actually got 692 votes.) *Time* and *U.S. News and World Report* also made such forecasts while, in the days immediately preceding the balloting at the convention, Associated Press issued periodic estimates of how many votes each prospective nominee was likely to get. During the 1968 Democratic convention, each day's newspaper reported the latest delegate count for Humphrey, all indicating a first ballot victory for him. Once the campaign started, CBS News regularly broadcast its changing projections of what the Electoral College vote might be, while *The New York Times* was only one of many newspapers that published forecasts of the probable Electoral College vote, based on the observations of its reporting staff. The likelihood that any legislation restricting these practices would be considered, and if enacted declared constitutional, is also limited.

The news media of 1968 also paid a good deal of attention to the possibilities that polls might be having an undesirable effect on the electoral process. Syndicated columnists, by-liners, and magazines all published articles with revealing titles:

"Do Polls Undermine Public Confidence?" Jules Witcover, *Long Island Press,* January 13, 1968;

"Polls and Pollsters—And How They Work," Lloyd Shearer, *Parade,* April 28, 1968;

"Could Polls Be Rigged?" Philip Meyer, *New Orleans Time Picayune,* June 27, 1968;

"The Polls and the Pols and the Public," *Newsweek,* July 8, 1968;

"The Abuses and Fears of Polling Power," John Pekkanen, *Life,* July 19, 1968;

"Can Pollsters Deliver the Vote?" *Business Week,* August 10, 1968.

In part informative, in that they described more or less accurately how opinion polls are conducted, these articles also typically expressed concern specifically about the role of private polls; for example, ". . . since they are for hire and not open to public scrutiny, [they] are the most susceptible to manipulation and abuse" (Pekkanen); "Private polls, of course, can be used to mislead the public" (Shearer); ". . . common is the use of private polls to scare up financial contributions" (*Business Week*). The recognition by the news media that private polls must be central to any discussion of the abuses of polls contrasts with the focus of legislative interest upon the published polls.

This concentration of legislative interest on the published polls also contrasts with the concern noted above of pollsters themselves about the manipulative use of private polls. Precisely because published polls function as independent investigators of public opinion there is concern among professionals that private polls could become a mantle for partisan interests or that the methodology of these polls could prove to be inadequate for their objective. It is also pertinent to observe that any "failure" on the part of published polls, such as in 1948, sends shock waves through political organizations with reverberations that continue two decades later. The performance of private polls, in contrast, goes largely unheralded except through rumor and hearsay. For example, in a closed meeting with party officials, one private pollster, often quoted in the press, commented, ". . . this year we have already picked our candidate on the basis of our surveys. We feel he had better win because if he doesn't I'll be out of a job."[42] Even though the candidate referred to was subsequently defeated, the pollster involved is still active and quoted in the press.

The most effective external constraint upon the possible manipulative use of private polls that has so far developed is the published public-opinion poll sponsored by the news media. These polls, such as those currently conducted by George Gallup, Louis Harris, Joe Belden (Texas), Mervin Field (California), Robert Coursen (Minnesota), and Glenn Roberts (Iowa), exert a constraint by presenting a disinterested standard against which any private poll can be evaluated. Since their accuracy is ultimately tested by actual election results, whenever two published polls differ in their reports their tested performance can serve as an objective criterion in choosing which one to accept.

Indicative of what might happen if published polls did not release the results of their final preelection surveys is the West German experience during their national elections in September, 1969. In reaction to criticism from some political leaders and commentators, the Association of German Market Research Institutes agreed not to publish any forecasts for that election. However, *The Times of London* commissioned Marplan Germany (a division of the United States-owned advertising public-relations firm Interpublic, Inc.) to conduct a preelection poll. The results of that poll were published in *The Times* and were widely circulated in West Germany. In addition, the results of privately commissioned polls reached the press, sometimes distorted or misrepresented in content. After the election was over, research organizations such as Emnid and Demoskopie released their actual findings, which had been deposited in sealed envelopes beforehand. While postelection release did provide information as to the accuracy of the preelection surveys conducted by these two organizations, this did not prevent out-of-country publication of one survey or distorted leaks to the press of private poll results.

The distinguishing characteristic of the published polls is that they are conducted as a form of journalism, to inform the public about the political world, and not for political intelligence. Some published polls are conducted by independent research organizations which release their reports in syndicated columns to subscribing newspapers. The Gallup Poll is archetypal of such polls. Others, such as the Minnesota and Iowa Polls, are owned by newspapers themselves, and their staffs are on the newspaper payrolls. A variant is the Harris Survey which is syndicated to newspapers through the *Washington Post* but which also reports through *Time* and *Life*. In all these instances the source of revenue is solely or primarily the news media.

Such a relationship can result in an over-emphasis on questions that have front page "newsworthiness," to the detriment of more fundamental analysis. Nevertheless, the relationship of public-opinion polls to journalism has had the effect of establishing them as independent, nonpartisan activities. Since the polls' most newsworthy quality is how accurately they measure voter preferences, the staffs of published polls have no choice but to make every effort to measure preferences as objectively and precisely as possible. This fact establishes published polls as a standard against which private polls can be measured, and which makes understandable the tendency that rumors about private polls are most apt to occur in elections which are not covered by published polls.

So long as the published polls remain the best criterion for evaluating all polls, there is every reason to expect that they will remain the primary target of public criticism, warranted and unwarranted. To the extent that such criticism of published polls diverts attention from the proliferating private polls, it beclouds the significance of the latter in the political process.

POLLS AND POLITICAL STYLE

Politicians have long expressed concern over their assumption that the publication of public-opinion poll results inevitably influences members of the electorate to change their views so as to conform to majority opinion. Correlatively, the demand for legislative control and regulation of opinion polls has derived largely from within political circles. Often ignored by politicians or relegated to secondary interest is the demonstrable effect polls have had on their own behavior.

As early as 1940, Representative Walter M. Pierce of Oregon asserted that "polls create opinion rather than measure it." By way of substantiation he claimed that Calvin Coolidge and Herbert Hoover were elected by larger majorities than would otherwise have been the case because the *Literary Digest* poll "molded" public opinion into believing each was a sure winner.[43] Almost thirty years later, Senator Everett Dirksen of Illinois wrote in a similar vein:

They [the polls] frequently become the conditioners of the public mind. . . . [W]hen the polls accentuate how a given candidate stands percentagewise with the voters of different age groups and different economic groups, the candidate and his background, his real mental ability and his attainments and spiritual equipment as a statesman, are somehow all interred in the statistical process.

. . . [P]olls, by their timing and the questions asked, and even by the very scanty comment that accompanies the summary of a poll, can and do influence the outcome of an election.

It could very well be that polls, which do not come under the interdiction of the [federal Corrupt Practices Act], could finally determine our political destiny.[44]

Although Dirksen comments on other aspects of how poll data may influence politics, the focus of his concern, like Pierce's, is on the assumed direct influence of poll reports upon the electorate. Thus, while Dirksen refers also to the possibility that poll results can spur on an underdog candidate or generate overconfidence in the favorite, his major argument centers on the supposition that published poll results may exert a greater influence upon voters than the combined effects of campaign "speeches, advertising in newspapers, on billboards and on radio and television."[45] It is his viewpoint that has dominated most public discussion about the manipulative use of poll data.

As we have seen, the weight of evidence is to the contrary. Empirical efforts to discover and measure the magnitude of bandwagon and underdog effects upon the general electorate have been at best inconclusive. If such effects do occur (and it is unreasonable to exclude the possibility that they may in some individuals), the incidence is so small that it has not proved susceptible to measurement. The negligible direct influence of polls is understandable if account is taken of what has been learned about the processes whereby vote decisions are reached. Repeated studies have shown that the interplay of social and economic factors (for example, familial and other primary group memberships, socioeconomic status, and religious or ethnic background) largely determine political loyalties and issue-orientation. It is this interplay that explains to the largest degree how the electorate selects among candidates.

We have also determined, in our review of the political functions of polls and of how their increased credibility has prepared the ground for those who try to use polls manipulatively, that the influence polls exert upon political leaders and party functionaries is considerable. In the 1968 Presidential election poll data undoubtedly comprised the single most important type of information used by political leaders to evaluate candidate strength and weakness within different sectors of the public, to determine the effectiveness of alternative campaign issues, and to assess the progress (or lack thereof) being made in campaigns. Decisions about over-all strategies and specific techniques (from the type of image to be projected to the selection of advertising media) were all conditioned by information obtained from surveys of public opinion. Moreover, candidate standings as reported by published and private polls became part of the campaign process. Each side cited or attacked published polls, depending upon whether or not the latest report was favorable, and each side leaked or buried private poll results accordingly. Most significantly, in the struggle for delegate strength at the nominating conventions, for financial backing both before and after the conventions, and in the effort to maintain party-worker morale, poll data were repeatedly cited as evidence of the political wisdom of supporting specific candidates. Finally, by making parties more responsive to majority opinion, polls have reinforced existing tendencies toward selecting middle-of-the-road politicians as candidates for office.

One important reason why many politicians pay such close attention to "what the polls are showing" is that career pressures require them to support a winner, if this is at all possible. Survival within a political party is contingent upon one's proximity to those centers of political power which dispense patronage and other political favors. Remaining in opposition to a successful candidate of one's own party for too long can be disastrous to a political career. However justifiable his stand may be in principle and however valuable to the polity in the long run, the politician who fights a victorious faction within his party places his own political career in jeopardy. Consequently, politicians themselves are extremely susceptible to bandwagon effects, however much they decry such effects in others. The archetypical example of the bandwagon effect is what happens once it becomes apparent who will be the ultimate victor at a nominating convention. Immediately politicians rush to jump on the bandwagon before it is too late and they are left in the political wilderness.

Since within their own world the publication of poll results may act to generate a bandwagon psychology, some politicians are prone to seeing everyone as subject to comparable influence. This proclivity for assuming that the public is as vitally interested in polls as are politicians, and consequently is as susceptible to influence by poll results, is an illustration of a "projective" mechanism—that is, the imputing of one's own traits to others. However, the general public's involvement in politics is of a different order from the politician's, so that behavior characteristic of the way many politicians react to polls is extremely rare among voters.

While public-opinion polls may be a source of bandwagon

behavior among politicians, this consideration should not detract our attention from the more basic impact polls have had upon political parties. As a direct result of the increasing reliance of political leaders upon polls, the style with which politics is conducted is undergoing a transformation that involves changes in the fundamental structure and functioning of political parties. Instead of relying for information upon the established network of grass roots contacts provided by county chairmen and precinct captains, candidates and other political leaders may now feel free to bypass these functionaries completely. We have noted that conducting a public-opinion poll properly requires a degree of professional and technical skill that only specialists can provide. The result is that those at the apex of the party hierarchy, or those who aspire to the apex, deal directly with professional survey researchers instead of operating through the party structure. The results of private polls are reported to persons in leadership positions, and only if the latter so decide are these results filtered down to rank-and-file party workers. Moreover, decisions based upon professional analyses of both published and private polls may differ considerably from recommendations made by local party workers who rely upon their own, on-the-scene judgments.

To the extent that those in decision-making positions come to rely upon poll data the party is bifurcated into a technically-oriented executive elite whose operative style is reminscent of the corporate business world, and a tradition-oriented rank-and-file membership which is threatened by its lack of participation and skill in this style. Allied with the latter are some high-ranking politicians who, for reasons of temperament, training, and/or loyalty find it difficult to adopt an executive style. Party functionaries who try to adjust to the new style find their role transformed so that their success is no longer contingent upon subjective qualities, but upon skill in implementing "objective," rationalized strategies. That is, instead of relying upon their personal abilities to develop loyalties which they can draw on in the struggle to win elections, party functionaries must learn to follow orders from technically oriented superiors who justify those orders by their access to "objectively" obtained and analyzed data. This development is now predominant in Presidential elections and is of growing significance in senatorial and gubernatorial elections in which poll information is being used more and more. On the other hand, in local elections, in which reliance upon personal knowledge and judgment is still the norm, this transformation is discernible only in isolated instances.

The significant impact of public-opinion polls on the political process is indirect but pervasive. Public-opinion polls are an application of the information-gathering methodology of behavioral scientists, albeit sometimes crudely executed. This methodology is used by politicians who want a more reliable channel of information from the electorate than existing party organizations can provide. To the extent that political leaders accept information transmitted by public-opinion polls as objectively valid and reliable, they can feel justified in rejecting contradictory advice based upon the subjectively derived judgments of party functionaries. Thus, the change in political style engendered by the use of public-opinion poll data leads to a "rationalization" of political parties analogous to the increasing rationalization of corporate business enterprises.

The communications flow in the political process, however, is two-directional. In addition to the need for an upward flow of information from the electorate there is the parallel need for a downward flow. One of the more important channels of communication from political leaders to the electorate is their election year campaigning. Such campaigning in recent elections, especially Presidential elections, has been characterized by the increased use of television and radio. In addition, leaders of both parties have come to rely upon these broadcast media to speak over the heads of party functionaries directly to the general public in the years between elections. This growing use of the broadcast media may also be influencing political style. Therefore, it is necessary to determine whether the use of such media is having a reinforcing or countervailing effect upon political style, particularly as such an effect compares with that of public-opinion polls. Furthermore, early broadcasts of election returns and computer forecasts on Election Night have been suspected of creating bandwagon effects in their own right. For these reasons, we now turn to the problem of identifying and measuring the impact that the broadcast media, and most importantly television, has had upon political style.

NOTES

1. Louis Harris, "Polls and Politics in the United States," *Public Opinion Quarterly* (Spring 1963), p. 3.

2. *Gallup Opinion Index,* no. 29 (November 1967), pp. 24, 25, 26.

3. *The New York Times,* November 7, 1967; Ted Lewis, *New York Daily News,* November 7, 1967; Robert J. Donovan, *Washington Post,* November 26, 1967; Philip Meyer, *Newark Star Ledger,* December 3, 1967; *Chicago Daily News,* December 4, 1967; *Philadelphia Inquirer,* December 6, 1967; Jules Witcover, *Long Island Press,* January 13, 1968; and "Can We Believe The Pollsters?" *The Reporter,* May 16, 1968, p. 16.

4. Louis Harris, *loc. cit.* p. 7.

5. *The New York Times,* July 7, 1967.

6. Rowland Evans and Robert Novak, *Philadelphia Inquirer,* October 10, 1968.

7. Lewis Chester, Godfrey Hodgson, and Bruce Page, *An American Melodrama: The Presidential Campaign of 1968* (New York: Viking Press, Inc., 1969), p. 711 *et seq.*

8. *The New York Times,* October 15, 1968.

9. *The New York Times,* October 10, 1968.

10. *Philadelphia Evening Bulletin,* October 10, 1968.

11. *The New York Times,* October 9, 1968.

12. Louis Harris, *loc. cit.,* p. 4.

13. The AAPOR conference was held at Lake George, New York on May 18–21, 1967. Citations are based on notes taken by Irving Crespi, who was in the audience.

14. The composition of the AAPOR Standards Committee at that time was Irving Crespi (Chairman), Rome Arnold, Helen Crossley, Raymond Fink, Robert Heyer.

15. Philip Meyer, *Newark Star Ledger,* December 3, 1967; and *Philadelphia Inquirer,* December 6, 1967.

16. News release issued June 30, 1968 (mimeographed).

17. Philip Meyer, "Truth in Polling," *Columbia Journalism Review* (Summer 1968), p. 23.

18. *Ibid.*

19. "Professional Pollsters Criticize Unscientific Surveys in Mass Media," news release (undated, mimeographed).

20. Warren Weaver, Jr., *The New York Times,* June 16, 1967.

21. Allen L. Otten, *Wall Street Journal,* June 16, 1967.

22. Homer Bigart, *The New York Times,* October 11, 1968.

23. Leo Bogart, "Social Sciences in the Mass Media" (mimeographed, undated).

24. "The Constituents Speak Out! A report on the 4th District response to Rep. Frank Thompson's Legislative Questionnaire as reported in the Congressional Record, September 12, 1968." (Received in the mail.)

25. "Public Opinion Survey in North Carolina's Eighth Congressional District," reprint from *Congressional Record,* September 6, 1968.

26. *The New York Times,* May 16, 1967.

27. Gallup Poll release, May 6, 1967.

28. *Newsweek,* July 10, 1967, pp. 20–21.

29. Confidential personal communication.

30. Philip Meyer, "Could the Polls Be Rigged?" *New Orleans Times Picayune,* June 27, 1968.

31. These remarks are excerpted from a typescript of Mr. Field's talk which he kindly made available.

32. Harris, *loc. cit.,* p. 7.

33. Theodore H. White, *The Making of the President 1960* (New York: Atheneum Publishers, 1961), p. 51.

34. Confidential personal communication.

35. John H. Fenton, *The New York Times,* March 23, 1967.

36. Thomas J. Fleming, "Selling the Product Named Hubert Humphrey," *The New York Times Magazine,* October 13, 1968, p. 45 *et seq.*

37. *The New York Times,* May 24, 1967.

38. *The New York Times,* May 21, 1967.

39. *Washington Post,* May 19, 1968.

40. Anthony Lewis, *The New York Times,* May 21, 1967.

41. House Resolution 485, "Relating to Opinion Polls," by Assemblyman Moretti; and House Resolution 568, "Relative to a Study of Political Polling," by Assemblyman Unruh.

42. Confidential personal communication.

43. Walter M. Pierce, "Climbing on the Bandwagon," *Public Opinion Quarterly,* vol. 4 (June 1940), pp. 241–243.

44. *The Sunday Bulletin* (Philadelphia), April 28, 1968.

45. *Ibid.*

Does Exposure to National Broadcasts of Election Forecasts and Results Affect Terminal Voting Behavior?

THE CONTEXT OF THE CALIFORNIA STUDY

Perhaps the first law of mass communications relates to the impact upon society of technological innovations in the means of communication. Simply stated, every major technological change in the means of communication produces profound changes in the ways people live; in the ways they spend their time and money; and in the ways they relate to each other and to their various social, economic, and political institutions. Each major change in the technological means by which a society communicates consequently produces its share of public issues, and the anxieties which are expressed with regard to these changes reflect one general concern—that is, that the new means of communication will exert undue (usually negative) influence upon audiences, and that ultimately this influence will damage both individuals and society. It was inevitable that the advent of television would generate anxieties about its alleged negative influences upon the political fabric of our society.

The new dialogues concerning the relationships between television and politics have pivoted on the allegation that exposing the public to televised, computerized election forecasts prior to

170

voting (particularly in the western portion of the United States) exerts undue influence on the subsequent outcome of the election—that is, that such exposure results in bandwagon effect. The anxiety over this possibility has resulted in numerous proposals before the Congress of the United States that are designed either to curb or to terminate the broadcasting of election forecasts in one way or another—proposals that raise further serious issues relating to the freedom of the press.

Whether or not one holds to the notion that bandwagon effects can be produced by exposure to television forecasts of election contests rests on the assumptions one holds relating to the image of man and to one's values regarding the power of communication media. Two distinct points of view can be noted on this matter.

One point of view exhibits a pessimistic image of man joined with an optimistic image of the power of mass communications. From Plato, who would banish the poets from the community because they might debilitate the young, to contemporary critics of mass communications such as psychiatrist Frederic Wertham, who charges the mass media with the "seduction of the innocent," the argument has been more or less the same: Man is weak and therefore vulnerable to manipulation by communications techniques. In politics, those who accept the "crowd" theories of Karl Marx, Gustave Le Bon, and José Ortega y Gasset have adopted the Platonic optimism regarding the power of communications and have come up with the proposition that the electorate (the masses) is a conglomeration of irrational, weak-willed numbskulls who can exhibit little or no immunity to the persuasive tactics of those who control the contents of communication media. Le Bon's observation illustrates this particular approach:

To bring home convictions to crowds it is necessary first of all to comprehend thoroughly the sentiments by which they are animated, to pretend to share these sentiments, then to endeavor to modify them. . . . [C]rowds are not influenced by reasoning, and can only comprehend rough and ready association of ideas. The orators who know how to make an impression upon them always appeal in consequence to their sentiments and never to their reason. The laws of logic have no action on crowds.[1]

This point of view is a most popular one; it is shared by ordinary citizens, politicians, intellectuals, and many social scientists alike. In essence, the contemporary popular "optimistic" impression of the effects of mass communications in formal political campaigns (even up to Election Night) is merely an extension of the crude psychological "learning model" that is rooted in classical behaviorist theory. Classical behaviorist theory avers that man is primarily a "responder" to stimuli from both within and without. Consequently, the theory asserts, when appropriate stimuli (in this case, political "messages") are hooked up to appropriate response-dispositions within appropriate "reward" contexts, the behavior of individuals can be manipulated, modified, induced, eliminated, or changed directly and immediately almost at the will of those projecting the stimuli.

In viewing the mass communication process, proponents of the behaviorist approach argue that individual items of mass communication (for example, television forecasts of election results) act upon individual members of an audience, as Paul Lazarsfeld has described the process, much like "hypodermic needles." Just as the serum enters the blood stream directly from the syringe to cause an appropriate effect, so too, continues the analogy, does a message enter the psychic apparatus of an individual to produce a direct effect. If a community of individuals is injected with hypodermic needles filled with an antitoxin, for example, a state of mass immunization is produced singly and additively. Likewise, goes the argument, if a political message containing the elements of persuasion is seen or heard by a community of individuals, actions appropriate to that "message" (for example, changes in voting behavior) will be induced directly on a community-wide, "mass" basis (in other words, the election of a candidate who might not have won had the messages been absent). This is to say, those who are schooled in the classical behaviorist psychological school would have us believe that the greater the number of "rewarding" messages a voter accumulates on behalf of one rather than another candidate, the more likely he is to vote for that candidate—even in the event that he originally did not intend to do so.[2]

Seen in this light an election represents merely the sum total of separate and individual actions that have been induced separately and individually by particular, specific campaign propaganda messages or messages regarding predictions of results to which voters may be exposed prior to actually voting. This view suggests that despite all the events that have occurred before a formal campaign commences, the object of any political campaign must be first to convince Voter W, then to do the same with Voter X, then with Voter Y, and then with Voter Z, in a linear series of progressions until eventually the number of separate individuals who are convinced singly and independently outweighs the number of Voters A, B, and C whom the opposition has managed to "convince." The argument further suggests that despite differences between the social status of Mr. X and that of Mr. Y; despite differences in their personalities, ways of life, perceptions of the world, their values, sentiments, and attitudes, their experiences in the past and their aspirations for the future, both Voter X and Voter Y can be induced similarly by the very same messages to vote for exactly the same candidate.

The second view of man and his relationship to mass communications simply does not buy the behaviorist's paradigm. The position of this second orientation reverses that of the Platonic school by viewing man optimistically and the power of mass communications pessimistically. Here, rather than seeing man as simply a "responder," he is seen both as a complex actor and as a reactor to complex stimuli. Proponents of this phenomenological or functional school suggest that there are many important influences other than exposure to the mass-communication message that impinge upon a voter as he proceeds to make up his mind about a particular candidate. These influences stem more from the totality of conditions of life that surround the voter both before and during a campaign than from the individual messages to which he might be exposed in the course of a campaign. On this point the observations of Elihu Katz bear repeating:

What research on mass communications has learned in its three decades is that the mass media are far less potent than had been expected. A variety of studies—with the possible exception of marketing campaigns—indicates that people are not easily persuaded to change their opinions and behaviors. The search for the sources of resistance to change as well as for the effect of sources of influence when changes occur led to the role of interpersonal relations. The shared values in groups of family, friends, and co-workers and the networks of communications which are their structure, and the decisions of members to accept or reject a new idea—all these are interpersonal processes which "intervene" between the campaign in the mass media and the individual who is the ultimate target. These recent discoveries, of course, upset the traditional image of the individualized audience upon which the discipline has been based.[3]

Whereas behaviorists view the effects of mass communications as analogous to those produced by a hypodermic needle, the phenomenologists' view is more analogous to an aerosol spray. If properly used and directed at a well-defined specific target the aerosol spray does hit some surface areas with some degree of accuracy. More often than not, however, much of the spray's potential effectiveness is dissipated as a result of many predisposing and intervening conditions such as bad aim, evaporation, or too much or too little pressure on the release mechanism. Most often one achieves wide coverage with the aerosol spray, but indeed very little of its contents succeeds in ever penetrating the surface.

Schooled in field physics, Gestalt psychology, and functionalist sociology, the phenomenologists see mass communication in political campaigns, particularly during the period of terminal decision-making, as merely one of many influences that may help the voter to arrive at his final decision. Among these influences, to name a few as examples, are the voter's socioeconomic status, his ethnic and religious background, his group identities, the voting habits of his friends, associates, and relatives, the issues in the campaign, the amount and types of cross-pressures bearing down on him, the candidates themselves, and the relevance of the election itself in his total life-space. Thus the act of voting is the end-product of many complex and interrelated influences that *in toto* make up what sociologists term the "definition of the (voting) situation."

If the phenomenologists' description is correct, it appears to make little sense to aver seriously that mass communication by itself contributes disproportionately to voting decisions directly. Yet the age-old anxiety that mass communication does affect voters' decisions directly, immediately, and unduly still persists; if anything it seems to be growing in strength rather than diminishing.

Despite this anxiety, if we consider mass communications to be but one of many complex influences that affect the voting-decision mix, it behooves us to examine the role of mass communications functionally rather than causally. That is, rather than assuming great power for mass communications as directly "causing" voting behavior, it is essential to delineate exactly what the unique purposes and functions of mass communications are within the totality of influences that affect voting choices. The theoretical underpinning for this particular viewpoint is called "functionalism."

Typically, within the phenomenological-functionalist perspective, the voter, who is a creature of past experience plus present concern and future aspiration, is first confronted with various attributes of candidates seeking political office, their platforms, the traditions of their political parties, and their formal campaigns. These variables are then evaluated by the voter in terms of his own group identifications and shared values, sentiments, loyalties, and goals; in terms of his core values, peripheral attitudes and belief systems, self-interest, political identifications, anxieties, fears, hopes, prejudices, "persuasibility," and a host of other influences that mediate between his exposure to formalized campaign propaganda and his ultimate reaction to it.

How the voter comes to his ultimate decision has been the concern of political and social scientists for some time now. In our own time the concern with these processes took on scientific significance with the pioneering work by Lazarsfeld, Berelson, and Gaudet, *The People's Choice,* which examined how voters in Ohio's Erie County arrived at their decisions in the 1940 Presidential campaign.[4] The examination was accomplished by a survey technique involving multi-interviews with the same "panel" of voters while that particular campaign progressed over time. The subtitle of *The People's Choice—How the Voter Makes Up His Mind in a Presidential Campaign—*pointed to a concern that still lingers in the political climate of our land to this very day. Hill comments on the significance of *The People's Choice* in diverting scientific attention away from the old behavioristic concern with the direct effects of mass communications upon voters' choices to the more sophisticated contemporary phenomenalistic approach to the problem:

> The unique contribution of *The People's Choice* was not verification of the [behavioristic] model's emphasis on the mass media. Quite to the contrary, the authors found that radio and print . . . "seemed to have only negligible effects on actual voting decisions and particularly minute effects on *changes* in vote decision." The most dramatic result of the study was the development of the concept of the "opinion leader" and the two-step flow of communications." Reduced to the simplest of descriptive statements, the three authors concluded that most vote changes were affected not by the mass media of print and radio, but by influential people acting upon the voter. The flow of information or persuasion was from the mass media *to* the opinion leader and then *to* his everyday associates.
>
>   . . . The most humanizing effect of this major finding was the discovery that between the mass media and the electoral results were people; the public, collectively, with interpersonal and intergroup communication. The development of public opinion theories until this time was undershot with the concept of the public, under pressure of urbanization and industrialization, as an atomized societal model, with only disparate exposure to interpersonal communication.[5]

To the extent that such studies as *The People's Choice* and subsequent research carried out at Columbia University and at the University of Michigan were concerned with the vote-decision process, they mainly focused their attention on how this process functions during the lengthy campaign period that commences with the nominations of national candidates and ends on Election Day. The issues raised in recent years regarding the alleged direct and immediate effects induced by exposing voters to televised forecasts of election results before they actually vote demonstrate the dramatic reduction of the time between exposure and possible influence—from the several months of the campaign's duration to the several hours or even minutes of the broadcasts' duration. In essence, it is argued that exposure to computer-based predictions of an election's outcome will unduly influence the outcome itself—even though only a few hours of time over-all are involved.

Is it possible to study not only the vote-decision process as it unfolds over the length of a Presidential campaign, but also the very termination or tail-end of the process that may occur within a span of hours or minutes just before votes are actually cast? A study attempting to do just this, concentrating on voting behavior and the possible consequence of television-induced bandwagon effects among a sample of California voters, was conducted by Mendelsohn in 1964.[6] In essence, the Mendelsohn investigation attempted to "freeze" a segment of the totality of factors that entered into the voting decisions of a sample of California voters and to examine rather circumscribed "last-minute" terminal influences that may have affected voting decisions immediately prior to the act of voting. In a sense, the Mendelsohn study represents a "continuity" in the more generalized research attempting to discover what roles are played by the mass media in making voters in national elections behave *as* they do *when* they do.

The impetus to concentrate on last-minute influences on voting behavior originated with concern over the allegations made by various writers, social observers, critics, and politicians that the broadcasting of election news from the eastern seaboard on Election Day causes western voters variously

1. to change their vote intentions in order to vote for the indicated winner;
2. to change their vote intentions in order to vote for the indicated loser;
3. to slacken their efforts to persuade others to vote;
4. to increase their efforts to persuade others to vote;
5. to vote, though they had intended not to vote;
6. to abstain from voting, though they had intended to vote.

Some allegations have been more or less sober and restrained, as witnessed by this statement by Robert Bendiner in the September 18, 1964 issue of *Life:*

In the end, for lack of initiative elsewhere, Congress will probably be left to wrestle with the basic question of whether or not these early television reports, projections and declarations do in fact appreciably affect the vote. And on this point it will need much more information than is now available . . .

Others have been somewhat far-fetched in the light of evidence that has been adduced on voting behavior in American Presidential elections. They epitomized the "optimistic" posture of the classical behaviorists. For example, in the September, 1964 issue of *Show*, Max Lerner, the well-respected historian, wrote,

> The public interest doesn't have to carry the burden of proof . . . to show beyond doubt that the TV early projections are necessarily harmful. It need show only what might and could happen. We know enough about voter behavior to know that the voter is highly suggestible, the American is a lonely person; he feels less lonely when he is joining others, especially on the winning side. Even granting that some voters are counter-suggestible, the two don't cancel each other out; in both cases the voter's mind is inflammable timber. The voter is modern man subject to pressures, riddled by anxieties, sometimes apathetic. He may come to the polling booth after a day's work, anxious to get home. It is crucial that he be allowed to resolve his inner debate by himself in the polling booth before he becomes the target for another attack—this time not on how he ought to vote or how others will vote, but on how others *have already voted.* [Lerner's emphasis]

Whether it is argued that election broadcasts create a bandwagon effect for the indicated winner, foster an underdog effect on behalf of the indicated loser, increase or inhibit persuasive efforts to "get out the vote," or alter a person's intention to vote or not to vote, one major assumption underlies the notion that voters may be influenced directly and immediately by election broadcasts prior to voting: Exposure to election broadcasts before voting is sufficient to lead the potential voter to behave on Election Day in a manner other than the way he had intended to behave immediately prior to the broadcasts.

The degree to which this assumption is scientifically viable rests not on subjective judgment, but on scientifically derived evidence. What evidence existed prior to Mendelsohn's California voter study in 1964 offered little or no basis for entertaining seriously the fundamental assumption posed.

Where the practical context for the study of possible bandwagon effects induced by election-broadcasts poses a problem of public concern that requires serious scientific investigation, the scientific, empirical context within which the California study developed laid down the fundamental research strategies wherein this particular investigation was conducted. The strategies bequeathed by past research encompass both theoretical frames of reference and methodology.

The evidence adduced in the investigations of voting decision-making that were conducted prior to the California study by social scientists at Columbia University and the University of Michigan generally agree that roughly nine out of every ten eligible voters make up their minds about whom they will vote for well in advance of Election Day. Indeed, there is evidence that indicates that far more voters decide upon a candidate in the very initial phases of a campaign when candidates are first announced than decide towards the last days of the formal campaign. The national survey data cited by Campbell, Converse, Miller, and Stokes and reproduced here serve as cases in point.[7]

Reported Time of Vote Decision	1952	1956
Knew all along they would vote	30%	44%
Decided when Eisenhower or Stevenson became a candidate or at time of conventions	35%	32%
Decided after conventions, during campaign	20%	11%
Decided within two weeks of election	9%	7%
Decided on Election Day	2%	2%
Do not remember	1%	1%
Not ascertained	3%	3%
Totals	100%	100%
(Base for Percentages)	1195	1291

The well-documented indications that the great majority of voters come to a final voting decision relatively early in the campaign are both synthesized and summarized by this observation by Kurt and Gladys Lang:

. . . the minds of most voters are closed before the campaign officially opens. At various places and at different times, this figure has been set at anywhere from 50 to 84 percent of the voters. But even if a voter arrives at a decision late in the campaign, he is not necessarily in a constant quandary, endlessly pulled in opposite directions by conflicting propaganda. Evidence from panel studies indicates that in most cases where the final decision comes late in the campaign prior leanings are crystallized into a firm intent. The impregnability of voting intentions as a whole limits drastically the number of people who are, so to speak, potential converts.[8]

The scientific evidence pertaining to the time at which the voting decision is made is diametrically opposed to that which is presented as mere hearsay in the popularized version of broadcast-induced bandwagon effect. Where the popular version of this concept suggests the possibility that substantial numbers of voters are swayed directly and unduly by external influences (in this case, national election broadcasts), the implication of the scientific data that has been gathered in the past is that only the smallest possible number of voters could be so swayed. Where the popular conviction of bandwagon effect claims that substantial numbers of voters have no minds of their own and react dramatically to each propaganda stimulus as if a hypodermic needle had been injected directly into their bloodstreams, scientific evidence on reactions to political campaign propaganda and information demonstrates that most voting decisions are "set" very early in the campaign, and that only the most earth-shaking events are capable of dislodging these tenacious commitments.

An additional fact gleaned from past studies of voting decisions highlights the differences between the popular and scientific perspectives on bandwagon effect. Simply stated, the great majority of voters vote in accordance with their intentions. These intentions in turn are functions of the position of the voter in the social structure and his political partisanship and interest in the particular election *plus* the specific appeals that are directed to him during the entire course of a given campaign; not necessarily at the very end of one. Considerable consensus exists among political and social scientists that the social and political predispositions of most voters generally outweigh the direct and immediate influences of mass communications in affecting final voting decisions.

A comment from the Berelson, Lazarsfeld, and McPhee study, *Voting*, is of interest here:

> . . . we have a general finding on [voting intention] implementation. Intentions supported by one's social surroundings are more predictably carried out than are intentions lacking such support. In the field of voting this can be formulated as the "rule of political predisposition." If we find at the beginning of a political campaign that certain demographic characteristics are correlated with a particular vote intention, then those who possess these predisposing characteristics are more likely than those without them to carry out this intention on election day.[9]

Thus, where the popularizers of bandwagon effect lay the greatest stress on the power of last-minute broadcast information to divert voting decisions away from voters' previous commitments—commitments that are known to both themselves and "significant others"—scientific evidence on voting decisions indicates that early voting commitments to self and group are so powerful that they can be expected to immunize most voters against last-minute, mass-media derived influences to switch choices.

The California Study

The circumstance resulting from the disparities between popular belief and scientific implication concerning the relationship of election broadcasts to bandwagon effect calls for some clarification of the issue. Certainly subjective argument can do little to clarify it, and the research conducted prior to 1964 did not concern itself *directly* with the specific problem of broadcast-induced bandwagon effect. The California voter study, along with others that were carried out in 1964 and in 1968, does attempt to clarify pertinent aspects of the problem explicitly by drawing upon the researches of the past and by focusing on voting-intention implementation—not over the span of an entire campaign, *but rather, over the span of the 24 hours intervening between Election Eve and Election Day.*

Essential to the investigation of the possible effects of election broadcasts on the terminal voting decision process, then, is an examination of whether, and, if so, in what manner, exposure to such broadcasts does indeed serve (1) to neutralize prior commitments so that the actual votes do not reflect previous voting plans and intentions, (2) to crystallize undecided votes in one or the other direction, and (3) to mobilize or depress voters' efforts to vote or to "get out the vote."

The Mendelsohn study addressed itself precisely to this question: Does exposure to election broadcasts before voting intervene to upset the otherwise supposedly almost perfect correlation between earlier commitment or lack of commitment to specific candidates and ultimate votes for those candidates?

This study was not intended to be a definitive, end-all investigation of bandwagon or underdog effects attributable to broadcasts. Rather, the research was conceived as a first-step, exploratory examination of the possible existence of these effects and of their influence, if any, on the vote under the particular circumstances attending the voting intentions and behaviors of a sample of Californians who were eligible to vote in the Presidential election of 1964.[10]

HOW THE STUDY WAS DONE

PAIRED INTERVIEWS

In order to ascertain the possible effects of exposure to election broadcasts on the relationship between voting intention and ultimate voting behavior it was necessary to obtain two separate sets of information from the voters who were studied.

First it was essential to obtain information concerning sample members' *intentions* to vote and to identify the candidates preferred *at the very latest possible time prior to Election Day* when prevoting exposure to election broadcasts might occur. These requirements made it necessary for the investigators to interview a sample of voters on November 2, the day *before* Election Day, 1964 as a first step. These interviews will hereafter be referred to as Wave I.

Second, in order to investigate whether persons contacted the day before Election Day had actually voted according to their intent and had or had not been exposed to election broadcasts before voting, it was necessary to *reinterview the very same persons after they had actually voted or surrendered the opportunity to do so.* Thus, the same individuals who were contacted in Wave I were *reinterviewed* after the polls closed on November 3, 1964, and during the morning of the following day. This second group of interviews will hereafter be referred to as Wave II.

The study employed the panel method; that is, the procedure which involves interviewing the same groups at separate points in time. Whereas most panel studies in the past covered relatively lengthy periods of time, the circumstances of possible alteration of voting-intention implementation via exposure to Election Day broadcasts here called for a drastic collapsing of the time between interviewing waves.

Telephone interviews were conducted with a total of 1,724 registered voters who resided in telephone-equipped households in fourteen of California's most populous counties. On Election Day, 1964, 84 percent of the registered voters in the state of Califronia were listed as residing in these counties. These same counties contributed 84 percent of the total votes cast in the 1964 general election in the state of California.

Of the 1,724 individuals who were contacted successfully in both Waves I and II, 1,704 said they intended to vote in the Wave I interview, and 1,689 of them reported they had indeed voted when contacted in Wave II.[11] This left a remainder of 15 people who had declared they would vote when contacted in Wave I, but who reported in Wave II that they had in fact not voted.

Most of the analysis that was conducted was based on various subgroups among the 1,689 voters who were interviewed both in Wave I and in Wave II, and particularly upon the 1,212 voters who specified intended candidate choices in Wave I.

The characteristics of the 1,724 respondents in the sample with whom interviews were completed both before and after voting took place were compared with 1960 census figures for California. This comparison showed that for the most part the sample was representative of all adult inhabitants of that state. It should be borne in mind, however, that the sample was based on eligible (registered) voters in California who resided in telephone-equipped households. These two factors introduced some elements of skewness in the sample in the direction of upper socioeconomic status characteristics (education, occupation, income).

ADJUNCT STUDIES WITH SUBSAMPLES

Supplementing the paired interviews with the 1,724 registered voters in the telephone sample were 20 personal intensive interviews done (during a period of two weeks following Election Day) with voters in Los Angeles who indicated in their telephone interviews that they had voted on November 3 after they had had an opportunity to witness Election Day broadcasts. These interviews were conducted in respondents' homes with voters who had been contacted in the main sample. The interviews were conducted by specially trained interviewers from the University of California at Los Angeles, and were designed to provide qualitative insights that might be of value in interpreting the quantitative data from the principal sample.

In order to substantiate the reliability of respondents' statements as to whether they had actually voted, and as to their claimed time of voting, a special study was conducted some time after Election Day among 201 respondents from the Los Angeles frame of the sample. This study entailed inspections of the actual voting records of subsample respondents in the office of the Los Angeles County Clerk. Two hundred of these persons claimed to have voted; one said he had not voted.

Interviewers were given the names of selected respondents who claimed they had or had not voted at specified times during November 3. Each of these names was then checked against the voting sign-in rosters for their precincts as determined by the addresses of the respondents. Although the sign-in rosters did not record actual time of voting, the sequence of identification numbers assigned to each signed-in voter provided a reasonably good indication as to whether a particular respondent had voted early or late in the day (those who voted early would have lower identifying numbers on the roster than those who voted late).

Of the 200 respondents in the subsample who claimed they voted on Election Day, 195 names were subsequently verified as having actually voted. Five names could not be so validated, nor was the name of the single alleged nonvoter uncovered. However, it must be realized that problems of illegible handwriting and a certain amount of human error in locating names on the sign-in rosters may have affected the loss of these names. Thus, it cannot be stated definitely that the six persons in question did not vote. Be that as it may, it is evident from the following figures that respondent testimony regarding voting (as well as time of voting) was generally quite accurate.

| | Respondents who claimed they— | | |
	voted before 2:30 P.M. *PST*	*voted after* 2:30 P.M. *PST*	*did not vote*
Total	*139*	*61*	*1*
Number of respondents whose names were located in Los Angeles County voter sign-in rosters	136	59	—
Number of respondents who could not be located in Los Angeles County voter sign-in rosters	3	2	1

In all cases except one, all respondents who claimed to have voted after 2:30 P.M. PST on Election Day—when exposure to national election forecasts became possible—were identified by higher actual sign-in roster numbers than were respondents in the same precincts who reported having voted before 2:30 P.M.

The one exception was a respondent who claimed to have voted after 2:30 P.M. but whose name on the sign-in roster was identified by an early number, indicating that he had obviously voted rather early on Election Day.

These data, indicating that at least 97.5 percent of the sub-sample who claimed to have voted actually did so, serve to assure the general reliability of the responses that were obtained in the over-all sample.

THE INFLUENCE OF PRIOR COMMITMENT TO CANDIDATES

In order to explore whether election broadcasts acted as an intervening influence between prior voting intention and ultimate vote it is necessary to examine the interrelationships of three major variables:

1. voters' commitments to specific candidates prior to Election Day;

2. the degree of exposure to election broadcasts prior to voting;

3. actual voting behavior.

Stated simply, votes and intentions must be compared according to whether or not voters were exposed to election broadcasts prior to casting their ballots.

The data from the California study confirmed previous research findings regarding early commitments to specific candidates among the majority of voters. In addition, the findings corroborate the findings of earlier studies regarding the tenacity of early voting commitments in the face of last-minute external influences that may be thought to upset them.

To illustrate, of the 1,212 voters in the sample who in Wave I reported an intention to vote for *a specific candidate,* 97 percent subsequently voted for that candidate. A total of 14 voters, representing one percent of the voters in the sample whose intended votes were known, switched their support to the opposition candidate. This one percent plus the two percent of voters who stated their intentions but refused to disclose their vote define the first and gross absolute limit of possible bandwagon or underdog effects. *Not more than three percent of the 1,212 voters could conceivably have been so influenced.* Furthermore, this three percent is obviously much greater than any actual effect, since not all were exposed to broadcasts nor did they all switch in the same direction. In fact, 5 of the 14 noted "Switchers" apparently changed their plans as a result of pressures from Election Eve campaign appeals and from personal persuasion.

The vast majority of the voters studied (at least 92 percent) made their decisions before Election Day. Seventy-seven percent of *all* the voters sampled (1,297 of a total of 1,689) declared that the candidate for whom they had voted had been their choice "since he was nominated at his party's convention," and an additional 15 percent reported having made their ultimate Election Day choice during the course of the campaign, but before Election Day. The remainder (8 percent) refused to answer the question about when they had made their final voting choice.

When the 1,297 voters who chose their candidates prior to Election Day were asked whether they had ever considered changing their minds during the course of the campaign, 81 percent (1,115) said that the possibility had never even occurred to them.

Now consider in somewhat greater detail the same data that were presented earlier. No less than 97 percent of the voters who had planned to vote for Johnson actually did so, and precisely the same percentage of voters who had planned to vote for Goldwater actually did so.

As noted before, 14 voters changed their choice between Election Eve and the time they actually voted. The net gain in switching slightly favored Senator Goldwater, the loser, not President Johnson. The Republican candidate managed to attract 12 voters, or somewhat over one percent of those who had declared for the Democrat in Wave I. In contrast, Johnson succeeded in attracting only two voters—less than half of one percent—from the previously announced Goldwater supporters. Approximately two percent of the announced supporters of each candidate refused to report whether they had switched or not.

Illustrative of the tenacity of prior commitment in its influence on subsequent voting behavior are the following quotations from the responses of two voters who were interviewed in the study.

This Californian made up his mind to vote for Johnson one whole year before he actually had a chance to do so:

I made up my mind to vote for Johnson when Kennedy was shot. I have always associated Johnson with the good works he did. He is for the old and the sick. Who wants to go back in history? Johnson has courage, experience. Goldwater wants to turn back the clock. Johnson is trying to do everything he can to wipe out poverty. That man has such feeling. You can tell he feels sorrow and wants to help the working people. The other candidate was against everything I believe in. He just wasn't my man. I didn't feel too well on Election Day. Maybe I was worried underneath about the silent vote. Everyone talked about the silent vote in the papers and on the TV. But I felt that Johnson would win. The highly educated and the intelligent voter would go for him.

Q: Do you feel there are many educated and intelligent voters?

A: More than people realize. Look at the vote. The silent vote didn't materialize. Probably it was because of the mess Goldwater made for himself at the convention. Goldwater cinched it for himself there. Coming out the way he did against civil rights made so many of the voters angry. Johnson is a new man since Kennedy died. He showed himself to be liberal and very capable. The way he handled himself in an emergency was very impressive. I loved Kennedy, and Mrs. Kennedy is a real lady. But since we can't have them, we are lucky to have the Johnsons. And Johnson picked a very good man to be the vice-presidential candidate. Who ever heard of that man Miller?

Q: Once you had made up your mind, were you confident or fearful of your decision?

A: I was somewhat fearful of the silent vote, but I knew I had made the right decision for me and the rest of the people.

This woman decided for Goldwater "halfway through the campaign" and saw her decision through on Election Day even though she claimed to be a "registered Democrat" and had heard of the possible Goldwater defeat prior to voting.

You can tell that Goldwater is a thinking man too. About halfway through the campaign, I realized that Goldwater was a thinking man. Sometimes his speeches were more cryptic than Johnson's, but I liked his ideas. I was never too sold on Johnson. He wasn't elected by the people and he didn't really have a right to have the job. I have to admit his speeches were more gentlemanly than Goldwater's. All my friends are for Goldwater, and my son and my daughter and her husband are for Goldwater also. I really never talked politics with my children, but my son-in-law who publishes the ———— which is really fair when it comes to politics kept saying to me, "You know, Mother, we must get that man out of the White House. He is ruining the country." Actually in some ways it was a toss-up since both men weren't really very good men. It seems to me that we should be able to do better in this country. That there must be somewhere in this country two men who would make really good presidents. Johnson obviously is a thief and Goldwater is a bit foolish with his talk about small atomic weapons, but I voted for him anyway because he was the lesser of the two evils. I knew I wasn't going to vote for Johnson as soon as he picked that man—what is his name (Humphrey) yes, Humphrey for his running mate. You know I am a registered Democrat, but I didn't care what the radio said. Actually by the time I went to the polls, it was still undecided. I wouldn't have cared. I made up my mind how I was going to vote and nothing I heard at that late hour would have changed it. Certainly I wasn't going to get on the bandwagon for Johnson, and I wanted Goldwater to have my vote.

Up to this point in the analysis, no evidence of bandwagon effect was apparent. The Goldwater plurality among Switchers suggested a possible tiny underdog effect, but whether any such effect can be attributed to Election Night broadcasts remains unsubstantiated at this time.

TIME OF VOTING

EARLY, MIDAFTERNOON, AND LATE VOTERS

Let us now consider the times of day at which the California sample voted. Together with other data, this information will provide some indication of the salience which voters attribute to Election Night broadcasts in the terminal decision-making process. The sample of 1,689 voters was divided into three groups, as follows:

1. *Early Voters,* who voted prior to 2:30 P.M. PST, *before* it was possible to attend election broadcasts. There were 1,044 persons (62 percent of the sample) in this group.

2. *Midafternoon Voters,* who voted between 2:30 P.M. and 4.30 P.M. PST, when it was possible for them to have heard only local, or cursory, inconclusive returns before actually voting. There were 170 such voters (10 percent of the sample).

3. *Late Voters,* who voted after 4:30 P.M. PST, and thus could have seen or heard sizable substantive tallies and predictions. There were 475 voters (28 percent of the sample) in this group.[12]

The important point to note here, of course, is that 62 percent of the sample of voters literally could not have been influenced by exposure to broadcast returns because they voted well before the broadcasts began. An additional 10 percent, who voted between 2:30 P.M. and 4:30 P.M., could have been exposed before voting only to relatively cursory election reports.

The 475 Late Voters could have been exposed to broadcasts including predictions and large tallies. But only 196, or 41 percent of them, actually *were* so exposed *prior to voting.* More than half of this group, who could have seen or heard substantive late broadcasts, simply did not. The ones who did see or hear such broadcasts represent only 12 percent of the total sample. But another way, only 12 percent of the sample made themselves available to substantive late broadcasts which could have induced vote-switches resulting in direct bandwagon or underdog effects.[13] These data do not indicate whether any significant number of intended late voters heard or saw broadcasts and as a result decided not to vote at all, a situation which would create indirect bandwagon or underdog effects. This question will be discussed a little later on.

THE INFLUENCE OF SOCIAL CHARACTERISTICS ON TIME OF VOTING AND EXPOSURE TO ELECTION NIGHT BROADCASTS

Social behavior such as attending to the media and choosing a time for voting are neither randomized nor monolithic in nature. They are governed by processes of selection in accordance with the various social statuses that voters and audiences occupy plus the variable of convenience. In the instance of voting, the time that ballots are cast can certainly be considered as relating more to the particular sex, occupational, and socioeconomic roles of the voters than to the voters' opportunity for finding out how the election is or may be turning out via broadcasts. The fact that some two-thirds of the voters in the California sample voted before they could have heard or seen any broadcast election data bears this point out succinctly.

Social roles play an important part in determining convenience. Since the casting of a ballot in a national election is out of the normal stream of daily activities, a special time outside the usual rhythm of daily ritual must be set aside for this unique activity. Such a time must be convenient. That is to say, it can be expected that voters will attempt to "fit in" time for voting with "normal" daily routines with as little disruption as possible. Thus, for example, it can be expected that mothers who experience a hiatus in the late morning hours when children and husbands are away from home will tend to find such a period more convenient for going out to vote than other times of day when they are preoccupied with family, in-home chores. Certain classes of workers (for example, agricultural or construction workers), who normally start the work day very early in the morning prior to the time that polling places open, will be compelled to vote late in the day, after their work has been completed. Ease of access to polling places, either on the way to or along the way from work, shopping, chauffeuring the family brood, social visiting, and such will also influence time of voting, and these activities in turn are reflections of social status and role.

The California voting study showed that social status did influence time of voting in California to some degree (Tables 1 and 2). For example, women showed some tendency to vote earlier in the day, while, in comparison, male voters were more likely to vote after 4:30 P.M.—either on the way back from work or after the evening meal and a chance to "wash up." The elderly (60 and over), who tire as the day progresses and prepare for sleep very early in the evening, were more apt to vote early in the day than were voters in other age groups.

Roman Catholic voters, who normally account for higher proportions of unskilled workers in trades that ordinarily start the

TABLE 1. Time of Voting by Sex, Age, Religion

	Early Voters (62% of total voters), %	Midafter-noon Voters (10% of total voters), %	Late Voters (28% of total voters), %
Sex			
Male (791)	59	9	32
Female (898)	64	12	24
Age			
21–29 (261)	52	10	38
30–39 (336)	60	10	30
40–49 (451)	55	11	34
50–59 (280)	61	11	28
60–64 (109)	78	8	14
65 and over (216)	84	8	8
Religion			
Protestant (1,033)	63	10	27
Roman Catholic (371)	55	13	32
Jewish (89)	65	6	29

work-day at very early hours, were the least likely of the major religious groups to vote early on Election Day. In fact, voters from families that were headed by unskilled workers, as compared with those from other occupational groups, were seen as the least likely to be Early Voters.

The data on socioeconomic status tend to confirm the hypothesis that time of voting is a function of convenience, the definition of which is reflected in the social status of the voter. Both relatively high socioeconomic status and relatively low socioeconomic status persons tended to vote early. The members of families whose chief wage-earner was a college graduate or better or whose occupation was either professional, or managerial, or in sales and service, or who earned $10,000 a year or more tended to be Early Voters. Note that these individuals characteristically reflected social and occupational positions that are either relatively flexible in start-work hours or allow the person consider-

TABLE 2. Time of Voting by Socioeconomic Status

	Early Voters (62% of total voters), %	Midafter-noon (10% of total voters), %	Late Voters (28% of total voters), %
Education of Chief Wage Earner			
8 years or less (152)	64	14	22
9–11 years (195)	57	11	32
12 years (591)	62	11	28
Some college (376)	60	10	30
College graduate (230)	65	7	28
Postgraduate (113)	66	7	27
Occupation of Chief Wage Earner			
Professionals (354)	64	9	27
Managers (209)	67	7	26
Clericals (151)	53	13	34
Sales (136)	68	7	25
Craftsmen (325)	45	13	42
Operatives, Semiskilled (64)	55	16	30
Service (91)	65	10	25
Laborers, Unskilled (66)	50	15	35
Students (18)*	78	6	16
Not in Labor Force; Retired (215)	83	8	9
Annual Family Income			
Less than $5,000 (304)	70	9	21
$5,000–less than $10,000 (671)	54	11	35
$10,000–less than $15,000 (351)	64	9	27
$15,000 and over (178)	69	8	23

* Base too small to be reliable for analysis.

able mobility outside the office or factory during early periods of the day (for instance, professionals or certain types of service and sales people). For such persons a half-hour to hour delay or work-break to cast a ballot does not reflect a serious breach of work mores. As a matter of fact, many employers in these categories allow time off for voting. Thus, getting the voting over with as early as possible in order to take advantage of the time off can be seen as a possible motivational factor here.

Lower socioeconomic status persons—particularly those "not gainfully employed" such as students and retired persons— were more apt to be among those who cast ballots before 2:30 P.M. in California on November 3, 1964. The high proportions of voters in these two groups account for the disproportionate incidence of persons in grammar- and high-school graduate households and in the lowest income bracket who were Early Voters. For students, who get busier as the day progresses and who are occupied with school chores in the evening, earlier hours of the day are apparently considerably more convenient than hours later in the afternoon and evening. It has been noted that for the retired-elderly earlier voting hours are more convenient due to progressive fatigue which sets in as the day wears on.

THE INFLUENCE OF PARTISANSHIP AND NEED
FOR POLITICAL GUIDANCE

Although it plays an important role in affecting time of voting, convenience alone cannot be considered as the principal variable. Certainly interest in the outcome of the election and political partisanship can be expected to have exerted some important influence on time of voting.

In this regard, it is quite conceivable that voters who had a high interest stake in the outcome of the election might have sought to exercise their choice at the earliest opportunity. This development is precisely what appeared to have taken place in the California sample. Voters who claimed to have been "more interested" in the 1964 Presidential Election than were their friends and acquaintances were more apt to vote early (64 percent) rather than late (36 percent) on November 3. Voters whose interest in the election can be termed either "average" (41 percent) or "weak" (41 percent) were more apt to vote later on Election Day.

It appears, then, that strong interest in the election was coupled with some urgency to cast votes early, while tepid or low interest in the election was accompanied by a more relaxed orientation to voting and resulted in late voting on November 3.

It has been observed that the 1964 Presidential campaign polarized the electorate well before Election Eve. That is to say, supporters of each candidate particularized their opinions about their man well before actual voting time had arrived. The consistently low frequencies of voters in the "Don't Know" categories of the various political polls that were taken during the campaign substantiate this observation.

The following article by California Poll Director Mervin Field which appeared in the November 2, 1964 edition of the *San Francisco Chronicle* illustrates this point. Under a caption announcing "Johnson Keeps Lead in State" (California) the item reports:

Despite one of the bitterest campaigns in recent history which has seen the two-party expenditures of money and effort in organization reach an all-time high, despite upheavals of major nature on the international scene, and despite such sensational revelations as the Jenkins case, the last eight weeks have seen virtually no change in the overall preference votes of Californians.

Lyndon Johnson still commands the same overwhelming majority over Senator Barry Goldwater that he had when the campaign started in earnest.

When the California Poll completed its survey of voter opinion on October 28 among a representative statewide sample of 1218 voters, the results were: Johnson 60 per cent, Goldwater 34 per cent, and 6 per cent were undecided. There is no significant difference between this result and the one obtained in early September, when President Johnson polled 62 per cent, Goldwater 33 per cent and 5 per cent were undecided.

If the undecided voters are set aside, the vote split becomes 64 per cent for Johnson and 36 per cent for Goldwater.

In particular, supporters of Senator Goldwater appeared to be increasingly more ardent and assertive about their candidate as it became more and more evident from the public-opinion polls— well before the election—that he would lose. Despite all the indications of potential defeat for their candidate, supporters of the Republican candidate continued looking to a major upset as election time approached. A "let's show 'em on Election Day" attitude was in ever-increasing evidence among Republicans (and, to some degree, Democrats as well) just prior to November 3, 1964. It is apparent that Republican partisans experienced a greater sense of urgency to vote early on Election Day than was in evidence among Democratic partisans.

As shown in Table 3, of the 428 persons who claimed in Wave I that it was "extremely important" that they vote for Senator Goldwater on the following day, 72 percent were classified as Early Voters in Wave II. Compare this with the 57 percent of the 629 voters who declared on November 2 a similar degree of personal concern about voting for President Johnson and who subsequently went on to vote early on November 3.

The study offers further corroboration for the hypothesis that in California, Republican partisanship rather than Democratic partisanship accounted for a considerably greater proportion of Early Voters on Election Day.[14] In contrast, Democratic partisanship rather than Republican partisanship accounted for a

TABLE 3. Time of Voting Compared with Expressed Concern

	How important is it to you to vote for Johnson tomorrow? (Asked in Wave I)		
	Early Voters (62% of total voters), %	Midafternoon Voters (10% of total voters), %	Late Voters (28% of total voters), %
Extremely/Very (629)	57	11	32
Somewhat/Not Too (65)	54	14	32

	How important is it to you to vote for Goldwater tomorrow? (Asked in Wave I)		
	Early Voters (62% of total voters), %	Midafternoon Voters (10% of total voters), %	Late Voters (28% of total voters), %
Extremely/Very (428)	72	7	21
Somewhat/Not Too (33)	58	18	24

considerably greater proportion of Midafternoon and Late Voters.

Seven out of ten voters in the California sample who voted for Goldwater as compared with less than six out of ten voters who cast ballots for Johnson did so *early* on Election Day. The same proportions of declared Republicans and Democrats voted in precisely the same early-late ratio on November 3, 1964.

In short, on Election Day, 1964, Republicans rather than Democrats in the California sample were more likely to be Early Voters, while Democrats rather than Republicans were more likely to be Midafternoon and Late Voters. This tendency substantially reduced the possibility of a major pro-Johnson bandwagon effect among potential Goldwater defectors.

The popular version of the bandwagon hypothesis suggests that influence from broadcast sources "just happens" to passive audiences. However, there is the possibility that certain types of voters may actively arrange their voting times so that their opportunity for exposure to election broadcasts may be maximized. In short, it is quite conceivable that some voters, particularly those who need guidance and advice regarding whom to vote for, might consciously arrange their time of voting to coincide with major election broadcasts that might help them to decide in favor of one candidate.

The California study revealed that explicit self-evaluation regarding the seeking of advice in making a voting decision did not affect time of voting. It made no difference whether the voter thought he needed guidance—more so than his peers, less so, or as much as the people he knew—as far as time of voting was concerned.

PREPLANNED TIME OF VOTING

The problem of voting time is critical to the discussion of the possibility of last-minute influences of voting behavior in the west by radio and television election broadcasts emanating from the east. In order to be influenced by such broadcasts voters must first be exposed to them and then go out to vote—not the other way around, obviously.

The data obtained in the Mendelsohn voting study indicate that time of voting is affected by both social status and partisanship. Thus, time of voting is not random; rather, it is generally planned purposive behavior.

The data in the study make clear the fact that close to nine out of ten persons (46 percent of all voters in the sample) who planned a day before to vote early on Election Day did so in fact. Nearly eight out of ten respondents (16 percent of all voters) who on November 2 planned to vote late on November 3 actually did so. Thus, whether a person will or will not be exposed to significant election broadcasts can be predicted with considerable accuracy *prior* to Election Day. Midafternoon voting behavior in California on Election Day was the least purposive. Consequently, midafternoon voting reflects a high degree of unplanned behavior. This suggests that midafternoon voting represented a residual opportunity for minorities of the California voters studied who could not exercise their franchise conveniently during either the early or later voting hours.

It is important to bear in mind the fact that nearly half the voters in the California sample, *through conscious preplanning of voting time,* literally removed themselves from the opportunity of being influenced by any election broadcasts that originated in the east on November 3, 1964. The consequences of these actions on the bandwagon phenomenon will be discussed in some detail.

PRIOR COMMITMENT, TIME OF VOTING, AND ACTUAL VOTES CAST

Worth noting at this point is the relationship between prior commitment, time of voting, and actual votes cast.

As previously noted, 97 percent of 1,212 voters in the sample actually voted for the person for whom they had intended to vote. There are only minor deviations from this figure when the voters are classified by time of day. Ninety-five to 97 percent of the voters voted in accordance with their previous intentions—regardless of whether they had high, low, or no opportunities to hear election broadcast coverage (Table 4).

TABLE 4. Voting Intention and Actual Votes by Time of Day

	Early Voters		Midafternoon Voters		Late Voters	
	Num-ber	Per-cent	Num-ber	Per-cent	Num-ber	Per-cent
Voted as intended	743	97	110	95	321	96
Switched from Nov. 2 intention	5	1	4	3	5	2
Intended to vote for either Goldwater or Johnson, refused to disclose actual vote	15	2	2	2	7	2
	763	100	116	100	333	100

This constancy of intention and vote holds even when candidates and time of voting are combined. As indicated in Tables 5 and 6, from 94 percent to 97 percent of those planning to vote for Johnson did so, regardless of time of day, and 96 percent to 98 percent of those intending to vote for Goldwater did so, again

TABLE 5. Intended and Actual Votes for Johnson by Time of Day

		Early Voters		Midafternoon Voters		Late Voters	
		Num-ber	Per-cent	Num-ber	Per-cent	Num-Per-	Per-cent
Intended to vote for:	Actually voted for:						
Johnson	Johnson	405	97	80	94	219	96
Johnson	Goldwater	4	1	4	5	4	2
Johnson	Refused to answer	8	2	1	1	4	2
		417	100	85	100	227	100

TABLE 6. Intended and Actual Votes for Goldwater by Time of Day

		Early Voters		Midafternoon Voters		Late Voters	
		Num-ber	Per-cent	Num-ber	Per-cent	Num-ber	Per-cent
Intended to vote for:	Actually voted for:						
Goldwater	Goldwater	338	98	30	97	102	96
Goldwater	Johnson	1	*	—	—	1	1
Goldwater	Refused to answer	7	2	1	3	3	3
		346	100	31	100	106	100

* Less than 1%.

regardless of time of day. The opportunity to hear returns in itself apparently had no effect on the constancy of voting intentions.

It may be noted that the twelve voters who switched from Johnson to Goldwater happened to be evenly distributed throughout the day, and that of the two voters who switched to Johnson, one voted early and one voted late. Here again, then, no evidence of bandwagon effect is seen as yet.

So far, however, only two major variables have been discussed: actual vote as compared with intention, and time of voting. It is time to introduce the third and most crucial variable: exposure to election coverage.

THE SALIENCE OF NATIONAL BROADCASTS

The fact that only twelve percent of the California voters studied made themselves available to substantive national broadcast coverage of the 1964 National Election *prior* to voting generally reflects the rather low salience that these broadcasts had as guides to voting behavior for the California electorate that was studied.

There is additional evidence from the study suggesting that the voters did not breathlessly await national broadcast election coverage, hoping that an inviting bandwagon would come along in time so they could modify their voting behavior accordingly. As to functioning as guides for as yet uncast votes, national election coverage broadcasts were greeted by the voters studied with what appears to be an attitude of general indifference.

For example, nine out of ten voters who *did not attend* election broadcasts before voting (88 percent of a total of 1,379) showed no regrets about not having availed themselves of such broadcasts beforehand. No more than three percent of this group voiced a desire to have had the opportunity to have heard or seen Election Day broadcasts prior to leaving for the polls. With respect to salience, these additional facts are worth noting.

Although the research did not attempt to explore why, before voting, voters preferred to watch or listen to specific broadcast outlets, it is evident that the reputation of a given channel or station for presenting predictions of the election's outcome was a factor that apparently motivated some 25 percent of the voters sampled in California to choose one election broadcast source over another. For the great majority (75 percent) of the prevoting election broadcast audiences sampled, the ability of one broadcast source to "scoop" a forecast of the election's outcome apparently made no difference in the choice of particular television channels or radio stations for getting early election news on Election Day prior to voting.

A pertinent footnote to this discussion of the salience of broadcasts in the decision-making process of voters concerns the voters' view of computer projections. All three networks place great emphasis on such predictions. Since these projections make up an important part of network Election Day broadcasts, all of the 1,689 voters were asked whether they thought such computer predictions were "usually right or usually wrong." A third (34 percent) of the voters queried were unable to offer an opinion on the matter, and an additional 10 percent stated that the computer predictions were usually wrong. Precisely what "no opinion" means in this case is somewhat difficult to determine. It is, however, interesting to note that in the fall of 1964, after computers had been used in Election Night broadcasts for several years, nearly half of the voters in the California sample were not ready to regard computer predictions as wholly trustworthy.

THE EFFECTS OF EXPOSURE TO ELECTION BROADCASTS

All in all, some 130 voters (8 percent) of the total of 1,724 who were surveyed claimed to have witnessed forecasts of an imminent Johnson victory either from television or radio prior to casting their ballots. The general reactions to these forecasts appeared to add up to nothing but a shoulder-shrug on the part of audiences. The following quotations from voters represent both typical confusion and reactions:

Q: What did you do on Election Night?
A: We turned on the set about 7 o'clock and watched until about 10. But it was silly, because I knew Johnson was going to win all along. I voted for Goldwater around 7:30.

Q: How did you feel about the electronic computing machines that forecast election results on television and radio?
A: I don't understand what you are talking about. Do you mean the computers that predicted that Johnson was winning before the polls had closed? (Yes.) That really isn't good, is it? It might keep the weak minded people from voting. If they thought their candidate was going to lose anyway, what would be the point to go vote. Now if people would be strong minded this wouldn't matter. I wanted my vote in this election counted, even though I knew I was on the losing side. I talked to people all day on the way to the polls—they were impressed by the returns. It didn't stop them, but it might stop someone. We should treasure our vote.

Q: Do you recall exactly what you saw on the broadcast before you went to the polls?
A: I remember that Johnson was winning, but that didn't matter because California wasn't in yet. I was interested more in the California elections, and I voted for Johnson.

Q: Did you hear anything about electronic computer machines?
A: Yes, I guess they were using them to count the votes. This

helped to show people what candidates were winning earlier because it made the vote counting easier. (One of the things these computers do is predict what the outcome will be. Did you hear any predictions?) Yes, I guess I must have. Do they really predict results? How do they do that? (I said it is done electronically.) Oh, that is interesting. Wonder how that is done? If you know ahead of time, who is going to win why bother to vote. Of course, I was more interested in the Congressional race. That they couldn't predict. I would have still voted, because once I make up my mind nothing changes it.

Let us look now at the basic group of 1,212 voters who declared a candidate preference in Wave I and who did in fact vote. Table 7 describes this group in terms of vote intention, exposure, and actual vote. The voters are not subclassified by time of voting here.

The data indicate that the intention to vote for a specific

TABLE 7. Actual Votes by Vote Intention and Prior Exposure to Election Broadcasts

| | Intended to vote for President Johnson and prior to voting were— | | | | | | | |
| | Exposed to election broadcasts | | Not exposed to election broadcasts | | Exposed to election broadcasts | | Not exposed to election broadcasts | |
	Num-ber	Per-cent	Num-ber	Per-cent	Num-ber	Per-cent	Num-ber	Per-cent
Voted for President Johnson	91	97	613	97	1	2	1	*
Voted for Senator Goldwater	2	2	10	2	56	97	414	97
Refused to disclose vote	1	1	12	2	1	2	10	2
	94	100	635	101**	58	101**	425	99**

* Less than 1%.
** Percents add to 101 and 99 due to rounding.

candidate was much more powerfully related to actual vote than was any possible effect of exposure to election broadcasts prior to voting. Both among those exposed and among those not exposed, 97 percent of those who intended to vote for Johnson actually did so. Precisely the same statistics hold for Goldwater. Switching involved two percent of the exposed as compared with one percent of the unexposed, but among the exposed Johnson and Goldwater each lost two percent to the other. In terms of the overall sample, then, no evidence of either bandwagon effect or underdog effect is apparent as yet.

So far only gross data have been presented. Investigation of the possible influence of election broadcasts on terminal voting decisions cannot be explored in gross terms alone. It is necessary to look for possible effects among specific types of voters as well as among all voters in the sample.

To obtain this information the sample was divided into two sets of subgroups: (1) according to the time of day at which they voted, as has already been indicated, and (2) according to the relationship between their stated voting intention and their actual voting behavior. Those in the latter classification were again divided into groups labelled

(1) *Persisters:* persons who voted for the candidates they intended to support (1,174, or 70 percent of the 1,689 voters);

(2) *Last-Day Deciders:* persons who were undecided in Wave I about whom they would vote for, but did vote for one or the other of the candidates on Election Day (161, or 9.5 percent of the sample);

(3) *Switchers:* persons who declared for a candidate in Wave I, but actually voted for the other candidate (14, or 1 percent of the sample).[15]

Clearly, the key groups for a study of possible broacast influence are the Switchers (who have been discussed previously), the Last-Day Deciders, and the Late Voters.

THE LAST-DAY DECIDER

Let us first consider the Last-Day Deciders—the 161 persons who, on Election Eve, had not yet decided for whom to vote, but who did in fact vote on Election Day. Theoretically, such people might be particularly susceptible to terminal influences of which election broadcasts might well be one. Strictly speaking, Election Day influences that may act upon Last-Day Deciders cannot be said to serve the prototypic function of bandwagon effect—that is, the function of conversion. Instead, last-minute influences on Last-Day Deciders can be seen as serving a crystallizing function, helping the voter to come to some decision immediately prior to the time he has to vote.

At what times of day did these Last-Day Deciders actually vote? Ninety-three Last-Day Deciders, or 58 percent of this group (6 percent of *all* the voters), cast their ballots early, before 2:30 P.M. Thus the majority of the voters who had not decided upon a candidate when interviewed on Election Eve not only apparently succeeded in doing so overnight, so to speak, but actually went out to vote for their final choices *before* they had an opportunity to avail themselves of election-broadcast information on Election Day. It is evident that prior to actually voting, the *majority* of the Last-Day Deciders, the most susceptible group of voters, *must have been exposed* to "crystallizing" influences other than television/radio broadcasts late on Election Eve or on Election Day itself. More on this point is discussed further on.

Eighteen Last-Day Deciders, or 11 percent of this group (1 percent of *all* the voters), cast their ballots between 2:30 P.M. and 4:30 P.M., during the period when the opportunity for exposure to significant election broadcasts was very low.

Fifty or 31 percent of the Last-Day Decider group (representing less than 3 percent of all the voters) voted after 4:30 P.M. at a time of high opportunity for election broadcast exposure. *However*, of these 50 voters only 18 (1.1 percent of *all* the voters) actually heard or saw broadcast election forecast returns prior to voting.

In sum, then, the Last-Day Deciders did not in general depend on broadcast election returns for voting guidance. Only about one in nine of them (eleven percent) heard or saw such broadcasts prior to voting. Let us now consider how Last-Day Deciders actually voted in reference to whether they were or were not exposed to substantive broadcast election forecasts and returns.

As indicated in Table 8, the late-voting Last-Day Deciders who had *not* been exposed and who reported their vote split exactly evenly between the two candidates. In contrast, those who *had* been exposed and who reported their vote favored Johnson over Goldwater.

TABLE 8. Late Votes of Last-Day Deciders in Relation to Exposure to Election Broadcasts

	"Undecided" in Wave I, and Prior to Voting Were—					
	Exposed to election broadcasts		Not exposed to election broadcasts		Total late voting Last-Day Deciders	
	Number	Percent	Number	Percent	Number	Percent
Voted after 4:30 P.M. PST, for						
President Johnson	9	50	11	34	20	40
Senator Goldwater	5	28	11	34	16	32
Refused to disclose vote	4	22	10	31	14	28
	18	100	32	99*	50	100

* Percents add to 99 due to rounding.

At first glance these data may appear to reflect some sort of rudimentary bandwagon effect. But considerable caution must be exercised in interpreting these data. In the first place, we are dealing with miniscule figures. The Johnson plurality among the exposed rests on the voting behavior of two people. Second, the proportion of Last-Day Deciders who refused to disclose their vote is so large that, were the votes of these people known, they could completely change the picture.

Finally, when the voting choices of Last-Day Deciders exposed to broadcasts are compared with those voters whose intentions as well as votes were known (Persisters) and who were exposed to election broadcasts prior to voting after 4:30 P.M., the proportion

TABLE 9. Late Votes of Last-Day Deciders and Persisters Who Were Exposed to Election Broadcasts Prior to Voting*

	Exposed to Election Broadcasts Prior to Voting			
	Last-Day Deciders		Persisters	
	Number	Percent	Number	Percent
Voted after 4:30 P.M. PST for				
President Johnson	9	64	91	62
Senator Goldwater	5	36	56	38
	14	100	147	100

* Persons refusing to disclose actual vote omitted.

of votes allotted to each candidate is virtually the same for the two groups. As Table 9 reveals, if refusals to disclose votes are omitted from the analysis, 64 percent of the Last-Day Deciders as compared to 62 percent of the Persisters who voted late after witnessing election broadcasts voted for President Johnson. Similarly, 36 percent of the Last-Day Deciders as compared to 38 percent of the Persisters who voted late after attending election broadcasts voted for Senator Goldwater. The 2-percent advantage for Johnson is meaningless, since a single voter represents 7 percent of the 14 Last-Day Deciders here under discussion.

THE LATE VOTER

It will be recalled that 475 persons in the sample voted after 4:30 P.M. PST on Election Day at a time when the opportunity to hear or see prevoting substantive election broadcasts was maximal. For this reason the Late Voters constitute one of the key groups in an investigation of possible broadcast-attributed bandwagon or underdog effects.

Analysis reveals that the Late Voters voted almost precisely as did the rest of the sample for whom adequate information is

TABLE 10. Late Votes for President Johnson by Intention and Exposure to Substantive Election Broadcasts

| | Intended to vote for President Johnson, and prior to voting were— | | | |
| | Exposed to election broadcasts | | Not exposed to election broadcasts | |
	Number	Percent	Number	Percent
Voted after 4:30 P.M., PST for				
President Johnson	91	97	128	96
Senator Goldwater	2	2	2	2
Refused to disclose vote	1	1	3	2
	94	100	133	100

TABLE 11. Late Votes for Senator Goldwater by Intention and Exposure to Substantive Election Broadcasts

| | Intended to vote for Senator Goldwater, and prior to voting were— | | | |
| | Exposed to election broadcasts | | Not exposed to election broadcasts | |
	Number	Percent	Number	Percent
Voted after 4:30 P.M. PST for				
Senator Goldwater	56	97	48	96
President Johnson	1	2	—	—
Refused to disclose vote	1	2	2	4
	58	101*	48	100

* Percents add to 101 due to rounding.

available. Tables 10 and 11 reveal that in the case of subjects voting for both President Johnson and Senator Goldwater, 96 percent of the Late Voters who were *not* exposed to election broadcasts before voting cast their ballots according to their previous intention, and 97 percent of those who *were* exposed did likewise.

Only five Late Voters defected to the opposite camp from their announced intention, and only three of these were exposed to election broadcasts before voting. Of these three, Johnson gained one and Goldwater two, which in percentage terms amounted to a two percent loss on each side. It should be noted that Johnson also lost two percent (two) of his previously announced adherents who were *not* exposed. This miniscule number of Switchers defies interpretation. There is no reliable evidence that switching is more common among those who witnessed election broadcasts (three persons, or two percent) than among those who did not (two persons, or one percent). If the switching among the exposed was due to the broadcasts, its two-directional movement cancelled out any net effects. In any case, to contemplate bandwagon or underdog effects on the basis of such figures is obviously meaningless, except to note that clearly neither effect occurred in any magnitude.

The absence of any clear effect even holds for Late Voters who recalled hearing radio or television tallies or predictions clearly forecasting a Johnson victory. The data are so similar to those which have just been presented that it seems purposeless to report them in detail here. In brief, each candidate lost one voter who had heard actual vote tallies, and each lost one who had heard forecasts or prediction.

It is interesting to consider why late-voting adherents of both Goldwater and Johnson continued to vote for their candidates even after they had heard that Johnson's victory was assured. It would seem that exposure to the election broadcasts wherein information regarding a Johnson victory was presented either had no effect upon such voters or served simply to reinforce preelection commitments in both camps. In particular, the fact that such information does not seem to have upset prior commitments to Senator Goldwater suggests the operation of a curious psychological phenomenon. Since well over nine out of every ten Late Voters who intended to vote for Goldwater carried out their commitments to the obvious loser, it is evident that knowledge of his impending loss was not assimilated psychologically as a meaningful reason for abandoning him. Qualitative data obtained from the twenty in-depth interviews indicated that witnessing broadcast predictions or actual announcements of an election winner may have either strengthened the determination among certain of the indicated loser's partisans to support him—come what may—or produced no ostensible effects.

The following interview protocols are illustrative:

Q: How did you expect the election to turn out?
A: Basically, I expected the same thing. I thought Goldwater may win a little bit stronger, but somehow he didn't. Big deals (laughs) Alabama, Georgia, I don't remember others. (Pause) But lot of people voted for him—twenty-five millions that's a lot of people.
Q: When did you know for sure who won?
A: About 7:30, after I voted. When I was voting Johnson was already leading in a few states, but by 7:30 or 8 it was almost certain and no question about it.
Q: Could any results or projections have affected you in any way?
A: (Reasonably strongly) No. I was determined to vote for Goldwater. (Matter of factly) I expected everything that was on TV; it wasn't surprising.

Q: What did you hear on radio or TV on Election Day, and how did you feel about it?
A: It didn't affect my voting—that was all figured out by over a week in advance. I kind of lost interest by the time it started to come around to the election. In fact, that night I turned off the radio and TV and just read.
Q: Did you hear any results before you voted?
A: Yes. (What were they?) A number of precincts back East were in. (Did you hear any projections?) Yes I heard a couple of predictions that Johnson would win. (How did you feel about that?) Well— I figured he would and (laughs) I was going to cast one vote that would help defeat him. (Did the projections and returns influence you in any way?) No. I think it's a person's duty to vote as he chooses.

Q: Whom did you vote for, Miss ———?
A: I voted for Barry. (I see. Were you disappointed when he didn't win?) No. You see I thought Johnson was the better man anyway, but I just thought it was important for him not to have it just given to him. (Would you have been disappointed if Goldwater had made it?) No. I don't think so. I believe that the government should stop doing everything for the people anyway. Besides, just before the election I

watched Ronald Reagan's speech on television, and it was pretty convincing. It made me realize how nice Goldwater really was.

Q: Did you know from hearing radio or television broadcasts who was ahead—before you voted?

A: Of course; I knew Johnson was winning before I voted.

Q: Were you excited because it was Election Day?

A: Excited no. I knew who was going to win, and so what was there to be excited about?

Q: How did you know who was going to win?

A: Well everyone said that Johnson was going to win. Now, I want you to know right now that I didn't vote for him. My husband did, but then we don't see eye-to-eye on politics. He tried to convince me to vote for Johnson but I am like Pamela Mason. Do you ever watch her on the TV? She has the right idea about women. She thinks women should be independent and think for themselves. Women shouldn't be patsies for their men. I sure get a bang out of her.

Q: What time did you vote?

A: About five o'clock.

Q: Was there any reason for you to wait until then?

A: No, I wanted to get my yard finished. The polling place was just two doors down and so I knew that I wouldn't have trouble getting there.

Q: Did you talk to anyone during the day?

A: No, I just worked on the yard.

Q: Did you have any idea when you went to the polling place who was winning the election?

A: Well, while I was working on the yard people kept coming by and telling me how things were going on television. Those for Goldwater and who knew I was too kept telling me to vote because Johnson was winning. All along I knew that Johnson was going to win, but I wanted to vote for my man, and besides that there were other things in California. The housing thing was important. I don't want my boy to be going to school with colored kids.

Here, then, is a psychological consideration arguing against the operation of broadcast-generated conversions. This consideration supplements the quantitative data which show that in California in 1964 explicit prior political commitment was capable of immunizing nearly all late-voting partisans—regardless of whether they were on the winner's or loser's side—to broadcast information about the developing resolution of the national election.

By way of review, we have now examined not only the large

sample, but also three key groups: the Switchers, the Last-Day Deciders, and the Late Voters. In none of these groups was there any evidence of either a bandwagon or underdog effect of any substance.

Occasional miniscule differences involving one or two voters which may or may not represent the manifestation of a tiny underdog or bandwagon effect have shown up. However, because of its exploratory nature, this study was not designed to possess the statistical power to interpret such small variations. Reliance on variations of this magnitude would require a panel study employing a sample of gigantic size.

OTHER TERMINAL INFLUENCES

All voters in the sample were asked in Wave II, "Did you see or hear anything or did anything happen in the past twenty-four hours or so (since Wave I) that had any effect on whether you voted or on the way you voted?" Of the 1,689 queried, 70 voters, or 4 percent of the total sample, answered "Yes." Indicative of the relative lack of importance that voters attached to network Election Day broadcasts of election forecasts or results is the fact that not one of these 70 mentioned exposure to them in response to this question.

Thirty-nine of the 70 voters claimed to have been influenced by last-ditch campaign appeals that were featured on television on *Election Eve,* the night *before* Election Day. Essentially, these voters were referring to appeals that were made either by the Presidential candidates or by their spokesmen. The data from the study show that 17 of these 39 voters ultimately voted for Goldwater, an additional 17 voted for Johnson, and the remaining 5 refused to disclose their final votes.

As the following responses indicate, a good number of these voters were reinforced in their initial choices by televised last-ditch campaign appeals on behalf of the candidates. Reinforcement occurred either through a favorable acceptance of one's own partisan line of argumentation or through rejection of the opposition's appeals.

"I was impressed with the Democratic thing they had on last night—all my favorite movie stars are voting the same way I am." (Planned to vote for Johnson, voted for Johnson.)

"I heard Senator Humphrey's speech on TV." (Planned to vote for Johnson, voted for Johnson.)

"I saw President Johnson's TV talk on Channel 7 and Ronald Reagan's impossible promises." (Planned to vote for Johnson, voted for Johnson.)

"I saw the movie actor Ronald Reagan speak. He told a few lies but didn't convince me, only made my mind completely up." (Planned to vote for Johnson, voted for Johnson.)

"The Duke [John] Wayne Show on TV was very interesting about the Viet Nam situation. After seeing this it made me more sure of my choice." (Planned to vote for Johnson, voted for Johnson.)

"Mr. Johnson's last TV speech confirmed my vote for Mr. Goldwater. Johnson was being unrealistic. He was talking about going hand in hand through a grass pasture into some kind of Utopia. It made me sick, really put me in orbit." (Planned to vote for Goldwater, voted for Goldwater.)

"Last night the Democrats said the polls were rigged and voters would be challenged by the Republican party. I felt this was a reflection on the Democratic party. I didn't like the mud-slinging of Senator Humphrey. I felt more than ever that I wanted to vote Republican because of the tactics of the Democrats." (Planned to vote for Goldwater, voted for Goldwater.)

"Ronald Reagan pointed out how gradually everything is being run by the monopolistic (sic) of our government. We are being told more and more what we can or can't do with our businesses or property. He mentioned what a mess the State Department has made of things. I liked the way it was presented and what was presented. It made me feel I must vote for Mr. Goldwater." (Planned to vote for Goldwater, voted for Goldwater.)

"John Wayne gave his slant on the candidate, based on his foreign policy." (Planned to vote for Goldwater, voted for Goldwater.)

"I heard Humphrey on TV and I decided I didn't want him for Vice President. Johnson has had a heart attack and looked tired on TV. That Humphrey is so terrible. I decided I didn't want to do one thing that would give him a chance at the White House." (Planned to vote for Goldwater, voted for Goldwater.)

Election Eve television appeals on behalf of the candidates served to crystallize the choices of a number of Last-Day Deciders—those voters who did not make up their minds about a candidate until the very last moment. The following responses illustrate how televised campaign appeals the day *before* Election Day helped a number of Last-Day Deciders to arrive at a decision.

"I heard a speech by Johnson on Monday evening and I liked his optimism." (Undecided initial interview, voted for Johnson.)

"I heard President Johnson's speech on TV last night. It really helped me make up my mind for him. His speech was very persuasive—how he is for us all. His speech was in Texas." (Undecided initial interview, voted for Johnson.)

"I heard a speech Johnson made in the Mormon Tabernacle. He said much of nothing but what a good guy he was. I decided right then he was a braggart and too darned conceited." (Undecided initial interview, voted for Goldwater.)

"Ronald Reagan was on TV Monday night and he explained Social Security. Before that I didn't know anything about it. This probably was the determining factor for my voting for Goldwater." (Undecided initial interview, voted for Goldwater.)

"I watched both on TV last night and saw their general feeling of sincerity. I made up my mind last night." (Undecided initial interview, voted for Goldwater.)

Two voters reported that the last-minute campaign appeals they had seen on television during a day's period before they voted helped them to "switch" from one candidate to the other. The voter who switched from Goldwater to Johnson said simply, "I heard Mr. Johnson's speech on TV Monday night." The voter who changed over from Johnson to Goldwater remarked, "I saw the TV program sponsored by the Republican Party. Ronald Reagan gave a good pitch for Goldwater."

Twenty-five voters mentioned spontaneously that they had been contacted by someone they knew who used personal persuasion on them effectively during the twenty-four hours that separated Waves I and II. Of these twenty-five voters who reported personal persuasive pressures, twelve ultimately endorsed Senator Goldwater, eight endorsed President Johnson, and five refused to disclose their vote. For the most part, successful personal pressures came from members of voters' families and from other intimate sources who served primarily to reinforce decisions that had already been made earlier.

The following responses are illustrative:

"My daughter is a Republican worker, and she influenced me." (Planned to vote for Goldwater, voted for Goldwater.)

"My daughter and her husband helped me to decide who to vote for." (Planned to vote for Johnson, voted for Johnson.)

"Friends of mine tried to get me to switch but I wouldn't budge. They said Goldwater lies too much. They said they saw him on TV." (Planned to vote for Goldwater, voted for Goldwater.)

"I was told Goldwater would win. An acquaintance of mine said he heard it on the radio." (Planned to vote for Johnson, voted for Johnson.)

For a number of Last-Day Deciders, pressure from personal sources on Election Eve served as an instrument for crystallizing some decision.

"My relatives and my husband emphasized how important it was to vote. I do not know whether their information came from TV or radio. They just believe their way." (Undecided in initial interview, voted for Johnson.)

"My husband and I discussed which candidate was the best and although I considered voting for Johnson, my husband convinced me to vote for Goldwater." (Undecided in initial interview, voted for Goldwater.)

"I heard from people who seemed to know more about both candidates, people who were better informed than I was." (Undecided in initial interview, voted for Johnson.)

"Some of my friends tried to get me to vote for Johnson." (Undecided in initial interview, voted for Goldwater.)

Personal pressures from family members and others known to at least three voters in the sample during the twenty-four hours before actual voting apparently resulted in ostensible "switches" from intentions to support President Johnson to an ultimate endorsement of Senator Goldwater.

"My husband told me if I voted for Johnson and he voted for Goldwater, we would just be cancelling each other's vote. He felt Goldwater would be the better man for his business so I went along with my husband. He is the breadwinner and he should know who was best. I'm sure some of his information he got from TV, but mostly from reading about the two men." (Planned to vote for Johnson, voted for Goldwater.)

"I was told that Goldwater would not get us into war any sooner than Johnson. This had been my chief objection to Goldwater." (Planned to vote for Johnson, voted for Goldwater.)

"My husband convinced me to switch, but no one else." (Planned to vote for Johnson, voted for Goldwater.)

Eleven voters mentioned having read newspaper items in the twenty-four-hour interim between Waves I and II which they claimed influenced their terminal decisions. And eight voters said radio appeals and commentaries of all sorts which they heard during the twenty-four-hour lapse between Waves I and II affected their decisions.

In summary, of the 70 persons who reported that they had been influenced during the twenty-four-hour lapse between Waves I and II, 39 claimed to have been influenced by last-ditch campaign appeals, 25 by personal persuasion, 11 by what they had read in the newspapers, and 8 by radio appeals and commentaries. (Totals add up to more than 70 because some voters mentioned more than one source.)

Of the eleven cases who claimed to have been influenced by what they had read in newspapers, five voters reported voting for Mr. Johnson and five for Mr. Goldwater. One of these voters refused to disclose his actual vote. Of the eight persons who claimed to have been affected by radio broadcasts, five voted for the former President, two for the Senator, and one refused to disclose his vote. For the most part, voters who claimed to have been influenced by either last-day political radio broadcasts or newspaper items were merely reinforced in their choices. A few Last-Day Deciders' choices became crystallized, and no switching was in evidence in these particular instances.

"Yes, I saw a cartoon in the paper. It showed a TV screen with a bunch of garbage all over the screen. It was explaining what a messy smear campaign this had been." (Undecided in initial interview, voted for Johnson.)

"Goldwater said all he needed was a little more time. He was just starting to get his point across. He made me more angry and convinced me even more to vote for Johnson." (Planned to vote for Johnson, voted for Johnson.)

Upon an uncritical examination of the actual votes that were cast by these 70 voters who claimed to be influenced by sources *other than Election Day broadcasts*, it could be readily concluded that those sources produced a bandwagon effect. Note that among these 70 voters 32 persons, or 46 percent, voted for President Johnson; 29, or 41 percent, voted for Senator Goldwater; and 9, or 13 percent, refused to disclose for whom they had voted.

The fact of the matter is that the variety of influences to which the "affected" voters were exposed served primarily to *reinforce* them in their previous commitments. This result was particularly true among Johnson supporters which accounts for his favorable position with this particular subgroup. In other words, whatever favored position Johnson enjoyed among the California voters was apparently already there *prior* to the Election Eve pressures that these voters experienced. In contrast, the external influences that impinged upon the Last-Day Deciders and Switchers in this particular subgroup failed to favor either of the two contenders significantly, although we may see vestiges of a superficial "underdog" effect here in favor of Senator Goldwater.

Of considerable interest is the fact that five of the fourteen Switchers in the sample apparently made their changes as a result of last-ditch campaign propaganda and personal persuasion pressures rather than as a result of exposure to election coverage on radio and TV on Election Day.

It is evident from the data that small groups of voters experienced a wide variety of pressures from various sources that mostly served either to reinforce their choices or crystallize a choice during the twenty-four-hour period prior to actually voting. In other words, the last minute barrage of campaign messages that permeated the 1964 Election Eve atmosphere in California fell on deaf ears for the majority of voters. Nevertheless, these messages seemed either to reassure some voters or to offer a rationale for others who were experiencing difficulty in making a final choice. Certainly there is no substantive evidence that the heavily saturated campaign-appeal atmosphere that characterized the Election Eve situation in California was successful in converting voters from one particular candidate to the opposition. The picture that emerges here is one of voters experiencing reassurance from the mass media and from personal sources even though many of the propagandistic messages that were being generated were actually designed to get them to change their decisions. Here is further evidence to indicate that the forces that operated to help voters come to a voting decision (primarily partisanship) "set" these decisions in the great majority of voters' minds well before Election Day. The decisions that are arrived at prior to voting time are tough and tenacious, and for the most part remain immutable. The tenacity with which these decisions are maintained serves to immunize the majority of voters who are prepared to act on their decisions from persuasive efforts that are designed to upset them. Consequently, last-ditch campaign-appeal propaganda merely serves to enhance the power of previously arrived at decisions for most voters who are subjected to these "pleadings of desperation."

It is extremely important to consider here that we have noted very similar "effects" on voting behavior among a subgroup of voters who were subjected to a variety of propagandistic influences prior to voting and a subgroup who were exposed to Election Day broadcasts primarily.

If voting behaviors are "influenced" similarly by both Election Day broadcasts and by pre-Election Day propagandistic communications, a serious question is raised regarding the validity of singling out Election Day broadcasts alone as the only possible "cause" of alleged bandwagon effect. Clearly, the possibility of bandwagon effect must be looked for within the *total context* of pressures that impinge upon some voters in the terminal decision-making process.

ELECTION BROADCASTS AND PERSONAL PERSUASION—GETTING OUT THE VOTE

Both my wife and I were active in the Johnson campaign. We tuned in television as soon as we could to see how the election was going. I had all the names of the registered Democrats for our district and my wife called them all afternoon (Election Day) and she was supposed to call me if any registered Democrat didn't vote. I called them before 8 o'clock, and (all smiles) our group turned out 100%. I also did a lot of campaigning at work. (How?) By talking to any people who could be influenced and trying to influence them my way.

The evidence from the 1964 California study indicates that considerable efforts in personal persuasion occurred on Election Day among the voters who were studied, regardless of whether exposure to Election Day broadcasts took place or not. Indeed, there is considerable reason to recognize the possibility that in some instances exposure to Election Day broadcasts may actually have enhanced the motivation for attempting efforts at personal persuasion rather than having inhibited them. Let us examine the data on these points.

It has been noted that a minority of California voters in the sample were actually influenced by pressures from a variety of propagandistic sources during the twenty-four-hour period immediately before they voted. It is evident from the study that additional influences were brought to bear on many California voters as well. These pressures were exerted through the medium of personal influence on Election Day. In classic two-step-flow manner, a number of persons who set out to influence voters in the sample made use of information they allegedly had obtained from election broadcasts to back up their arguments.

Of the 1,689 voters in the sample, 257 or 16 percent reported that they had been personally contacted by someone on Election Day, someone who stressed to them the importance and desirability of simply voting in the Presidential election.[16]

Table 12 indicates that these efforts may have served to increase the proportion of total votes that were cast ultimately for Mr. Johnson. In other words, it appears that efforts that were

TABLE 12. Partisanship and Personal Persuasion

On Election Day, did anyone personally try to convince you
that it was important to vote? (Refusals omitted)

Influence exerted on persons who voted for:	YES		NO	
	Number	Percent	Number	Percent
President Johnson	165	64	707	59
Senator Goldwater	92	36	490	41
	257	100	1197	100

designed to encourage the voters in the sample simply to vote—
through the medium of personal contact—may have resulted in a
disproportionate, slightly larger vote for the former President.

Personal pressure to vote appeared to benefit the Arizona
Senator somewhat among voters who were undecided about their
choices on November 2 (Table 13). Similarly, what miniscule
switching was in evidence appeared to favor Goldwater—among
Switchers who reported being contacted on Election Day by
people who urged them to vote.

TABLE 13. Personal Persuasion and Actual Vote

On Election Day did anyone personally try to convince you
that it was important to vote? (Refusals omitted)

Intended to Vote for:	Actually Voted for:	YES		NO	
		Number	Percent	Number	Percent
Johnson	Johnson	132	52	566	48
Goldwater	Goldwater	72	28	396	33
Undecided	Johnson	9	4	53	4
Undecided	Goldwater	13	5	39	3
Refused	Johnson	24	9	86	7
Refused	Goldwater	4	1	46	*
Goldwater	Johnson	—	—	2	
Johnson	Goldwater	3	1	9	1
		257	100	1197	100

* Less than 1%.

Of the 257 voters in the sample who said they had been asked to vote by persons who called them on Election Day, 27, or 11 percent, reported that the individuals who attempted to persuade them just to vote mentioned election broadcasts in the course of their arguments. Thus, in 11 percent of the reported 257 instances of personal influence on sheer voting, election broadcasts were alleged to have backed up the persuasion process in typical two-step-flow fashion.

Among the 27 voters who said they had been urged to vote by persons who mentioned Election Day forecasts and results, 10 persons had planned to vote for President Johnson, and actually did so; 9 persons had intended to vote for Senator Goldwater, and eventually did so; 1 each had been undecided, and ultimately supported either Johnson or Goldwater; and the remaining 7 refused to disclose for whom they had actually voted.

Voters in the sample were asked whether on Election Day anyone had tried to convince them *not* to vote. Of the 1,689 voters queried, 25 or 1.5 percent reported that they had in fact been subjected to such urgings. Of the 25 voters who were urged *not* to vote, 9 reported that the persons who had so urged them had resorted to the forecasts and results they had allegedly heard via Election Day broadcasts. Five of the voters who were asked *not* to vote by persons who used election broadcasts of predictions and results as bases for persuasion voted for Senator Goldwater in line with their intention to do so; 2 voted for Johnson as intended, and 1 each had been undecided on November 2 and subsequently decided in favor of either Johnson or Goldwater. The fact that all those who had been urged *not* to vote by individuals who contacted them on Election Day did in fact vote, indicates the utter failure of those efforts.

Some 223 voters (13.5 percent of the 1,689 sampled) averred that they had been contacted on Election Day by persons who urged them to vote for the candidates of the subject's own choice (Table 14). Although these persuasive attempts did not appear to influence votes disproportionately for either candidate in terms of total votes cast, Table 15 indicates that some minor increases in determination may have resulted among voters who eventually voted as they had planned.

TABLE 14. Personally Persuaded to Vote

Did anyone personally remind you (on Election Day) to vote for your own candidate? (Refusals Omitted)

Influence exerted on persons who voted for:	YES		NO	
	Number	Percent	Number	Percent
President Johnson	132	59	709	59
Senator Goldwater	91	41	498	41
	223	100	1207	100

TABLE 15. Personally Persuaded to Vote for Chosen Candidate

Did anyone personally remind you to vote for your own candidate (on Election Day)? (Refusals Omitted)

Intended to vote for:	Actually voted for:	YES		NO	
		Number	Percent	Number	Percent
Johnson	Johnson	119	52	581	48
Goldwater	Goldwater	77	35	392	32
Undecided	Johnson	7	3	55	4
Undecided	Goldwater	7	3	45	4
Refused	Johnson	8	4	72	6
Refused	Goldwater	3	1	51	4
Goldwater	Johnson	—	—	1	*
Johnson	Goldwater	2	1	10	1
		223	99**	1207	99**

* Less than 1%.
** Percentages total 99 due to rounding.

Of interest is the fact that 10 of 223 voters who reported being contacted with arguments to vote for the candidate they favored said that the persons who made the contacts alluded to broadcasts of election forecasts and/or results to bolster their arguments. Five of these voters voted for Johnson as planned; two voted for Goldwater as intended; one each refused to state their intention, but eventually voted for either Johnson or Goldwater; and one refused to disclose his ultimate vote.

Data from the study show that 94 voters (5.5 percent of the total 1,689) experienced pressure from persons who contacted them on Election Day to change their vote. Table 16 indicates

TABLE 16. Personally Persuaded to Switch Vote

Did anyone personally try to convince you (on Election Day) to switch your vote to the candidate who was not your choice?

Influence exerted on persons who voted for:	YES		NO	
	Number	Percent	Number	Percent
President Johnson	49	52	811	60
Senator Goldwater	45	48	535	40
	94	100	1346	100

that proportionately more citizens who were urged to change their vote—as compared with those who gave no indication of such conversion efforts—ultimately voted for Senator Goldwater. The reverse held true for those who voted for President Johnson.

It is unlikely that these facts indicate totally successful conversion efforts on behalf of Goldwater's candidacy. Rather, these data show a high degree of "boomerang effect" (Table 17). That is to say, it is apparent that efforts to persuade some Goldwater partisans to switch to Johnson mostly tended to bolster Goldwater votes among those who already supported him. Indications are that these efforts to convert voter choices through personal contact did indeed benefit Senator Goldwater's candidacy overall more so than that of President Johnson. The boomerang aspect of the efforts to convert Goldwater partisans is highlighted further by indications that radio and television forecasts and results were used by persons attempting to change the decisions of the voters in the sample. Nineteen, or 20 percent of the 94 voters who said they had been asked to change their votes by others asserted that the persons who attempted to persuade them to switch alluded to Election Day broadcasts to back up their

TABLE 17. Personally Persuaded to Switch Vote
Compared with Actual Vote

Did anyone personally try to convince you to switch your vote
to the candidate who was *not* your choice (on Election Day)?
(Refusals omitted)

Intended to vote for:	Actually voted for:	YES		NO	
		Number	*Percent*	*Number*	*Percent*
Johnson	Johnson	36	38	651	48
Goldwater	Goldwater	38	40	429	32
Undecided	Johnson	6	6	56	4
Undecided	Goldwater	4	4	48	3
Refused	Johnson	7	8	103	8
Refused	Goldwater	1	2	48	4
Goldwater	Johnson	—	—	1	*
Johnson	Goldwater	2	2	10	1
		94	100	1346	100

* Less than 1%

arguments. Of these 19, 13 ultimately voted for Goldwater in accordance with their intention to do so; 4 voted for Johnson as planned; 1 had been undecided but eventually voted for Goldwater; 1 had refused to indicate his intention, but ultimately cast a ballot for the former President.

The potential influence of election broadcasts on Election Day behavior can be viewed in a light that is perhaps different from the ordinary. Ordinarily attention is focused on the possibility of direct and immediate influence of such mass communications on the voter alone. The two-step-flow hypothesis suggests the possibility that the mass media have potential effect on an audience that extends beyond those whose contacts with the media are direct and immediate. The 1964 California study investigated the possibility that voters who were exposed directly to broadcasts of election forecasts and/or results might use this information to persuade others in a variety of ways. The data that were gathered suggest that for many voters Election Day broadcasts did in fact serve as ammunition for their own efforts at personal influence.

TABLE 18. Personal Persuaders Within the Sample

As a result of the Presidential election returns or forecasts that you yourself heard on radio or TV (on Election Day)—

	YES		NO		NO REPLY	
	Number	Percent	Number	Percent	Number	Percent
Did you personally try to convince anyone that it was important for them to vote?	341	20	1244	74	104	6
Did you personally suggest to anyone that they need not bother to vote?	3	°	1579	94	107	6
Did you personally remind anyone to vote for the candidate they had already chosen?	235	14	1344	80	110	6
Did you personally try to convince anyone to switch their vote to the candidate who was not their choice?	102	6	1478	88	109	6

° Less than 1%.

Table 18 shows that, contrary to the popular suggestion that Election Day broadcasts serve to inhibit voting, the exact opposite may be the case. This is evidenced by the fact that a full fifth of the voters in the sample reported that as a consequence of personally attending undifferentiated Election Day broadcasts they personally urged others of the importance of simply voting. Conversely, only 3 out of the 1,689 voters studied admitted that after hearing Election Day broadcasts they tried to convince others *not* to vote. Of these, 2 voted for Johnson; the other voted for Goldwater.

Election Day broadcasts may also have been "used" in the sample to some degree of importance by persons who reminded others to vote either for the subject's chosen candidate or for the opposition candidate.

It has been indicated that many Goldwater partisans in the sample, more so than Johnson supporters, may have been spurred on to an ever-greater determination to vote for their favorite in the face of information that they received from a variety of sources—including Election Day broadcasts. It is evident that Election Day broadcasts may not only have served to inspire many of the Senator's supporters to vote for him in the face of impending defeat, but may also have operated to motivate such partisans to attempt to stem the tide of defeat by resorting to personal influence.

TABLE 19. Actual Votes and Personal Attempts to Convince Others of the Importance of Voting—After Attending Election Day Broadcasts (Refusals Omitted)

| | ACTUALLY VOTED FOR: | | | |
| | President Johnson | | Senator Goldwater | |
	Number	*Percent*	*Number*	*Percent*
Personally attempted to convince others of the importance of voting	161	20	141	26
Did not attempt to convince others of the importance of voting	661	80	403	74
	822	100	544	100

The data in Tables 19 to 21 point up the last-moment efforts that voters made on behalf of their favorites as a result of claimed exposure to Election Day broadcasts. Proportionately more Goldwater partisans than Johnson partisans were involved in these attempts at last-moment personal influence, whether voters who had been attending Election Day broadcasts (1) attempted to convince others merely to vote, (2) tried to remind others to vote for the candidates they had already decided upon (efforts to reinforce), or (3) sought to persuade others to abandon their favorites and support the opposition candidate

TABLE 20. Actual Votes and Personal Attempts to Remind Others to Vote for the Candidate Already Chosen—After Attending Election Day Broadcasts (Refusals Omitted)

	ACTUALLY VOTED FOR:			
	President Johnson		Senator Goldwater	
	Number	Percent	Number	Percent
Personally attempted to remind others to vote for chosen candidate	117	14	99	18
Did not attempt to remind others to vote for chosen candidate	701	86	450	82
	818	100	549	100

TABLE 21. Actual Votes and Personal Attempts to Convince Others to Change Their Votes to the Opposition Candidate—After Attending Election Day Broadcasts (Refusals Omitted)

	ACTUALLY VOTED FOR:			
	President Johnson		Senator Goldwater	
	Number	Percent	Number	Percent
Personally attempted to convince others to change their vote to the opposition candidate	33	4	60	11
Did not attempt to convince others to change their vote to the opposition candidate	786	96	495	89
	819	100	555	100

instead (efforts to convert). Within the design of the 1964 California voting study, however, there was no way of knowing to what degree, if indeed any, this apparently greater activity on the part of Goldwater adherents was stimulated directly by the broadcast returns, and to what degree it simply reflected a more vigorous campaign than the Johnson adherents were waging.[17]

It can be stated with some validity that as a result of the election broadcasts a considerable number of people spoke to others about voting on Election Day, 1964. These would-be persuaders urged others to vote far more often than they urged them not to vote. They also urged people to stay with their chosen candidates far more often than they urged switching.

ABSTENTION FROM VOTING

Q: Did you follow the election on radio or TV?

A: Oh yea, gee, on Election Day I got up. I didn't read the paper; went to work. A few people had the returns on. I just passed by and listened to how they were going—it was just going on the way I expected it. Then when I came home I watched it for 15 or 20 minutes, it was still going the same way. Then I went out to dinner. That's all, I didn't see any more that day. (After dinner?) (R laughs) It was kind of late when I got back.

I guess I should start off by telling you that I ended up and I didn't vote at all. I was busy and I didn't take time off. It was the same as a normal day; nothing out of the ordinary.

Q: When did you decide not to vote?

A: I hadn't really decided to vote or not to vote. I thought I may vote. I registered for the first time. I followed the elections, it isn't that I haven't followed the elections—it's just I haven't seen much difference; they've both been good men—I'm not a one party follower or anything.

Q: Did you think about voting during the day?

A: I didn't think about it, really.

Q: Did you think you would vote?

A: No. I thought about it but I knew I wouldn't vote. I was mainly interested in Proposition 14, and the way I looked at it either way you voted you came out wrong. I don't think it was properly done.

Q: Did you discuss the election with anyone that day?

A: Well there was a general discussion. Most people at ———— (advertising agency where R is employed) are Democrats—maybe two or three are Republicans. Everyone told me how important it was that I vote and they just kept it up and kept it up.

Q: How did you feel about being urged to vote?

A: If they felt it was that important and they wanted to vote, fine. But I wasn't going to vote anyway.

I didn't particularly like Johnson but I didn't think he was that bad.

I thought Goldwater was a good man but I didn't like him that much. I thought they'd both do about the same job—both have the interests of the country at heart. I don't think it would have made too much difference.

Q: Did you ever feel that you ought to vote?

A: Not really, or I probably would have.

Q: How did you feel about not voting?

A: I didn't feel any guilty feeling about it. If I had felt I would have hurt the country or that one person (candidate) would really hurt the country I would have voted. But I never felt that way.

The data obtained in this study offer no reason to believe that exposure to election broadcasts kept eligible voters who had intended to vote for a President from actually doing so.

Of the 1,704 people who stated in Wave I that they *intended* to vote, 15, or approximately 1 percent, subsequently *failed to vote*.[18] Of these 15 persons five had stated that they would vote for Senator Goldwater, three had planned to vote for President Johnson, four were "undecided" about whom to support, and three refused to disclose their preferred candidate. It must also be remembered that of twenty persons in Wave I who *said they would not vote* or *did not know if they would vote, 9 subsequently did.*

To determine whether exposure to election broadcasts had led to abstention by the fifteen persons who *intended* to vote but did not vote, these fifteen persons were asked in Wave II, "What, if anything, happened in the past twenty-four hours or so that made you *not* vote?" In reply, not one of the fifteen mentioned exposure to election broadcasts. Only six had, in fact been exposed, and these abstainers stated that the election returns they had heard had had no influence at all on their decisions not to vote.

The reasons for abstaining that were given by the fifteen abstainers in the sample fell into five general categories:

1. *Physical or psychological incapacity*

"I was just too tired and didn't feel up to it. My wife died six months ago and I'm all alone and a little sad."

"I've been ill for some time and confined to the house."

"Nothing, except I am laid up in bed."

"I knew I couldn't vote. I'm too blind to go out. If someone votes for me, I'm not sure they would mark my ballot the way I tell them."

2. *Preoccupation with other matters; delay in getting to the polls*

"I had an embryology exam and could not get to the polls. It was either take the exam or flunk it."

"Well, I should've gone to vote before work because I was delayed at the office until it was too late. My boss really needed me, that's all."

"I was working and couldn't get away."

3. *Ineligibility*

"I went with a friend to San Diego and I had no transportation back home. I thought I could vote in San Diego. This was my first time to vote and I didn't know. I feel real bad today that I didn't get to vote."

"I wasn't in the precinct."

4. *Indifference*

"I decided to go fishing."

"Nothing happened. I just didn't feel like voting."

"Nothing happened in the last 24 hours. I made up my mind several days ago not to vote for President. It doesn't matter to me one way or another. I'm in business for myself and it just doesn't matter."

5. *Disenchantment*

"The things I read—I swayed back and forth and was displeased with both. Then on Election Day I read about the civil rights issues and felt Goldwater was impossible. I couldn't accept Johnson so I decided to withhold my vote."

"I reviewed both candidates and I don't like the campaign. They're not handling it well. I don't like either one, they can't run the government."

It should also be noted further that at least five of the fifteen abstainers revealed little interest generally in national politics; three had not voted in 1960, though eligible to do so, and two others said they had voted in 1960, but could not remember for whom.

The report of the California voting study concludes with these remarks:

It is clear that among the Californians studied exposure to election broadcasts on November 3, 1964 did not create discrepancies between prior commitments and ultimate choices. Nor was any evidence found that election broadcasts deterred persons who planned to vote for a President from actually doing so.

By and large well over 9 out of every 10 voters in the study (actually 97%) who had committed themselves to either presidential candidate before Election Day voted accordingly, regardless of whether or not they heard election broadcasts prior to voting. Negligible switching, which occurred in both directions, could not be traced to pre-voting exposure to election broadcasts. Nor can the trivial advantage in vote accorded Johnson by the handful of lastday deciders exposed to election broadcasts be regarded as indicative of a bandwagon effect in any meaningful sense of the term.

The conclusion that stands out is that there is no evidence from the research to support the contention that Eastern network coverage of the unfolding national voting pattern on November 3, 1964, was responsible for either a bandwagon or an underdog effect among the voters studied.[19]

A study that focused on a number of problems which were explored in the Mendelsohn research was conducted by Douglas A. Fuchs, then of the University of California, and arrived at very similar conclusions: "Neither voting turnout nor vote switching in our three western areas seem to have been affected by the early 'declarations of victory' last November 3 [1964]."[20]

There is no doubt that the election in 1964 could not have been changed by any amount of bandwagon effect in California. Of the total votes cast in 1964 general election in the state of California, 59.2 percent were cast for Lyndon Johnson (voters in the California study cast 52 percent for Johnson and 13 percent refused to disclose actual votes cast) and 40.8 percent for Barry Goldwater (35 percent in the California sample reported voting for Goldwater and 13 percent refused voting disclosure). The Johnson victory was decisive and overwhelming regardless of any possibility of "undue influence" on the part of election results broadcasts. To comprehend the extent of Johnson's victory, it should be pointed out that Johnson attracted votes among the California sample

1. from the majority of both male and female voters studied;
2. from *most* voters below the age of 60;
3. from *most* Catholic and Jewish voters;

4. from *most* voters who were Negro or Oriental, and from *half* the Caucasian voters;

5. from *most* voters with a grammar school education and from *most* of those who had some high school, who had graduated from high school, or who had postcollege graduate schooling;

6. from *most* voters who were either clerks or craftsmen or who worked in either semiskilled, unskilled, or service trades, or who were students;

7. from *most* voters whose yearly total family income was less than $10,000.

In effect, the California voting study reaffirmed the viability of the phenomenological position on the effects of mass communications on voting behavior—at least as far as the 1964 general election in California is concerned. There is no doubt that the majority of voters do indeed make up their minds about their ultimate preferences well in advance of Election Day. Similarly, it is clear that these early commitments are considered practically sacred by most voters, and that efforts to dislodge them immediately prior to actually voting serves most often to harden and reinforce rather than to weaken and convert. That exposure to Election Day broadcasts per se plays no peculiarly significant role in the terminal voting-decision process is clearly a good bet from the data in Mendelsohn's California research.

ADDITIONAL STUDIES

The Mendelsohn study was one of five studies, published independently, which conducted research efforts designed to explore the possibility of broadcast-induced bandwagon effects in 1964. Thus we have the opportunity of examining not one, but five separate substantive studies of the same phenomenon—a rarity indeed in the social sciences. Brief descriptions of the studies that were conducted independently from the Mendelsohn research follow.

1. A. R. Clausen. "Political Predictions and Projections: How Are They Conducted? How Do They Influence the Outcome of

Elections?" Survey Research Center, University of Michigan, 1966. Pamphlet published in *Grass Roots Guides Series on Democracy and Practical Politics—A Service of the Center for Information on America.*

Sample and Design: A national sample of adults of voting age was used. Interviews with the same 1,450 people were conducted before and after the 1964 national elections. Respondents were asked to state their preferences prior to Election Day. After Election Day they were asked to indicate for whom they had actually voted. Additional information was collected regarding respondents' awareness of televised predictions, how much attention they paid to such predictions, when they had decided upon their choice of candidates, and the time at which they had voted vis-à-vis the times at which televised predictions were witnessed.

2. D. A. Fuchs. "Election-Day Radio-Television and Western Voting." *Public Opinion Quarterly,* Summer 1966. Pp. 226–236.

Sample and Design: A panel of some 2,700 registered voters residing in Seattle, Washington and in Alameda and Orange Counties, California, was interviewed during the week preceding November 3, 1964, and was reinterviewed during the week following Election Day. The author reports setting up a control sample in East Lansing, Michigan, but because of deficiencies in this sample the data from this group are not included in his report.

3. K. Lang and G. Lang. "Ballots and Broadcasts: The Impact of Expectations and Election Day Perceptions on Voting Behavior." Paper presented at the American Association for Public Opinion Research Annual Conference, May 1965. Later published as a book, *Voting and Nonvoting.* Waltham, Masachusetts, Blaisdell Publishing Co., 1968.

Sample and Design: Two samples were used. One was composed of 364 registered voters in the state of California who by 4:00 P.M. on Election Day, 1964 (when election broadcasts emanating from the east had begun) had as yet not voted. The other, a control sample, consisted of 116 voters in Ohio who had no opportunity of being exposed to election broadcasts prior to visiting the polls. Both samples were interviewed after Election

Day, 1964. The study placed a special emphasis upon nonvoters as well as voters.

4. W. E. Miller. "Analysis of the Effect of Election Night Predictions on Voting Behavior." This is a special analysis of the Survey Research Center data reported by A. R. Clausen performed for the American Broadcasting Corporation and submitted as evidence to the Pastore Subcommittee on Communications, July, 1967.

All five of the major published studies show a remarkable degree of consistency regarding their principal findings:

Finding 1. Because the vast majority of voters (more than nine in ten) make up their minds about a candidate well before Election Day, relatively few voters are potential targets for persuasion via exposure to Election Day broadcasts of predictions or results.

The University of Michigan Survey Research Center study indicates that some four percent of all the voters sampled nationally reported having made their voting decisions on Election Day. The Langs found a similarly small proportion of "Last-Day Deciders" (four percent). As previously reported, Mendelsohn uncovered a group representing some eight percent of all the voters sampled in California who reported having reached their terminal voting decision on the day of the election.

Neither the Langs nor Mendelsohn found any discernible effects of exposure to Election Day broadcasts upon these last-day deciders.

Finding 2. The potential proportion of voters who may be influenced by exposure to Election Day broadcasts is relatively small.

The Survey Research Center study shows that eighty-eight percent of the voters, nationwide, cast their ballots in 1964 *before* TV network coverage began (7:00 P.M. EST). In actuality, the Survey Research Center study indicates that on a national basis no more than five percent of the voters reported having witnessed Election Day broadcasts prior to casting their ballots. Thus the nationwide maximum *potential* proportion of persons who conceivably could have been influenced by election broadcasts in 1964 was fifty in every thousand.

The studies conducted in the maximum potential influence areas on the west coast by Mendelsohn and by Fuchs show that well over eight voters in ten went to the polls *before* the opportunity to be exposed to Election Day broadcasts became a reality.

Finding 3. Even though small proportions of voters theoretically could have been influenced by exposure to Election Day broadcasts, the researches show that over-all, last-minute switching to candidates not previously chosen was miniscule.

On this score, Clausen reports that, nationwide, five percent of the voters sampled in the 1964 studies claimed to have switched preferences on Election Day. As previously reported, one percent of the voters in the Mendelsohn study revealed a last-minute change of heart. Fuchs reveals that Election Day choices for opposing candidates affected some four percent of all the west coast voters he had studied.

Finding 4. Given the relatively small proportions of voters who conceivably might have seen Election Day telecasts prior to voting, the amount of last-minute vote-switching among those who were exposed to such broadcasts as compared to those who were not was so negligible that it manifested no statistical significance.

As stated previously, Mendelsohn showed that switching occurred among one percent of the voters who reported no prior-to-voting exposure to Election Day broadcasts, as compared to a two percent occurrence among voters who claimed prior exposure. However, his data revealed further that from among those who claimed both prior exposure *and* vote-switching, both Johnson and Goldwater lost an equal proportion of votes to the other.

In a similar vein, Fuchs' data show that vote-switching in the 1964 Presidential election was slightly higher (although not statistically significant) among voters who reported witnessing televised election forecasts and results before they went to the polls. With regard to voting for senatorial and gubernatorial candidates, however, Fuchs paradoxically noted a slightly smaller amount of vote-switching among voters who reported prior exposure to Election Day broadcasts as compared with voters who claimed no prior broadcast exposure.

Clausen states that reported vote-switching among persons who claimed prior exposure as compared with those who made no such claim was about equal—"approximately one out of every 20."

Finding 5. All five studies could uncover no discernible effects of exposure to Election Day broadcasts upon voter turnout. In other words, the major research efforts in 1964 on possible broadcast-induced bandwagon effects found no meaningful evidence that viewing election forecasts and results on television either stimulated or inhibited voter turnout.

The only possible conclusion to be reached from reviewing these reports is that there are no bandwagon effects produced by viewing Election Day broadcasts prior to voting—surely, as far as the 1964 election was concerned.

In his testimony before Senator Pastore's Senate Subcommittee in 1967, Dr. Warren E. Miller of the University of Michigan's Survey Research Center indicated that he had examined the principal research that had been conducted on broadcast-induced bandwagon effects and arrived at the very same observation:

My own conclusion . . . is even in the most unusual circumstances, it would be most unlikely that TV predictions would contribute significantly to any election result.

. . . All of the studies that I have examined . . . show that even at the level of concern for individual behavior, the largest and most detailed studies fail to disclose any substantial evidence that any voters or non-voters have been influenced by election night projections. With this as a basic conclusion it of course then follows that the net impact on the election outcome is insofar as one is able to provide appropriate statistical measurements, zero.

SOME ISSUES RAISED BY THE "UNDUE INFLUENCE" DOCTRINE

Although the authors of this book generally agree that the likelihood that exposure to election broadcasts can produce a

significant bandwagon effect is remote beyond serious consideration, a number of other serious observers still suspect the possibility of "undue influence." Fuchs and the Langs, for example,
still remain skeptical. Although their suspicions cannot be validated statistically, these scholars argue that the broadcast-
induced switching (or nonvoting) of even relatively small
numbers of voters could possibly change the over-all results of
"close" elections. K. and G. Lang suggest that

[i]t is altogether possible that in the future, in areas where early returns are available long before polls close, voters will learn to estimate
the utility of their vote before voting. Imagine, for instance, a very
close election where early returns indicate that California—or Oregon,
or Hawaii, or Alaska—would supply the electoral votes necessary for
victory. With the electoral votes in other states already accounted for,
attention would turn to the West and what voters there would do. If
the expectation of a close race had been widespread and if many people were undecided about whether to vote or for whom to vote, large
numbers of people might delay going to the polls until they had first
heard how the election was going. The fact that few voters waited
around in 1964 does not mean that more might not do so in some
future election.[21]

The Langs readily admit to the "if" quality of their speculations,
and point to the lack of probabilities of occurrences of this sort.
Yet there is a nagging anxiety that "it could happen here."

The election that took place in 1968 was among the "closest" of
all the national elections that have occurred in the United States.
This particular election affords some opportunity to examine the
speculations of the pessimists. "The Influence of Television Election Broadcasts in a Close Election," a study conducted by the
National Broadcasting Company, addressed itself precisely to the
problem of undue influence in a close election.[22]

Drawing on the designs and findings of the 1964 studies, the
NBC research was conducted via face-to-face interviews with a
probability sample of 1,455 registered voters in the Pacific Time
Zone and with a control probability sample of 517 registered
voters in the Eastern Time Zone. Both samples were interviewed
several days before Election Day, 1968, and were reinterviewed
during a two-day post-Election Day period. Reinterviews were
completed with 91 percent of the original respondents. The

objectives of the research were to obtain information on two questions:

First, did prior exposure to television election returns affect *voter turnout*—did exposure cause people who had previously planned to vote to decide not to go to the polls, and vice versa?

. . . Secondly, did the TV broadcasts affect *candidate-switching* —did exposure cause people to switch from their preelection choice to another candidate?

Consistent with the 1964 findings of Mendelsohn and the other researchers, the NBC research reports that 62 percent of its western sample voted on November 5, 1968 *before* network telecasts of the election began at 3:00 P.M., Pacific Standard Time. The opportunity for exposure to Election Day telecasts consequently was limited to 38 percent of the voters *in toto*. However, this figure represents the *potential* audience, not the actual one. In reality, no more than 6 percent of the western sample was exposed to election telecasts prior to voting. In the east, prevoting exposure to election telecasts was limited to 1 percent of the total.

On the matter of voter turnout, among the *unexposed* group in the west, 3 percent claimed that they had changed their minds regarding whether they would vote or not in the interim separating the pre- and postvoting interviews. "In short," the report observes, "even if there were no television broadcasts, one would expect some 3 percent of voters in the west to make changes in voting turnout plans." Among those who had viewed coverage of the election before going to the polls, 4.3 percent claimed to have altered their turnout plans. The difference in turnout between western voters who had been exposed to election telecasts before voting and those who had not was not statistically significant. Among the eastern control sample, the level of change in voting-turnout plans within the subgroup which was not exposed to telecasts about the election prior to voting (the exposed group was too small to warrant analysis) was 7 percent—a statistically significant difference vis-à-vis the western voters.

With regard to the role that exposure to election broadcasts may have played in motivating voters to switch choices for candidates, the NBC study found that among western voters 6.7

percent of those who had been exposed to televised election coverage had changed their choices. However, among the unexposed group the level of switching was 6.1 percent. Additionally, 5.6 percent of the voters in the eastern sample who had not witnessed election telecasts indicated that they had switched choices during the several days separating the pre- and postvoting interviews. The differences in vote-switching among the three subpopulations were not statistically significant.

In attempting to summarize all the data on switching behavior—whether they related to changes in voting-turnout plans or to choices of candidates—the study found that among unexposed western voters the level of change was 8.9 percent *in toto.* Among the western voters who witnessed election coverage via TV prior to voting the total change level rested at the 10.6 percent mark. The difference between the two groups was found not to be statistically significant. When the eastern data was compared with that obtained in the west, it was learned that a total of 12.1 percent of the unexposed voters in the east exhibited some change. The difference between the unexposed group in the east and that in the west was statistically significant. The study indicates that this difference "reflects the fact that the eastern voters were more likely to change their voting turnout plans."

Worth noting is the observation from the NBC study that the number of persons in the western sample who witnessed televised election coverage prior to voting and manifested any kind of change in voting intentions added up to 10 voters—0.7 percent of the total sample of registered western voters. The actual margin of victory for President Nixon in the west was 2.8 percent.

In this context, it is evident that even if all exposed voters who changed voting plans were caused to do so by the TV election broadcasts, and even if their changes were all in Humphrey's direction—both assumptions not true—there were still far too few of these people to have affected the outcome of the election in the West.

The NBC study seriously challenges the allegation that exposure to televised election coverage affects voting behavior, particularly in close national elections such as the one in 1968:

Summing up, the principal finding of our study is that there are no statistically significant differences in levels of change in voting plans between exposed and unexposed voters in the West. Moreover, even when we control for time of day of voting, by comparing the exposed voters to unexposed *late* voters, we still find no significant difference. These findings clearly indicate that exposed voters registered essentially "normal" levels of change.

When the results of this study on the 1968 election are examined in the perspective of the prior . . . studies on the 1964 election, we can conclude with a high degree of confidence that television election broadcasts have no detectable influence on voting behavior—in *close* elections, as well as in *landslide* contests.

The NBC report does not treat an important point regarding exposure to Election Night television coverage in "close" elections. The point relates to televised forecasts of "winners." On Election Night, 1968, voting for the two major candidates was so close that it was impossible to determine—either through statistical projection or from reports of actual tabulations of votes—what the eventual outcome would be until well after the entire electorate had actually voted. Here, literally, there was no way even for the most arduous follower of Election Day broadcasts to glean any notion whatever, prior to casting his ballot, of who the winner might be. Thus, the possibility of being influenced by Election Night coverage in 1968 remained entirely in the realm of viewers' subjective fantasy evaluations of the outcome. It appears, then, that under circumstances of very close elections where it is literally impossible to determine outcomes early enough to be broadcast prior to the closing of all the nation's polls, the possibility of broadcast-induced bandwagon effect is seriously diminished (if not eliminated entirely) rather than seriously enhanced.

CONGRESSIONAL PROPOSALS FOR CONTROLLING ELECTION BROADCASTS

As a consequence of the expressed concern over the possibility that even small numbers of voters might conceivably be influenced by exposure to Election Day broadcasts of voting results and projections, a number of bills designed to control such a possibility have been introduced in the Congress of the United

States in recent years. The restrictions suggested fall into four categories, and the bills cited exemplify these categories:

1. *Prohibit releasing election returns until a specified time.* S. 3115, 88th Congress introduced by Senator Prouty on August 12, 1964. This bill would make it a federal crime to release or publish information concerning the election of a President, Vice President, or member of Congress prior to a prescribed hour.

2. *Prohibit the broadcasting of predictions before all polls are closed.* H. R. 11648, 88th Congress, introduced by Congressman Gubser, June 17, 1964; and S. 2927, introduced by Senator Mundt, on June 19, 1964 sought to amend the Communications Act of 1934 in this manner.

No licensee shall broadcast the results including any opinion, prediction, or other matter based on such results, of any election of electors for President and Vice President of the United States or Senators or Representatives in Congress in any state or part thereof until after the latest official closing time of any polling place for such an election in any other state on the same day.

3. *Voluntary restraint by broadcasters from predicting election results before all polls are closed.* Resolution 94, 88th Congress, August 12, 1964, by Senators Salinger, Bartlett, Gruening, Inouye, McGee, and Moss would "express as the sense of Congress" that news-gathering organizations and the media refrain from disseminating predictions based on electronic computers in any election for federal office until the last polling place in the nation is officially closed.

4. *Provide for a uniform closing time for all polling places.* S. 3118, 88th Congress, August 16, introduced by Senator Javits, would establish a uniform closing time for polling places during elections for federal offices—11:00 P.M., EST; 10:00 P.M., CST; 9:00 P.M., MSP; 8:00 P.M., PST; 7:00 P.M. in the Yukon time zone; 6:00 P.M. in the Alaska-Hawaii time zone; and 5:00 P.M. in the Bering time zone. A bill similar to S. 3118—S. 36—was introduced by Senators Curtis, Mundt, and Thurmond in the 90th Congress on January 11, 1967.

It is the general conclusion of authorities on the Constitution that legislation designed to restrict in any way the dissemination of voting results either as forecasts or as tabulations would be in direct conflict with the First Amendment guaranteeing freedom of speech.

On this matter a case in point is the Federal Communications Commission's memorandum, "On the Constitutionality of Prohibiting the Broadcast of Federal Election Results, and Predictions Based Thereon, Until the Polls Are Closed in All of the States," February 1, 1967, which concluded:

The prohibition involved would be directed specifically at the content of speech and the harm thought to flow from it, not at conduct whose regulation only incidentally affects speech. Further, although the restriction would be only for a limited time, it would prevent the free flow of election news at a time when interest is at its height, and thus, in a very real sense, the restriction is at odds with the underlying assumption of the First Amendment—that the widest possible dissemination of information from diverse sources is essential to the welfare of the public; and the ban on predictions is total in its scope, and is thus a complete suppression of informaton. In these circumstances, even if it were assumed, *arguendo,* that there existed a grave substantive evil, imminently to be feared from the exercise of the speech here involved, the restraint would raise the most serious questions in this freedom of speech context.

Clearly the proposals regarding restrictions on dissemination of election-result information are fraught with the dangers of censorship, and consequently it can be presumed that they would be declared unconstitutional in court tests.

It is apparent that the constitutional problems involved in attempting to control the dissemination of election forecasts and results on Election Night—even before all polling places in the nation are closed—are of such a magnitude that the Senate Subcommittee on Communications has not recommended any legislation to the United States Congress on this matter as of Spring 1969.

Undoubtedly some voters are affected in some ways by a variety of influences on Election Day. A voter on his way to the polling booth sees a newspaper headline reporting the latest survey forecasts of victory for the opposition; he receives a telephone call from his shop steward urging him to vote for the opposition candidate; his son who is an opposition party worker makes a last-minute bid for a vote; he passes an opposition billboard on the way to the voting site; the matchcover used in lighting his cigarette while he is waiting his turn to cast his ballot extols the virtues of the opposition candidate. Each of these sources can be considered to wage "undue last-minute influence." What are we to do, then? Must we place the entire electorate in an isolation chamber for twenty-four hours prior to vote-casting on Election Day? Within this total context of last-minute influences, Election Day prediction broadcasts must, of necessity, be considered as just one among many. But by what manner of argument can such broadcasts be singled out as *the one important single* last-minute influence in the total array of such influences to which the voter may be subjected immediately before he actually exercises his franchise? Surely the answer does not lie in curbing such broadcasts until the polling places in the western section of the country close down.

The president of CBS, Dr. Frank Stanton, has commented on this question before Senator Pastore's subcommittee saying, "We see any curb on the press whether radio or television, newspapers or magazines—as the worst solution—and, in an opinion CBS has obtained from eminent counsel as an unconstitutional suppression."[23]

Instead of attempting to suppress Election Day broadcasts— but not other potential influences—Dr. Stanton suggested the institution of "a 24-hour voting day throughout the country, with all polls opening and closing simultaneously"—regardless of time zones. With this plan all voters in the country—regardless of region—could exercise their franchise conveniently at any local time during the uniform twenty-four-hour period. The uncertainties generated by the reporting of partial election returns and their possible effects on western voters would be eliminated under the plan, since results would be based on simultaneous, nationwide tallies rather than on early, scattered, regional votes. This would eliminate any possibility of one region's voting results exerting "undue influence" upon another.

The Stanton proposal and similar plans to control closing times of polling places throughout the nation on some uniform basis (for instance, S. 3118) fall clearly within the power granted to Congress to determine when federal elections are to be held. On this score, Article II, Section 1, clause 4 of the Constitution provides that, in the election of the President and the Vice President, Congress may determine the *time* of choosing the electors and the *day* on which they shall give their votes, which day shall be the same throughout the United States. On the matter of electing members of Congress, the Constitution (Article 1, Section 4, clause 1) provides that *the times, places, and manner of holding elections* for senators and representatives shall be prescribed by the legislature of each state individually, but that Congress may, by law, make or alter such regulations.

The specific proposal for a twenty-four-hour voting day or similar plans could lay to rest for all time the question of whether or not eastern-originated Election Day broadcasts present the danger of producing bandwagon effects in the western sector of the nation.

Even though this particular issue may be resolved ultimately, we shall still remain confronted with the larger question of how television does influence, albeit indirectly, the conduct of politics in the United States of America.

NOTES

1. Gustave Le Bon, *The Crowd* (New York: Viking Press, 1960), pp. 112–113. (Published originally in French, Paris, 1895).

2. For a full discussion of the trends in research on the direct effects of mass-communications campaigns see E. Katz and Paul F. Lazarsfeld, *Personal Influence* (Glencoe: Free Press, 1953), Part I, pp. 15–42.

3. E. Katz, "Communication Research and the Image of Society," *American Journal of Sociology*, 65:5 (1960), pp. 435–440.

4. Paul F. Lazarsfeld, B. R. Berelson, and H. Gaudet, *The People's Choice*, 2nd ed. (New York: Columbia University Press, 1948).

5. Ruane B. Hill, "Political Uses of Broadcasting in the United States in the Context of Public Opinion and the Political Process, 1920–1960," unpublished doctoral dissertation (Evanston, Illinois: Northwestern University, 1964).

6. Harold Mendelsohn, "Election-Day Broadcasts and Terminal Voting Decisions," *Public Opinion Quarterly*, vol. 30 (1966), pp. 212–225.

7. Angus Campbell, *et al.*, *The American Voter: An Abridgment* (New York: John Wiley and Sons, Inc. 1964), p. 41.

8. Kurt Lang and Gladys Lang, "The Mass Media and Voting," in E. Burdick and A. Brodbeck, eds., *American Voting Behavior* (Glencoe: Free Press, 1959), pp. 218–219.

9. B. R. Berelson, Paul F. Lazarsfeld, and W. N. McPhee, *Voting* (Chicago: University of Chicago Press, 1954), p. 283.

10. Source: *State of California Supplement Statement of Vote—General Election, November 3, 1964,* compiled by Frank M. Jordan, Secretary of State.

11. Twenty of the 1,724 said they did not intend to vote or did not know whether they would vote. Ultimately, nine of these people did vote, and eleven did not. Nine of these eleven nonvoters said they did not intend to vote when they were first contacted in Wave I. The other two did not know in Wave I whether or not they would vote. Two of the nine voters had said they would not vote in the Wave I interviews, and seven did not know whether they would vote.

12. According to *The New York Times,* the National Broadcasting Company presented the first conditional forecast at 3:49 P.M. PST, stating that President Johnson would probably receive between sixty percent and seventy percent of the popular vote. At 6:04 P.M. PST the Columbia Broadcasting System announced the first substantive "Vote Profile Analysis" of a conclusive Johnson victory.

13. Although twelve percent of the sample was exposed to substantive late network broadcasts, some nineteen percent *in toto* (310 of 1,689 cases) claimed they had attended all kinds of broadcast returns during Election Day prior to voting including scattered local returns reported in morning and early afternoon broadcasts that were aired in California.

14. Note that Republicans ordinarily have higher socioeconomic statuses than do Democrats. It has been mentioned that high socioeconomic-status persons tended to vote early on Election Day.

15. Because they refused to name candidates in either Wave I or II or both, 19.7 percent of the sample could not be classified within these subgroups.

16. It is altogether likely that these persons were urged to vote for a particular candidate. Thus, considerable overlap between Tables 12, 14, and 16 may have occurred.

17. There is some evidence that indicates that Republicans are more likely than Democrats to attempt personal persuasion during national election campaigns. On October 17–21, 1968, the Gallup Poll reported that twelve percent of its national sample of households claimed to have been contacted by Republican partisans, as compared to eight percent of the householders who reported having been contacted by Democratic workers.

18. Of the nine people who did not know in Wave I whether they would vote for a President or not, seven did vote and two did not vote. Of the seven who ultimately voted, five voted for Johnson, one for Goldwater, and one refused to disclose his vote. Of the eleven who, in Wave I, said they

would not vote, two subsequently did vote. One voted for Goldwater and the other refused to disclose his vote.

19. Mendelsohn, *loc. cit.*, p. 225.

20. Douglas A. Fuchs, "Election-Day Radio-Television and Western Voting," *Public Opinion Quarterly*, vol. 30 (1966), pp. 226–236.

21. Kurt Lang and Gladys Lang, *Voting and Nonvoting: Implications of Broadcasting Returns Before Polls Are Closed* (Waltham, Mass.: Blaisdell Publishing Co., 1968), p. 165.

22. Prepared by Thomas E. Coffin and Sam Tuchman, and presented at the 1969 Annual Conference, American Association for Public Opinion Research, May 17, 1969 (mimeographed).

23. Statement of Dr. Frank Stanton before the Subcommittee on Communications, United States Senate Commerce Committee, July 20, 1967.

12345

Indirect Political Effects
of the Mass Media

If the vast majority of the votes cast in a Presidential election are not influenced directly and immediately by the mass media in hypodermic fashion, what, then, are the effects of mass communications upon the political process in America?

For those who view man as a predominantly cognitive being—as truly Homo sapiens—the mass-communication media are seen as the great liberators. Prior to print and electronic means of communications, it has been averred, the common man was shackled by his own ignorance and by the unavailability of the kinds of political information that could serve to liberate him. Without pertinent political information man could neither recognize his own plight nor, if he were aware of it, do something about it. Political information in print and the electronic media serve cognitive man by making him aware of candidates and issues and by providing him with the kinds of information which are useful to him in making the decisions democracy demands of him. In the long run, it is argued, man uses this information wisely in the expression of public opinion both prior to vote-casting and at the polls. Without the media of mass communication, the classical syllogism goes, there can be no public opinion, and without an informed public opinion there can be no democracy. Putting it more succinctly, the classicists have taken the position that the mass media enhance the direct participation of the common man in the democratic process.

247

Political polls and research on the effects of mass communications have indicated that the arguments presented by the classicists are only partially true. These studies have shown that, for the most part, the electorate is composed of various subgroups whose concern about, awareness of, and participation in politics varies, and varies mostly as a function of their socioeconomic statuses and psychopolitical predispositions.

Thus, the classical Jeffersonian image of the voter as a purely rational being who seeks out political information which will guide him in making rational choices among issues and candidates on the basis of merit alone is an idealized one that applies only to a very small minority of voters. Beginning with *The People's Choice* (Lazarsfeld, *et al.;* see Chapter 4 above), much subsequent research has shown

. . . that people in the U.S. range on a scale from "social" on one extreme (characterized as indifferent to public affairs) to "ideological" on the other (absorbed in affairs, but rigidly, in a highly partisan manner). In the center is "political man", with only a moderate interest in politics.[1]

The classical view of the role of mass communications portrays the media as presenting "all points of view" on given political issues and candidates. The electorate, exposed to "all points of view," is supposed to weigh each one independently on its own merit and to adopt only those that will be of benefit to all—in utter disregard of private, selfish needs and interests. Massive research evidence indicates just the contrary. Typically, most voters appear to sift out from the mass media only that particular information which will bolster and reinforce their own objectives and already-held attitudes and opinions. Very little *actual change* in political attitudes occurs among voters as a *direct* consequence of exposure to political information alone. Certainly it is clear from the evidence which social science has compiled thus far that the injection of high doses of political information during the frenetic periods of national campaigns does very little to alter the deeply rooted, tightly held political attitudes (or prejudices) of most voters. Indeed, a small number of the confused, the disinterested, the indifferent, the uninformed, and the uncommitted among the electorate actually may alter their attitudes and opinions during a given campaign. But these "independents," as we euphemistically call them, are reflective of a minority of voters, not the majority. It would be folly to ignore this subgroup which has the potential to "swing" its support, particularly in close contests. The fact remains, however, that most voters vote according to their sociopsychological predispositions rather than according to their thoughtful weighing of the political information they might receive from the mass media. At most, as Pool indicates, the mass media focus voters' attention on salient issues and on images of the candidates.

Various experimental and survey results suggest that the mass media operate very directly upon attention, information, tastes and images. Election studies, for example show that the campaign in the mass media does little to change attitudes in the short run, but does a great deal to focus attention on one topic or another. It also affects the saliency of different issues. Television studies have shown that TV has relatively little direct effect on major attitudes, but it does develop tastes (good and bad) and provides much image material to stock the mind of the viewer.[2]

It has been argued that the "new" electronic media (radio and television) have resulted in "greater participation" in politics by the "masses" in America. The assertion that increases in the proportions of eligible voters who actually cast ballots is the single most important measure of increased political participation appears to be refuted by the facts. For example, in 1896, fully 80 percent of the eligible voters in the United States actually cast ballots. The low in actual voting behavior in the United States was reached in 1920, when the franchise was extended to women. Only 49 percent of the expanded electorate went to the polls that year. In recent national elections, including that of 1968, the percentage of actual voters as a proportion of all persons of voting age has hovered just a trifle above the 60 percent mark.[3]

Many factors other than the mass media contribute to voter participation (or lack of it) in national elections. As we shall soon see, radio does indeed appear to have resulted in some increases in voter participation in national elections, while surprisingly, television has not. But is it sufficient to apply the criterion of increased votes alone to determine the effects of modern mass communications on the political process? Is the vote-increase argument not simply another version of the hypodermic-needle analogy?

We cannot predict man's behavior solely from the stimuli that may strike at him directly as an individual physical being. How man ultimately behaves is always a consequence of how both individual stimuli and his total environment impinge upon him in any given circumstance. Some years ago, the distinguished social psychologist Kurt Lewin demonstrated the futility of merely directing propaganda to persons in order to get them to change their ways.[4] One does not expect juvenile delinquents to surrender their antisocial behavior as a result of simply being urged to do so, argued Lewin. Rather, one way to eliminate such behavior is to provide better housing, better nutrition, and better educational and employment opportunities as a total environmental package for the youths who experience inadequacies in these regards. In other words, alterations in the environmental circumstances in which an individual finds himself might very well have a greater chance of changing his behavior than specific bits of persuasive information to which he may be exposed. In politics we assume that the mass media are far more powerful in altering the political environments in which voters function than in actually changing their voting as such.

As time goes on and we begin to move away from the early classical behavioristic images of political man, our attention is increasingly turned away from efforts to merely correlate simple exposure to the mass media with direct, consequential, behavioral manifestations.

Not all of us who read and hear about the nuclear bomb capabilities of the Soviet Union and Red China install bomb shelters in our homes. Yet the mass media serve the social function of warning society of imminent peril. Not all of us dash out to purchase an automobile when we come across its shiny, brilliant visage in the advertisements of our brightly colored mass circulation magazines. Yet the mass media help us to know what our production economy is making available to consumers. Not every female in America wears miniskirts and not every young man allows his hair to grow à la Buffalo Bill simply because he has seen TV personalities attired similarly. Yet the mass media serve to transmit the social norms and cultural happenings of a society to its members.

It should be clear from these examples that it is not necessarily fruitful to study the specific behavioral manifestations of individuals alone in attempting to determine the effects of social institutions like the mass media of communication. Regardless of whether more voters actually vote, or whether actual votes cast are influenced directly and unduly by the mass media, mass communication, and radio and television in the particular, have affected the political fabric of contemporary American society.

Before we turn to some of the ways in which modern mass media have affected our political lives, let us look into two reasons why political "campaigns" as such usually fail to change many votes directly during their course. We have already noted that the main reason why most voters do not switch their allegiances during political campaigns is related to their personal characteristics and predispositions.

Failure of individual national campaigns to switch large numbers of votes is due to still another constant—the flow of news, information, and entertainment that normally emanates from the mass media. In his normal state the voter is enmeshed in complex nets of mass-mediated communications that together produce his normal "mass-communications situation." Ordinarily this "mass-communications situation" is characterized by large doses of unserious entertainment fillers (for example, advertising) which do not make demands of significant consequence on the viewer. These fillers do not require him to work. And even though they often contain considerable amounts of propaganda that is designed to induce him to act on a variety of matters ranging from the purchase of spot removers to joining the Marine Corps, the mass-communications "messages" which the ordinary voter is generally exposed to can be ignored with considerable impunity. Not so with the serious business of political campaigns that require voters to make explicit decisions of consequence.

Every four years the "normal" mass-communications situation is interrupted and changed drastically for the ordinary voters. Rather than affording them their usual psychological immunity, with regard to the serious matters of blatant political encounter, the media turn into intense assault weapons operating on the psyches of their audiences. The effects of this sudden assault can be viewed as twofold. First, because the new set of symbols that interrupts the old mass-communications situation is so incongruous with what is experienced normally, it stands out as naked "propaganda." Propaganda labeled as such is to be guarded against vigorously. Up go the voters' defenses against being "propagandized"—especially by the opposition political party. The result is often tune-out rather than turnout.

Second, because the mass media suddenly plunge the voter into serious political encounters that may result in serious consequences for him, the voter's level of anxiety may rise. Where he previously expected "play" from the mass media, he is suddenly confronted with "work" (at least on a psychological level). Anxiety quickly translates itself into resentment that is directed against both the media and the candidates (particularly of the opposition party). Once again, tune-out has been the consequence in the past.

Another reason for the failure of national political campaigns to directly and immediately persuade large numbers of voters to change their votes is due to the relatively short duration of the campaigns. In the normal flow of mass communications to which we are all subjected from early childhood, national political campaigns can be viewed as the briefest of momentary interludes. It is axiomatic that mass persuasion of true political consequence must be not only intense, but also long-lived.

Rather than bowling the voter over into the opposition camp, the very brevity of national political campaigns make them stand out like the proverbial sore thumb. This brevity frequently results in increasing rather than lowering the resistances of voters. Worth noting in this regard are the observations of Jacques Ellul.

[Effective propaganda] is based on slow constant impregnation. It creates convictions and compliance through imperceptible influences that are effective only by continuous repetition. It must create a complete environment for the individual, one from which he never emerges . . .

. . . Having no more relation to real propaganda are the experiments often undertaken to discover whether some propaganda method is effective on a group of individuals being used as guinea pigs. Such experiments are basically vitiated by the fact that they are of short duration. Moreover the individual can clearly discern any propaganda when it suddenly appears in a social environment normally not subject to this type of influence; if one isolated item of propaganda or one campaign appears without a massive effort, the contrast is so strong that the individual can recognize it clearly as propaganda and begin to be wary. That is precisely what happens in an election campaign; the individual can defend himself when left to himself in his everyday situation. This is why it is fatal to the effectiveness of propaganda to proceed in spurts with big noisy campaigns separated by long gaps. In such circumstances the individual will find his bearings again . . . The more intense the propaganda campaign the more alert he will become—comparing this sudden intensity with the great calm that reigned before.[5]

Political campaigns seem to be peculiarly impotent in moving the masses of voters away from their original choices. A small proportion of voters who are interested in politics make use of any source of information to satisfy their desire for additional knowledge, but these voters seek to educate themselves mostly about their own choices of candidates. Apart from this minority, the "great majority" of us ignore most sources of political information. The result remains a stand-off. The campaign media merely add to the knowledge of those who already are motivated. The unmotivated remain relatively politically naive, and all the pleadings of press, radio, and television appear to fail in their missions of direct persuasion-conversion.

In reviewing the literature on mass communications and politics it becomes increasingly clear that the mass media have political effects different from and broader than the wielding of sheer, direct influence on voters during campaigns. Our experience with the mass media as a socializing agent is a dynamic, life-long process. The process is one that continues as life itself continues. Unlike those of life itself, however, our experiences with the mass media are constellational rather than linear. That is to say, our experiences with the media occur as totalities over long periods of time. Precisely when and how the process begins or ends is almost impossible to tell. Thus, political campaigns operate within contexts composed of previous campaigns and all the events that have taken place between campaigns. Over time, each campaign becomes yet another input in the total constellation of inputs which ultimately influences both the structure of politics in this country and the political behavior of its citizens.

At this point, Ithiel deSola Pool's cogent note merits attention:

> The voter is not a passive target of the messages of mass media. Rather he is a repository of countless bits of previous information. He retains within him a lifetime of earlier messages that have been structured into a series of predispositions. The new message adds one more, but its net effect in changing the balance is infinitesimal compared to its effect as a trigger to responses already determined by predispositions. At any one moment the voter's predisposition is likely to be a far better predictor of his response to a stimulus than the character of the stimulus.[6]

The lessons from the past have not been unheeded. Campaigns in the future will be shaped more and more to become congruent with the over-all life experiences of voters. Efforts will be made to blend more and more the sheer manipulative aspects of political campaigning with the precampaign mass-communications experiences of audiences.

In order to examine how the mass media—particularly the electronic media—operate within and upon the political process in America, it is essential to forego the notion, which is nothing more than a value judgment, that the media simply exert undue direct influence on voters' choices of candidates during campaign time. The undue-influence doctrine is not only evaluative, it is eminently tautological. What, after all, is the purpose of political campaigns via the mass-communication media other than the attempt to exert undue direct influence on behalf of candidates? Pursuing the logic of the undue-influence doctrine leads to the simple-minded conclusion that successful candidates are better at exerting undue direct influence on voters than are unsuccessful ones.

The direct manipulation of populations via mass persuasion can occur only where preconditioning has previously taken place. Thus, as just one example, it is impossible to persuade people to buy a particular brand of toothpaste before they have learned to believe that brushing one's teeth is important to their health. The mass media of communications have proved to be outstandingly successful in the preconditioning process—certainly in the realm of advertising. Concededly, politics and advertising are quite different. Yet in both the market place and at the voting polls, mass communications have demonstrated that they are far more effective in shaping environments, creating needs and expectations, demonstrating the rewards to be experienced from suggested behaviors, and structuring predispositions in general than they are in "making sales" *per se.*

In Lewinian terms, then, and as expressed most recently in Marshall McLuhan's work, the impacts of mass communications upon a society and upon the groups and individuals that comprise it are far more indirect than direct, are far more covert than overt, and are far more subtle than obvious.

Fundamentally, the electronic media—and particularly television—have worked to shape new political situations in America which are yet to be defined fully. In so doing, it appears less important that the media be concerned with how the voter may or may not react to direct, persuasive entreaties. Rather, the important problem is how the media present to the voter political situations over-all, in terms of a new set of "definitions" which serve to orient him to particular candidates without the voter being consciously aware that he is being so oriented.

In this regard we do not wish, either by assertion or implication, to suggest a conspiratorial theory of the effects of mass communications on politics, although such a possibility cannot be foreclosed entirely. Instead, we suggest that simply by being there, the electronic media have altered the customary routines of politics in this country in ways that go considerably beyond the exertion of undue direct influence upon voters' choices; and, in doing so, those media have created a set of new and consequential issues which transcend the more mundane concerns such as the alleged direct effects that the mass media may induce upon the electorate.

The issues presented by the utilization in politics first of radio and now of television are integral aspects of the dialogue concerning "the new politics." We propose to examine a number of the issues that have been evolving from this dialogue by first taking a look at the roles that radio played in changing traditional politics in America, and then by exploring some of the more important political consequences that have resulted from television's emergence on the political scene.

RADIO AND THE MAKING OF THE PRESIDENCY

The ubiquity of television today makes it difficult for us to remember that radio once occupied the same preeminent position in the public's attention. In 1922 the total number of radio receivers in use throughout the United States was a mere 400,000. Within a decade the radio-receiver saturation figure in the United States was 18,000,000. By 1942, in the era prior to television, the figure stood at a peak of 59,340,000.

The first major study of the public's reaction to radio was published in 1946—*The People Look at Radio*, by Harry Field and Paul F. Lazarsfeld.[7] This study revealed three important facts worth noting about radio-listening in the peak years of the mid-forties, before television's advent:

1. On the average, the American public listened to radio for some 2.5 hours every day.

2. Vis-à-vis other social institutions such as churches (rated favorably by 76 percent of the population), newspapers (rated favorably by 68 percent of the population), public schools (rated favorably by 62 percent of the population), and local government (rated favorably by 45 percent of the population), radio's acceptance as a social institution by the general public was the most favorable (82 percent).

3. By the mid-forties radio had established itself as the major daily news source for nearly two-thirds (61 percent) of the population.

A further indication of radio's grip on the nation's attention was reflected in the study by Field and Lazarsfeld. Asked which they would rather give up, reading newspapers or listening to the radio, 62 percent of the nationwide sample that was studied elected to forego reading newspapers.

Franklin Delano Roosevelt first took the oath of office as President of the United States on March 4, 1933. F.D.R. died on April 12, 1945, in the early part of his fourth term as President. During the span of these twelve years tremendous changes occurred in the political life of the nation, particularly in the role of the Presidency. Radio, which began the age of electronic mass media, played no small part in affecting these changes.

During Roosevelt's administration the opportunity for reaching the masses of American voters via radio was ever-increasing. In the period 1932–1943, for example, the number of radio-equipped homes in the United States doubled, while the total sets in use tripled, and eight million American automobiles became equipped with radios.

It has been noted by some observers that radio may indeed have had a direct effect on voter participation in national elections. For example, Neville Miller points to an apparent relationship between increased radio-receiver saturation and increases in total votes cast in the national elections of 1920, 1924, 1928, 1932, and 1936:[8]

Election		Total Radio Sets in Use	Total Votes Cast
Harding	1920	400,000	26,705,346
Coolidge	1924	3,000,000	29,022,261
Hoover	1928	8,500,000	36,879,440
Roosevelt	1932	18,000,000	39,816,522
Roosevelt	1936	33,000,000	45,646,817

Campbell is also convinced that a correlation exists between early radio saturation and increasing voter turnout.

Turn-out in the early 1920's rose substantially when women received the vote and reached a new high point in 1928, a level that was maintained in 1932. Between the elections of 1932 and 1940, however, the turn-out records jumped more than 8 percentage points; the off-year congressional vote increased even more markedly—from 33.7 percent in 1930 to 44.1 percent in 1938.

These increases in the national vote, as radio reached the less educated and less involved sections of the population, are impressive . . .[9]

It should be remembered that radio's initial growth began to accelerate during the Great Depression when the nation was in the throes of social, economic, and political disquietude. This set of circumstances did not inhibit the growth of radio saturation. Ownership of sets actually increased during the periods between 1929 and 1933. It was during this time that total employment dropped from 96.2 percent of the labor force to a low of 73.1 percent. Nevertheless, during the very same period of time, the percentage of families owning radio receivers nearly doubled from 34.6 percent to 62.5 percent.

DeFleur makes note of the seemingly paradoxical inverse correlation between unemployment and the ownership of relatively expensive radio receivers during the 1930's.

But in spite of the hardships of the times, radio seemed to thrive on the depression! Advertising revenues, instead of drying up, grew at an ever increasing pace. The number of radio sets owned by Americans about doubled every five years. Families who had reached the limit of their financial resources would scrape together enough money to have their radio receiver repaired if it broke down. They might have to let the furniture go back to the finance company or to stall the landlord for the rent, but they hung grimly on to their radio sets.[10]

Why was this so? In line with the functional paradigm of mass-media effects developed by Lasswell, Wright, and Mendelsohn,[11] radio proved to be particularly potent in offering respite (in other words, entertainment) from the heavy woes of everyday life, and, via its news and information services, proved to be effective in reassuring the nation that all was not lost.

Franklin Roosevelt was well aware of the two major functions that radio was serving during his time. He placed the greatest emphasis on the use of radio to reassure the public. Even before his ascendance to the Presidency, F.D.R. began to experiment with radio while he was governor of New York. His early local experimentation with radio was designed to overcome the hostile opposition to his policies in the New York State Legislature, as this letter written on March 28, 1932, attests.

Time after time in meeting legislative opposition in my own state, I have taken an issue directly to the voters by radio, and invariably I have met a most heartening response. Amid many developments of civilization which lead away from direct government by the people, the radio is one which tends, on the other hand, to restore direct contact between the masses and their chosen leaders.[12]

It is apparent that very early in his public executive career Roosevelt came to view radio as a potent instrument for rallying public opinion because of the direct communication it made possible between the executive and the electorate. In this process the executive could by-pass the machinery of strictly local politics and opposing legislators to appeal directly to the public for support.

Roosevelt developed a technique for controlling the opposition of an adverse legislature by taking his appeals for support of his bills directly to the public via radio. These appeals usually included requests for listeners to pressure their legislators for support. Here were the beginnings of the famous "fireside chats." Grace Tully reports on how effective these early radio efforts were:

> Mr. Roosevelt first took to the radio as a field of battle when he became ensnarled with a recalcitrant legislature in Albany a year or so after becoming Governor. Fed up with the pulling and hauling of customary political bargaining, he declared curtly: "I'll take the issue to the people." The issue in this first instance was over his request for appointment of a commission to consider revision of the laws pertaining to the control of utilities.
> He did, by radio over a New York State chain, and the results were immediate. Mail came flooding into Albany, most of it in support of the Roosevelt position and most of it addressed to the working level of the legislature. It was a convincing demonstration and from that time on F.D.R. made it a more or less regular practice to take his problems "to the people" in this manner.[13]

Burns, in his political biography of Roosevelt, also points to the use made of radio during F.D.R.'s first gubernatorial term.

> Roosevelt also began his famous "fireside chats" during his first term. Direct and pleasing in tone, these radio talks were aimed especially at upstate New Yorkers, who got most of their information through the Republican press. Radio still faced a host of technical difficulties, and Farley had to send questionnaires throughout the state asking local Democrats how good the reception was from various

stations. Roosevelt, of course, began the first of his talks with the claim that they would be nonpartisan reports. Actually, most of them were highly partisan thrusts at the Republican legislators.[14]

Radio not only served Governor Franklin Roosevelt as a means of by-passing the opposition of his legislature, but, as Friedel points out, the then governor of New York soon realized that the opposition press could be neutralized equally as effectively by the new radio medium.

Among those people, whether in the city or in the country, who had radios, Roosevelt hoped further to circumvent the virtual Republican monopoly of the press through monthly addresses in which either he, the Lieutenant Governor, or the Democratic legislative leaders would discuss developments in Albany. In these talks he could, if need be, speak more openly as a Democrat. Or if he were faced with a legislative impasse, he could use the microphone, as Governor Charles Evans Hughes had once used the newspapers, to make an appeal to the people. The Democratic party contracted for an hour of radio time a month on a statewide hookup.

Long since, Roosevelt had grasped the significance of radio as an invaluable political medium for the Democrats which would enable them to break through the paper curtain of the publishers and appeal directly to the voters.[15]

The lessons learned in Albany were soon to be applied to the Washington, D.C. scene with startling impact.

Even before F.D.R. won the Presidency, the use of radio by candidate Roosevelt during the campaign served to produce two important effects that were interrelated. His use of radio reduced the previous power of the print media in the political arenas of the United States, and it propelled national political campaigning into the twentieth century.

Mott estimated that 59 percent of the daily newspapers in the United States and 55 percent of the weeklies were opposed to F.D.R.'s Presidential candidacy in 1932.[16] In order to overcome this majority press opposition, the Democrats allocated 17 percent of their total 1932 campaign expenditures of $1,170,000 for radio. The Republicans countered by spending 20 percent of their total campaign expenditures of $2,670,000 on radio time. Roosevelt polled 22,813,786 votes to Hoover's 15,761,000 in 1932. He became the first Democratic President in eighty years to attain a clear majority of the popular vote—57 percent. In the Electoral College, F.D.R. garnered 472 electoral votes to Hoover's 59.

The radio campaign of 1932 saw the demise of the torch-light parade, the "front porch" campaign, the focus on local speech-making, and exclusive dependence on the printed page. A new technique for appealing directly to millions of voters was projected into national politics. No longer would the American national political campaign be waged almost exclusively in unfamiliar public surroundings that were boisterous, emotion-arousing, and crowd-dominated. The new arena now was the familiar, quiet, private setting of the potential voter's own home. With radio, the foundation for "the new politics"—participatory politics—was set in the voter's living room.

Mr. Roosevelt was well aware of the changes that radio had wrought in national political campaigning when he advised a *New York Times* reporter on July 31, 1932:

I hope during this campaign to use the radio frequently to speak to you about important things that concern us all. In the olden days, campaigns were conducted amid surroundings of brass bands and red lights. Oratory was an appeal primarily to the emotions and sometimes to the passions. It always has been my feeling that with the spread of education, with the wider reading of newspapers and especially with the advent of the radio, mere oratory and mere emotion are having less to do with the determination of public questions under our representative system of government. Today, common sense plays the greater part and final opinions are arrived at in the quiet of the home.

F.D.R.'s promise of talking matters of public concern over with the people directly via radio came to fruition the very first year of his administration. The newly-elected President took to the air waves no less than 84 times between March, 1933 and January, 1934.

At the time F.D.R. made his momentous first inaugural address, the country was engulfed in economic and social disaster—unemployment was at its peak, factories were idle, banks began to go under, and hungry people roamed about in aimless desperation. Roosevelt sought to reassure a nation that was edging over the dark pit of catastrophe; he did so by resorting to what

McLuhan has called the new "tribal drum"—radio. The manner in which the new "tribal drum" beat out messages of hope to eliminate the despair that clung to the nation is highlighted in this observation:

On March 4, 1933, people huddled around radios with desperate intensity. Unable though they were to see the wire-taut muscles in Roosevelt's face while he delivered his inaugural speech, their response to his confident voice and message turned despair into hope edged with excitement. . . .

Never before in all human history had a speech been heard by so many people; never before had an address produced such an immediate, widespread, or profound impact upon a nation's psychology. A new mood of hopeful expectation had been achieved through the alchemy of a man, his message, his rhetoric, and the far-flung radio audience.[17]

Soon came the era of the radio "fireside chat." This public-communication device, refined from its crude beginnings, was designed to inform the nation, to reassure it, and, in the process, to begin to develop the Presidency into the awesome position of power it now enjoys.

During his tenure as President, F.D.R. delivered a total of twenty-eight fireside chats, usually on the critical issues that confronted the nation. The same techniques Roosevelt utilized as Governor of New York he now employed on a nationwide basis. The responses to F.D.R.'s national radio appeals were massive. As many as 80,000,000 Americans heard these radio talks at one given time. Roosevelt's radio chats generated an average of five to eight thousand letters daily to the White House from listeners all over the country.

Wrage and Baskerville highlight the important role that the fireside chats played in freeing the Presidency from obstinate congressional control—particularly throughout the reforms and changes that characterized the Roosevelt era. The Roosevelt "radio personality" proved to be most effective in this regard.

The fireside chat proved to be a brilliant invention because of Roosevelt's keen appreciation of the value of communication, his gift for the popular idiom, and his incomparable radio voice and personality. Through the fireside chat he made the affairs of government warm, interesting, and personal; he created a public opinion on issues to which few congressmen dared remain indifferent. The fireside chat was Roosevelt's supreme achievement, thought Gerald W. Johnson, for it "gave him the power to accomplish all his other works."[18]

No doubt Roosevelt's successful use of radio was due to a combination of personality and a great deal of savvy about how the radio medium worked.

There can be no question that F.D.R.'s personality was his most potent political weapon. His fireside chats projected this personality to the fullest. Witness the amazing finding of a 1938 American Institute of Public Opinion poll that 80.3 percent of the public "liked" Roosevelt's personality.[19] Not only did F.D.R.'s use of radio break the traditional weakness of the Presidency, but also, as assuredly he laid the groundwork for the emergence of a new criterion for the public to use in judging the President of the United States—the acceptability of his personality.

The dynamics of the effective means by which the charisma of a powerful political leader can be projected through the radio medium to kindle the imaginations of listeners is explained succinctly by Marshall McLuhan:

Radio affects most people intimately, person-to-person, offering a world of unspoken communication between writer-speaker and the listener. That is the immediate aspect of radio. A private experience.[20]

The powerful combination of a strong-willed, attractive personality and a visionary understanding of the dynamics of radio's impact produced many changes in American politics. It changed campaigning; it broke the traditional political influence of the press; it began to weaken the traditional power of political machines and political parties. Most important of all, it provided the base from which the modern powerful office of the American President emerged.

This latter development cannot be overemphasized, as Mendelsohn indicates:

The seemingly minor use of radio by Franklin D. Roosevelt to reach directly into the home of the ordinary citizen produced one of the most profound political changes of our time. This single stratagem permanently enhanced the power of the President as a strong *individual* initiator of political policy. At the same time, the new ability of the President to act on his own as a political organizer of the national electorate marked the beginning of the end of local and regional power wielders. Now in the age of television, national politics are indeed national, with the locals thoroughly dependent—and not the other way around, as it was not more than forty years ago in the age of print.[21]

TELEVISION AND THE EMERGING CULTS OF POLITICAL PERSONALITIES

The law of technological displacement applies to mass communications just as it does to other sectors of society. As new innovations in the technical means for mass communication are introduced they rapidly displace the previous most popular media. Thus, in 1950, 95 percent of America's households contained at least one radio, and 7 percent owned one television receiver. In seven short years, by 1957, 82 percent of all the households in America were equipped with television sets and 98 percent with radios. A television revolution had taken place.

In a very short period of time television not only became America's major source of entertainment, but also, according to a series of controversial public-opinion polls that have been conducted by Roper Research Associates, it had begun to displace all other media as a "primary" news source for the majority of the public (51 percent) as early as 1959.[22] By 1967, according to the Roper studies, television was cited as the primary news source by 64 percent of the American public.[23]

On the role of television in politics the Roper report shows television to be a preeminent source of political information on the national and state levels but of secondary influence on the local levels. The report concludes that

. . . the farther a candidate was removed from "here in town," the stronger television was as the source of a person's political information . . . newspapers are number one as the public's source of information about candidates for local offices although [in 1967] television is only 12 percentage points behind newspapers as against the 15 points by which it trailed newspapers two years ago [32 percent use television; 44 percent use newspapers]. At the state level, television is the number one source of news about candidates as it was in 1964.[24]

Not only has television displaced newspapers and radio as a major source of news for most Americans, but by 1961 the news presented on television was considered to be more believable by more Americans (39 percent) than either newspapers (24 percent), radio (10 percent), or magazines (10 percent). By 1967 television continued to rank first in credibility—this time among 41 percent of the population.

Worth noting in particular are figures from the 1964 Roper research which showed an inverse correlation between age of the viewer and his willingness to believe what he sees on television. Here, where 36 percent of those sampled in the 50-and-over age bracket considered TV to be the most believable medium, fully 52 percent of the 20-to-25 "new voter" age group thought television to be most believable.

The contemporary young voter is an entirely new breed from the standpoint of mass communications. Whereas his parents derived most of their entertainment, news, and information primarily from radio, he now gets all these mostly from television. The television experience is unique. Although it calls for near-complete involvement of the audience, this involvement is with the medium, but not necessarily with the voting process.

Professor Angus Campbell concludes from a number of surveys of voting behavior that were conducted by the University of Michigan that television, with its powerful grip on modern day audiences, nevertheless has not apparently stimulated greater voter participation in national elections. Campbell notes:

. . . comparisons of the national elections during the era of television raises serious doubt as to whether this new medium, despite its tremendous audience, has greatly altered the basic relationship of the electorate to its national government. In its first decade, it seems neither to have elevated the general level of political interest nor to have broadened the total range of political information. It has greatly extended the purely visual dimension of political communication; the public no doubt finds it easier to form an image of its political leaders than it did through the older media . . .[25]

It is precisely in the area of building the public's imagery of political leaders and the political process that television's impact on American politics has been felt most strongly. The introduction of the "personality" ingredient into the selection and election (or rejection) of national political candidates begun by F.D.R.'s assiduous use of radio has become a most significant development in our contemporary age of television.

McLuhan points out that television is a "low intensity" medium that forces audiences themselves to fill in details of television "images." This process calls for a high degree of audience involvement with television's simultaneously occurring "mosaic mesh." This mosaic quality produces, in turn, a "stress on [audience] participation, dialogue and depth." From the kind of personalized involvement that the television medium (regardless of its contents) calls for, subjectively defined profiles of the personalities who appear on television emerge as "extensions of reality." For personalities to be accepted by television audiences their projected "images" must be as open-ended as the medium itself. McLuhan calls this lack of image definition "cool." The formula he offers suggests that a "cool" medium such as television calls for the projection of a similarly "cool" personality on the TV screen. If an individual's appearance on television openly asserts his singular status and role position (McLuhan refers to this phenomenon as "hot") he will fail to catch the attention and interest of viewers. "Anybody who looks as if he might be a teacher, a doctor, a businessman or any of a dozen other things all at the same time is right for TV."[26] Extending the dictum to politics, we might say anyone who *appears* physically attractive, sincere, diligent, tough-minded, poised, bright, assertive, and at the same time *appears* to be of Presidential timber will ultimately have a very strong go at the office. The reluctance of many office-seekers to declare their candidacy early in an on-coming campaign reflects their concern with the danger of establishing the singular "hot" role image of "candidate" only.

What television accomplishes most effectively, then, is the shaping of the viewers' images of national political figures, both as those figures perform in office and as they project themselves in bidding for office. Thus, television has provided the electorate with a new set of criteria which enable viewers to shape expectations of what an American President should be and help them to make judgments of a particular President as he is. These criteria are not lost upon seekers or holders of high political office. Considerable anxiety about the projection of the "right" television image to the electorate is exhibited by politicians in the knowledge that a "correct" projection can make them successful, while the "wrong" projection can doom them to failure.

The following excerpt from a *New York Times* interview with Mrs. Lyndon B. Johnson touches on the former First Family's concern with the televised public projection of Mr. Johnson's Presidential image:

[Q] Do you think that the news media like radio and television project the President as you see him? You know, some people's personality comes over on television very accurately, others don't.

[A] I do think that he is at his best in a small group of people where he simply talks straight from the heart. There's a pungency and a color and a humor and a force in meetings of that sort, and it may be equally as good in a face-to-face confrontation with a larger group. It is somewhat diluted and restricted when it gets to the mechanics of TV and the great invisible audience. I do not think it is quite as good as face to face. I think it's perhaps because he's used to and likes that bond of looking at people and feeling their response. Nevertheless, I have seen him lots of times on TV when I thought, "That is the real flavor of the man coming through."

[Q] Why at times doesn't that flavor come through?

[A] I simply think that the sheer mechanics and the absence of the audience make it somewhat more difficult for some people. He's a human man and not a machine man.

[Q] Do you think he is somewhat afraid of these machines?

[A] No, not at all. He just is not responsive to them. He responds to humans.[27]

President Johnson's difficulties with mastering the communicative power of the television medium has been underscored by the former Chief Executive himself, and in Eric Goldman's phrase, this failure to take advantage of the medium effectively contributed substantially to "the tragedy of Lyndon Johnson."

The capability of television to project relatively unknown politicians into full-blown national figures was first realized as early as 1951 when the hearings of the Senate's Special Committee to Investigate Crime in Interstate Commerce—the so-called Kefauver Committee—were aired on network television. With national television reaching audiences ranging from twenty to thirty million viewers, "Estes Kefauver, as chairman of the committee looking into the activities of organized crime in the United States was raised by the magic eye from the status of just another United States Senator to the very verge of the Presidency, from being an interesting 'comer' from Tennessee to a pinnacle of national popularity and international interest."[28]

Although the televised Kefauver hearings gave viewers some impressions of the extent of criminal activities in the United States, it did not accomplish much in implementing its manifest function—the generation of new crime control legislation. Instead, the hearings fulfilled two quite unexpected latent functions. First, they demonstrated that politics, as viewed in progress on television, can project the necessary dramatic elements for affording entertainment. Second, because viewers can become involved (even though vicariously) in an unfolding political process as it appears to be actually happening, they can experience the same identifications with hero figures and vent the same kinds of emotions against villainous characters as they would in witnessing fictionalized dramas.

Here lies the true political power of television. Whereas the print media can merely describe the results of complex political-legal processes such as United States Senate hearings, testimony, and cross-examination of witnesses, television allows the viewers to literally *see these processes in action*. How the various participants (the actors) in such a process comport themselves soon becomes a measure of the men themselves. These public judgments quickly become crystallized into psychological sets—composed of sentiments, attitudes, and opinions—the sum total of which emerge as "images." Generally these images or impressions revolve about a man's physical appearance, his poise, assertiveness, determination, reaction to pressure, and all the various complex attributes that go into making up his particular "style." As already stated, when a man's style and role participation match the peculiar exigencies of the television medium he can be launched as a prominent political personality quite literally overnight. This happened in 1964 when an obscure motion-picture actor took to the television air waves several nights before Election Day with an impassioned plea for Californians to cast their ballots for Barry Goldwater. The very next day Ronald Reagan was launched into the political waters that won him the governor's chair in California and then propelled him as a serious contender for the Presidency of the United States in 1968.

The ability of television to push political personalities into national prominence was realized all too well by Senator Joseph McCarthy when, as Chairman of the Senate Permanent Subcommittee on Investigations, he began what we now commonly refer to as the "Army-McCarthy hearings" on television on April 23, 1954. The Senator's guess that television would provide him with a massive public sounding board was realized on the very first day of the activities when fully 63 percent of all the TV sets in New York City were tuned into the hearings.

What McCarthy did not realize, however, was that both in his personality and in the highly unorthodox manner in which he conducted himself lay the ingredients for the emergence of a highly negative image of the man. McCarthy apparently was unaware that his personality and his performance were, to use McLuhan's terms, "hotting up" a "cool" medium. The results were disastrous for McCarthy. Instead of emerging as a tough, patriotic, anti-Communist dragon-slayer, McCarthy's image as projected on the television screen, came through as an unshaven, ill-mannered, nasty, unprincipled, brow-beating bully. The Army-McCarthy hearings sounded the political death-knell for Wisconsin's then junior Senator. Laymen and politicians alike experienced their first realization of the boomerang power of television to tear down a political personality. The demonstration in the televised Kefauver hearings of television's build-up power, it was soon realized, told only part of the story.

Wedged in between the 1951 Kefauver hearings and the Army-McCarthy hearings of 1954 was the national Presidential campaign of 1952. Twenty-seven million Americans in that year, from the vantage point of their living-rooms had the opportunity to take an intimate glimpse into the selection of a President from the preconvention primaries right through to the final vote tallies.

As matters finally developed, the 1952 campaign boiled down

to a "personality" battle between a revered, simplistic, avuncular, war-hero General and an urbane, intellectual, unknown, divorced Governor of Illinois. Television was the major weapon that was used in this battle.

Hill makes the following observation:

The 1952 election was the first to . . . completely adapt broadcasting to its purposes. Never before were so many of the aspects of the political process so completely exposed to public view. The comparative novelty of television guaranteed viewer interest and assured a viewer-fascination with proceedings, bordering perhaps on naivete . . . Clearly, too, television indelibly affected the political process itself, by the nature of the public's response to the new medium. Image and charisma were apparent political factors.[29]

It was during the 1952 Presidential campaign that the full impact of television on the political process was felt. Beginning with television coverage of the state primaries, proceeding through the coverage of the nominating conventions, and continuing through the campaign itself, the full panoply of political televisionalia—advertising agency participation, remote coverage, "meet-the-press" type of interviews, "spot" commercials, "in-depth" news documentaries, and paid, full-length political telecasts—was in near-ubiquitous evidence.

Just as F.D.R.'s use of radio in political campaigning drastically altered the traditional process of selecting a President, so the new television medium in 1952 rendered unique and lasting changes in this process. D. W. Brogan noted:

Just as the radio and more recently, television have begun to change the character of the conventions, radio and still more television have changed, and will increasingly change the character of the campaign . . . The most effective introduction of the candidate to the voters is now made on the air. It is not necessary for him to show himself personally to scores of small towns and hundreds of "whistle stops." His chief job is to present himself on the air. It may still be worthwhile to make a great speech from a big city, capital of a region. The television appearances go down better if they are part of a meeting and not mere studio jobs. The loyal party members who fill the auditorium provide the necessary warmth; but the real audience is elsewhere. Both candidates in the 1952 campaign went through the motions of the old traditional campaign. But their effective appeal to the voters was in great meetings seen by millions.[30]

While Stevenson, in 1952, attempted to encourage voters to address themselves to rational considerations of the issues, he only succeeded in pinning the high-brow, "egg-head" label on himself. In contrast, Eisenhower focused least of all on political matters and mostly on his own personal, folksy image by appealing to voters who, as Hyman and Sheatsley point out, "placed less emphasis on ideology and more emphasis on personal qualities in their choice of a candidate."[31]

In a study of what images of the two candidates emerged during the 1952 campaign, Ithiel de Sola Pool concluded that "*both* candidates were regarded as fine and great men by people on *both* sides of the political fence . . . It was not a struggle of good versus evil but of good versus good."[32]

Pool found that the predominant images of Eisenhower held by his supporters as a consequence of exposure to the mass media during the campaign (expressed by over 70 percent of the sample studied) was that the General was good-natured, sincere, honest, cheerful, and clear-headed. Even majorities of the Stevenson supporters (over 50 percent) who were surveyed believed Eisenhower to be likeable and good-natured.

In contrast, over 70 percent of the Stevenson supporters studied considered the Illinois candidate to be clear-headed, sincere, brilliant, likeable, honest, and refined. Eisenhower advocates thought Stevenson to be clear-headed mainly (in over 50 percent of the cases). Thus, where Eisenhower warmed up his previous public image as a tough soldier, Stevenson succeeded in converting himself into a potent *intellectual* political power from a starting point of near anonymity. In 1952—during a period in our history when an alleged "mess in Washington" was supposed to have dominated the national political vista—the times apparently were not such as to warrant the electorate to respond positively to the egg-head approach to politics.

It is important to note here that in the United States in 1952, the mass media, and television in particular, began to focus voters' attention on personalities and away from the issues in national political campaigns, a trend which became most discernible in 1968. From 1952 on, the national political wars were waged on the basis of the very good guys versus just the good guys or versus the bad guys, as the case may be. James Reston noted in *The New York Times* on October 30, 1958, "Instead of the old-fashioned emphasis on what a candidate thinks, or what he says, the emphasis now seems to be on how he looks, especially on television, and on what kind of personality he has."

What radio was for Franklin D. Roosevelt in 1932, television was for John F. Kennedy in 1960. As Theodore White, the chronicler of the 1960 national election observed, television had rendered "a revolution in American presidential politics." By that year nearly nine out of ten American homes (40,000,000, or 88 percent) were equipped with at least one television receiver. The new importance of television as a political device was noted in the expenditures that both parties were to make for national network broadcast time on television—$3,006,100 ($1,900,000 spent by the Republicans, and $1,106,000 by the Democrats). Outlays for national radio network time during the 1960 campaign were to be cut by no less than 75 percent. It was clear that the new Presidential candidate had to be blessed with an abundance of funding as well as with personal appeal.

Mr. Kennedy entered the 1960 Presidential lists with a mixed set of positive attributes and negative handicaps. On the positive side he was youthful, independently wealthy, articulate, physically attractive, and he was bestowed with a personality that was fresh, charming, and free of the stilted politician's posture. In describing his reaction to Senator John F. Kennedy in 1959, Douglas Cater wrote,

. . . he shows a restraint of manner that is unusual among politicians. Both in public and private conversation he eschews cliché with the contempt of a man for whom words are precise instruments. He does not retreat behind the high wall of pomposity that most politicians erect on occasion to protect themselves from interlopers.[33]

It was clear from the start that John F. Kennedy possessed all the "cool" attributes that television required for projecting a positive image.

On the negative side, Mr. Kennedy's Catholic persuasion and Irish-American background were considered to be definite political handicaps. His opponents would try to turn his youthfulness into an image that denoted "lack of experience," and his Boston

Brahminism could be used to identify him with the "privileged classes."

John Kennedy's task was clear in 1960—above all he had to establish himself as a *serious* contender for the Presidency of the United States. He had to convince the electorate that he could and would be a strong Chief Executive. The image he wished the public to develop of him was sketched in early 1960 by Mr. Kennedy himself in an address before the National Press Club when he suggested that contemporary Americans needed

. . . a vigorous proponent of the national interest—not a passive broker for conflicting private interests. They demand a man capable of acting as the commander-in-chief of the grand alliance, not merely a bookkeeper who feels that his work is done when the numbers on the balance sheet come out even. They demand that he be head of a responsible party, not rise so far above politics as to be invisible—a man who will formulate and fight for legislative policies, not be a casual bystander to legislative process.

Kennedy accomplished the projection of this image through public encounter with opponents within the Democratic party in the Wisconsin and West Virginia State Primaries; through his appearances before Protestant ministerial and lay groups in which he outlined explicitly his position on the separation of church and state; through his performance at the Democratic Nomination Convention; and, perhaps most importantly of all, through the way he conducted himself during the tradition-breaking Nixon-Kennedy "Great Debates." All this was made available to multitudes of television viewers throughout the land.

Although political observers and researchers alike agreed that neither Mr. Kennedy nor Mr. Nixon "won" the Great Debates in terms of influencing opposition votes, the four televised confrontations accomplished two major objectives. The first was the direct involvement of the electorate once again in an important part of a political process as it actually occurred. Audience measurements tallied the viewership of the first debate at between 70 and 75 million, of the second debate at between 51 and 62 million, of the third at between 48 and 60 million, and the fourth at between 48 and 70 million.

The second over-all effect of the Great Debates was the elevation of John F. Kennedy as a serious Presidential contender in his own right. Democrats became convinced that with Mr. Kennedy as their standard bearer the possibility of a November victory was real. Republicans came to the realization that they indeed had a tough battle on their hands. That the debates helped to crystallize allegiances in J.F.K.'s own party was evidenced after the first encounter with Nixon on September 26, 1960. The very next day the "Ten Southern Democratic governors" relayed a telegraphed message to Mr. Kennedy proclaiming, "We the undersigned Governors . . . wish to congratulate you on your superb handling of Mr. Nixon and the issues facing our country. It is the consensus of the Governors . . . that the masterful way in which you controlled this debate further accelerates the movement to the Kennedy-Johnson and Democratic ticket." How many heretofore "undecided" Democratic voters left their television sets that night with the same feeling is unknown.

In a November 5, 1960 *Nation* article titled "Asking for a Job," Alan Harington summed up the broad impacts of the Great Debate encounters on voters' assessments as primarily those of the candidates' projected television personalities:

. . . A political speech made before an admiring audience that will surely applaud the candidate, or a cozy chat issuing from his library, has never given us an approximation of the whole man. Now thanks to the Kennedy-Nixon TV confrontations, we are appreciably closer to the valid, intuitive "take," the wholly human—even though sometimes mistaken—feeling we have about someone whom we are going to accept or reject for a job.

After his elevation to the Presidency, Kennedy used the device of the televised, "spontaneous" press conference to reach the people directly, much as Franklin Roosevelt used radio to accomplish similar purposes through his fireside chats. The new President's charisma, developed in his televised precampaign and campaign performances, accompanied him into the White House. It was estimated that some 65 million people viewed President Kennedy's first televised news conference.

The televised news conferences helped to reinforce the charismatic attributes that previously were merely in embryo. Suddenly television brought forth an exciting new star in the nation's political firmament. The cult of the Kennedy personality was developing through the unprecedented attention that the mass media was giving both to the President and to members of his family.

Bernard Rubin comments on the role that Kennedy's televised press-conference performances played in propelling him into the attention and admiration of millions of Americans:

Television displayed a most personable leader, able, and forthright. These conferences provided the President with a most adequate display case for his talents. He was quite capable of humor, but his major interests were to register his opinions and to state what he and his Administration would or could do about various foreign and domestic problems . . . Before long, the press conferences were eliciting a tremendous mail response largely because of television coverage. It should not be forgotten, however, that television only partially satiated the vast public curiosity about the President. The young man was a center of national attention virtually every day of his tenure in office. A substantial portion of the citizenry, their appetites whetted by all of the mass media, placed John F. Kennedy and his family in a hero-worship category formerly reserved for movie-stars and the like . . . Revealed to the nation was a terribly vigorous, aggressive, dynamic, and yet deeply introspective personality. Television suited him well, and he seemed made for it—a true partnership of man and medium.[34]

Television had presented America with a new genuine political hero. The power of this new personality was used once again to strengthen the office of the President, to weaken traditional party encumbrances, and to promote the office-holder's own programs and aspirations.

In its ability to create in its audience the illusion of involvement through what Horton and Wohl term "para-social interaction," televised presentations of President Kennedy seemed to create more and more public curiosity about the man as more and more was written and broadcast about him. Although neither the media nor the public seemed to be sated with the abundant coverage that Mr. Kennedy was accorded, a certain degree of alarm began to be voiced regarding the "dangerous" precedent that was being set. It was argued that overemphasis on the "trivia" of the President's life might very well divert the public from the pursuit of the "serious" aspects of politics. The dangers of "hero worship" were pointed out succinctly in an article written by Sister Mary Paul Paye in *The Nation* (August 11, 1962), titled "The Kennedy Cult":

> The gentleman smiles, the youngster sidles up to a pony on the lawn, the lovely lady bows. Cameras click, tape-machines whirl. I protest—vehemently, vigorously, apolitically and almost alone.
>
> Three threats are inherent in this constant projection of the personal image of the President: the suppression or obscuring of significant news; the amassing by the President of personal power; and most insidious of all, the irrational world-wide identification of him with the country as a whole. We all—mass media and mass audience—could well pause to assess the ramification of what less sophisticated societies termed hero worship, a phenomenon that in our own electronic age, has become more complex and more potent.

In our own time, then, television has created new political experiences for the electorate which are not fully understood. Because these experiences are emotional rather than purely cognitive they have powerful impact upon the election process, particularly in the selection of candidates for national office. As the voter is embroiled in the daily unfolding of the political process on the TV screen, he develops over time his own subjective, private percepts of the process and of its participants. The development of these percepts occurs quite imperceptibly and unconsciously. In McLuhan's words, "Everybody experiences far more than he understands. Yet, it is experience rather than understanding that influences behavior."

The television build-up of political personalities is the major new mass-communications effect upon contemporary politics in our time. As yet we have not been able to measure what this will do to our future political lives. Mendelsohn has attempted several speculations:

> . . . we should [now] expect a new breed of politicians. They will not necessarily be a bunch of well-poised, good-looking, vacuous types, as some observers have conjectured; nor will it be impossible for an ugly man to become President, as some have warned. The recent emergence of Hollywood actors on the political scene reflects a rather crude temporary response to the demands of television in contemporary politics. Rather, we can expect the new generation of politicians to respond to the "low intensity" demands of the TV medium in

order to procure the greatest possible degree of viewer involvement well before the national conventions are convened officially. Regardless, then, of whether they fit the Cary Grant or the Anthony Quinn pattern, the professionals of tomorrow must project a "cool" image.

This image will be cultivated and polished over considerable periods of time—during which every opportunity for television exposure will be exploited. Testing grounds for developing this particular sort of imagery will be young audiences who . . . are peculiarly sensitive to the televised mode of political communication.[35]

Between the appearances of *The Making of the President 1960* and *The Making of the President 1964,* a political event of the gravest tragic importance occurred—the assassination of President John F. Kennedy. No American can forget the incredible experience of an entire nation participating in this disastrous event through a medium of mass communication—television. Reports published by the Nielsen Audimeter Service, a television audience measurement service, revealed that in New York City, which comprises 10 percent of all the television households in America, 70 percent of the television households had tuned in to view the arrival of the late President's body at Andrews Air Force Base in Washington, D.C. on the night of his murder, Friday, November 22, 1963. Throughout the next day, Saturday, November 23, estimates indicate that nearly 50 percent of all the households in the United States had their television receivers tuned in, marathon fashion, for nearly twelve hours. On Sunday, November 24, during the ceremonies in the Capitol Rotunda, it is estimated that 85 percent of all the TV homes in the United States were tuned in, and on the following day, Monday, November 25th, an unbelievable 93 percent of all television households in the United States—representing more than 100 million persons —became witness to the funeral and burial services for President Kennedy via television.

Television's ability to involve the nation in near-total, psuedo participation in a calamitous national political event was demonstrated as it had never been before. Theodore White noted two important consequences of this psuedo participation by the American people:

The political result of this participation, of this national lament, was a psychological event which no practical politician will ever be able to ignore. Out of it began the Kennedy myth and the Kennedy legend . . .

Beyond the beginning of the myth one must stress another political result . . . By concealing nothing; by sharing all; by being visible when their private natures must have craved privacy, Jacqueline Kennedy first above all, then the grief-stricken Kennedy family, then the new President permitted television to give strength and participation to the citizens.[36]

Well before the 1964 national election, then, it was clear that the personalities of a popular, martyred President and his successor, as projected primarily through television coverage of the assassination, would play significant roles in the contest that was to occur a year later.

In assuming the Presidency upon Mr. Kennedy's death, Lyndon B. Johnson afforded the nation the essential reassurance that no doubt played a critical part in his 1964 victory. First of all, by virtue of the quiet, steadfast manner in which he took the reins of government, he demonstrated both ability and stability at a time when such traits were critically necessary to the tranquility of a nation that had experienced a brutal sense of loss, despair, and anxiety. Theodore White writes,

There is no word less than superb to describe the performance of Lyndon Baines Johnson as he became President of the United States [upon the death of President Kennedy].

All the accounts of his behavior through the week of the tragedy—his calm, his command presence, his doings, his unlimited energies—endow him with superlative grace. Yet such stories limit the tale only to his positive deeds. To measure the true quality of his take-over, one must consider not only these positive acts, but what did *not* happen. So much might have gone wrong—yet did not.[37]

Second, President Johnson, during the period in which he assumed the Presidency in 1963, did nothing to abrogate the Kennedy legend that was emerging and becoming full-blown with unsurpassed rapidity and over-all public acceptance. Johnson indeed pledged to continue the Kennedy orientation to politics, and in actuality both exploited and reinforced the legend simultaneously.

Against this backdrop, the Republican party in 1964 presented the junior Senator from Arizona, Barry Goldwater, for consideration by the American electorate. From the very moment of his nomination, Mr. Goldwater suffered a severe image problem with the voters—a problem which stemmed primarily from the personality of the man plus the rigid ideological stance he assumed. This image was both projected and reinforced in rather negative terms throughout the 1964 Presidential campaign by television and the other media of mass communication.

Goldwater used rough-house tactics at the Republican National Convention in 1964. He obstinately refused to accommodate to the Party's moderates. This refusal was reinforced by the capstone pronouncement in his acceptance speech—"Extremism in the defense of liberty is no vice . . . Moderation in the pursuit of justice is no virtue!" He suggested the possible use of low yield nuclear weapons in Vietnam. He questioned social security funding. And he publicly mused about the possible sale of the Tennessee Valley Authority. All of these factors served to fashion an image of the Republican candidate as a hard-nosed, irresponsible, trigger-happy, calloused, militaristic, anti-civil-rights politician who represented a dangerous threat to all that the legenary John F. Kennedy had sacrificed his life for.

Where Johnson offered continuity in the tradition of Kennedy, Goldwater presented the possibility of an abrupt and explicit break with that tradition. Where Johnson offered social progress in the Kennedy manner, Goldwater offered what appeared to be a regression from Kennedy's social concerns. Where Johnson offered an image of reassurance, ability, and stability, Goldwater offered untried ideology, radical change, and a seemingly careless and casual approach to government that conflicted sharply with the Kennedy style.

Nor did the rather massive television campaign launched by the Goldwater forces seem to be able to rescue what was rapidly solidifying into a disastrous image for the Arizonan. (The Republicans are estimated to have spent $12,800,000 for national radio-TV time in 1964 as compared to $5,100,000 expended by the Democrats.) Although five major television network half-hour programs designed to project the Goldwater image in more favorable terms were presented during October and on Election Eve, 1964, the largest number of viewers attracted to any one of these offerings never topped the 7 million mark. Contrast this to the estimated 100 million viewers who witnessed the Kennedy-Nixon debates just four short years before.

The utilization of television in the 1964 campaigns once again drove home the risks that are involved in "hotting up" the medium with political ideologies and with the old fashioned images of the so-called conservative brand of politics (for example, explicit super-patriotism). The 1964 campaigns also pointed up television's inability to project a favorable image of a candidate whose disfavor with the electorate had become hard reality by virtue of the man himself and his rigid adherence to his stand. As Theodore White put it, "The fundamental Goldwater problem was himself."

Even before convention time in 1964, a top aide to Barry Goldwater, Richard Kleindienst, commented on the Senator's reluctance to place himself completely in the hands of the image-makers, even though it appeared that his candidacy might have benefited substantially from doing so:

The advertising people just love to get their hands on a guy like this. They treat him like a block of wood, cutting him into the shape they want. Barry just won't put up with that. If it means losing the nomination because he won't adopt the image they want, then he'll lose.[38]

What Goldwater appeared to be saying to the electorate in 1964 was, "If you don't like me the way I am, to hell with you." By the time 1968 rolled around, Richard Nixon in effect was promising the American voter, "If you don't like me the way I am, I'll change."

The lessons of 1964 were not ignored as 1968 began. Enmeshed in the complex events relating to America's participation in its most unpopular foreign war and to its internal upheavals, and overwhelmed by his admitted difficulties in turning the image-building, sustaining power of television to communicate with the electorate effectively, the hero of 1963-1964 became the villain of 1968. Rather than risking a Goldwater-like humiliation at the polls, President Johnson withdrew voluntarily from the 1968 Presidential race. It can be said perhaps that in 1968, the "fundamental Johnson problem was himself."

Richard Nixon was far more optimistic about overcoming his particular image. Burdened by past allegations of opportunism, of conservatism (and even reactionary orientations), of allegiance to the special interests of Wall Street, of a propensity to "shoot from the hip," and by his actual record as a political "loser," Mr. Nixon unabashedly and straightforwardly presented himself to the American electorate in 1968 as "the new Nixon." The new Nixon image was to be projected primarily through the medium of television, the instrumentality by which the 1968 Republican candidate had in the past experienced both his greatest triumph—the famous "Checkers" performances—as well as his deepest humiliation—the "Great Debates" against John F. Kennedy.

Nixon's effort to put across the new Nixon together with the poignant attempt of his opponent, Hubert Humphrey, to convince the electorate that the latter was indeed "his own man," both efforts primarily taking place via the television route, ushered in a new and strangely frightening development in American politics—the pseudo campaign.

TELEVISION AND THE EMERGENCE OF THE PSEUDO CAMPAIGN

On the national level, with the advent of television as a major means of political communication came a ritualistic, stylized orientation to national political campaigning, the product of which looks like the genuine, honest-to-goodness, real thing, but in essence is not. The psuedo campaign as presented by television merely simulates political reality, but it is as far from the real thing as the girl in the Revlon ad is from the bucolic young creature next door.

In the psuedo campaign candidates appear to be chosen by explicitly observable democratic processes of selection taking place before the television cameras on the floors of the conventions, when in actuality all the selective action takes place behind closed doors, where the cameras are barred. The campaign trail looks as if the candidates are addressing themselves to vital issues of the day in every nook and cranny of the land, but, in fact, most of those pathways are carefully prearranged and are "coordinated" to the demands of nighttime television news shows whose deployment of equipment and reporters dictate to a large degree where a candidate goes and when he will appear. Additionally, what the candidate says must be carefully tailored to fit the cleverly captioned three-minute "lead story" that can be easily inserted into those very same news programs. The spontaneous reaction of the crowd is the lifeblood of actual campaigning, and in the psuedo campaign the crowds are paraded before the television cameras with their "spontaneous" reactions properly cued in to be filmed. The psuedo campaign thrives on the visual "body count" because, if the candidates themselves appear dull and uninteresting, at least the "crowd" can be made to appear visually stimulating. Instead of spending substantial amounts of time in solely elucidating the issues involved, the positions taken, and the specific actions they intend to put in motion after Inauguration Day, candidates are compressed into ten-, twenty-, thirty-, and sixty-second commercials that hawk their attributes much as if they were frozen fruit pies.

The components of the televised psuedo campaign are succinctly described by Robert MacNeil:

Day by day campaign reports spin on through regular newscasts and special reports. The candidates make their progress through engineered crowds, taking part in manufactured pseudo-events, thrusting and parrying charges, projecting as much as they can with the help of make-up and technology, the qualities of youth, experience, sincerity, popularity, alertness, wisdom and vigor. And television follows them, hungry for material that is new and sensational. The new campaign strategist also generate films that are likely syrupy documentaries; special profiles of the candidates, homey, bathed in soft light, resonant with stirring music, creating personality images such as few mortals could emulate.[39]

The psuedo campaign of today is a direct response to the exigencies of television. As McLuhan has pointed out, the television medium involves the viewer kaleidoscopically in a "mosaic mesh" which forces audiences to absorb disparate bits of information at tremendous rates of speed. After two decades of maximum exposure to television fare, viewers have either trained themselves or have become trained to absorb, often simultaneously, increasingly large numbers of these information bits at increasingly high speeds. As a consequence television commercials have become shorter and more numerous; news programs have become "tighter" and considerably more concentrated (all the news items featured on a typical nighttime half-hour telecast can be fitted into the front page of the New York Times); and even the very essence of TV fare—the variety show—has undergone drastic changes, as an adjustment to this situation, in terms of speedy, quick-changing imagery. A case in point is the top-rated "Laugh-In" show that has been featured on the NBC network. In a cover story about "Laugh-In" in its October 11, 1968 issue, *Time* noted that the typical "Laugh-In" program was the end-product of some "350 snippets of video tape" that had been "stitched together." The article observed further,

What appeals is the program's extraordinary ambiance; it has an artful spontaneity, a kind of controlled insanity, emerging from a cascade of crazy cartoon ideas . . . It features no swiveling chorus lines, no tuxedoed crooners. Just those quick flashes of visual and verbal quality, tumbling pell-mell from the opening straight through the commercials till the NBC peacock turns tail.

What is remarkable about "Laugh-In" is that the ordinary viewer has very little trouble in absorbing these "350 snippets of videotape per hour." A parenthesis worth noting is that "Laugh-In" has become so identified with "what's happening" in America's television subculture that, as a campaigner in 1968, President Nixon made a momentary appearance on "Laugh-In"—just long enough to sternly query the show's key identifying line, "Sock it to *me?*" No doubt this appearance was part of the effort to project "the new Nixon" to a "new" audience. Looking back at the 1968 national campaign, it appears that Presidential politicking in America has begun to emerge as the political counterpart of "Laugh-In." This mixture of serious politics with "show biz" will be touched on more fully later on.

The overwhelming demands of television for individuals skilled in its use and application in entertainment, news, and particularly in the mass-persuasion process has introduced a new breed—the "campaign strategists"—into the political process in the United States. The new campaign strategist is generally a man versed in the arts of advertising and public relations. He usually has some knowledge of the structures and functions of the mass media; is generally an amateur psychologist dabbling in the intricacies of individual "motivations" and mass behavior. He is familiar with the techniques of show business; has vague insights into the workings of public-opinion polls and into some of the grosser aspects of sociological research; and, above all, is not embarrassed to be cast in the role of an overt manipulator (or aspiring manipulator) of public opinion on behalf of paying clients who are determined to win an election. More often than not all these attributes do not reside within one man, but are found to be distributed with more or less abundance among the bevy of campaign management and consulting firms that has sprung up with amazing proliferation throughout the nation during the past two decades.

The process whereby, as campaign strategist *par excellence* Joseph Napolitan put it, "[W]e decided it was time to take politics away from the lawyers," began in 1952 with the candidacy of Dwight D. Eisenhower. In their book, *Electing the President,* Ogden and Peterson record the beginnings of this significant shift in campaigning strategy and procedure:

In 1952 . . . Rosser Reeves, a representative of a small New York advertising firm, strongly recommended a television campaign for General Eisenhower featuring maximum penetration through the use of numerous short spot announcements. The General himself was to appear in each announcement.

Three basic arguments were advanced for such an innovation. The cost would be low per thousand homes reached. Spots, unlike full-length programs would reach people not already for a candidate. Spots would allow concentrated efforts in the relatively few critical states which could not be counted in either candidate's column.

Ultimately, 50 spot announcements of 20 seconds each were prepared, and approximately $1.5 million was spent on their presentation. The contents of the spots were statements of concern and general promises, each of which helped reinforce the favorable image of experience, kindliness, and sincerity which Eisenhower enjoyed as a result of his command positions during World War II.[40]

It was soon learned that viewers who normally would be reluctant to engage in sustained eye-to-eye contact with a candidate over lengthy periods of expository exposure did not appear to mind the miniscule perceptual brushes with candidates that were afforded by "commercials" in which their candidacies were featured. Out went most attempts to present issues in their fullest exposition; in came more and more "snippets" of persuasion.

By 1964 the resort to television commercials as campaign instrumentalities had escalated to major proportions. Theodore White reports in his coverage of that campaign that throughout the year 1964 fully 29,300 TV commercials on behalf of candidates were repeated over and over again as were some 63,000 on-air radio commercials. These figures contrast sharply with the 9,000 political commercials that were repeatedly telecast and the 29,000 spots that were broadcast over radio throughout the year 1960.

In order to mount campaigns of such magnitudes, Presidential campaigners have begun to rely more and more heavily upon the resources, know-how, and counsel of professional advertising and counseling agencies. Thus, for example, some sixty professional advertising men from a large variety of agencies such as J. Walter Thompson; William Esty Company; Ketchum, McLeod and Grove; Young and Rubicam; Ted Bates and Company, under the overall management and administrative supervision of Fuller and Smith and Ross serviced the advertising needs of the 1968 Republican Presidential contenders. The switching of agencies in midstream by the 1968 Democratic ticket made front page news in the advertising and media trade press in October of that year. The Humphrey-Muskie account was moved from Doyle, Dane, and Bernbach and was set up in a newly formed operation, Campaign Planners Associates, an offshoot of Lennen and Newell. An estimated twenty-five professionals serviced the account at Campaign Planners Associates.

In actuality, advertising agencies afford political campaigns a variety of prosaic services that are concerned mostly with the purchase of advertising time on the electronic media and space in print. The "brains" and "creative" influences for the actual advertising strategies and content are provided by specialists who may or may not be employed by a standard advertising agency. In a lead article in *The New York Times Magazine* of October 13,

1968, titled "Joe Napolitan Packages Candidates: Selling the Product Named Hubert Humphrey," Thomas J. Fleming explains the set-up for the Democratic national candidacies:

> Joseph Napolitan is the former public-relations partner of Larry O'Brien, whom Hubert Humphrey installed as head of the Democratic National Committee after the Chicago convention. O'Brien, the man behind Humphrey's successful nomination drive, and the political engineer of the Kennedy 1960 victory and the Johnson 1964 triumph, had Napolitan on the job within a week, installed in an office next to his own at National Committee headquarters in Washington. Doyle, Dane Bernbach were out the door a week later.
>
> . . . To fire it some nine weeks before Election Day with the Nixon radio and television campaign already achieving a steam-roller impact would seem at first either an act of high courage or sheer madness on Joseph Napolitan's part.

Napolitan is quoted as proclaiming "I am the only one ordering stuff. Campaign Planners are mostly just buying time."

Backing up Napolitan were so-called creative units among which were such groups and individuals as Tony Schwartz, described by Fleming as the "American advertising world's acknowledged King of sound . . . a disciple of Marshall McLuhan"; Vision Associates, film producers; Harry Muheim, a television-film writer; and Shelby Storck, a producer of motion pictures.

One recent political outcropping worth mentioning here is the full-blown emergence of campaign news as reported assiduously in the trade press of both the advertising and the media industries. To the advertising and media fraternities Presidential campaigns represent substantial business, both in terms of actual cash and attendant prestige value. The contemporary student of the new politics would do well to refer himself to such sources as *Advertising Age* and *Broadcasting* during the course of Presidential campaigns along with the more orthodox *New York Times* (do not by-pass the daily advertising and television columns) and the *Wall Street Journal*.

Preliminary figures released by the Federal Communications Commission on January 2, 1969, reveal that in 1968 the Republicans spent an estimated $2.5 million on television commercial announcements, and the Democrats spent $844,313 for *national network "spot" time alone.* These figures are a bare minimal estimate since they do not include monies spent on behalf of national candidates by various business interests, labor unions, and the like. They exclude expenditures to local television that is not affiliated with any of the three national networks. And these figures do not include expenditures for talent, production, and placement on television by advertising agencies (costs for the production of one sixty-second commercial alone average about $20,000). Similarly excluded from these estimates are expenditures for radio commercials and print advertisements on behalf of the candidates.[41]

The same FCC report indicated that the 1968 expenditures for all *political advertising time on national network television* alone reached an unprecedented high of $5 million on behalf of the Republican national ticket and $3 million on behalf of the Democratic national ticket. Again, these estimates represent a bare minimum for the reasons cited. Ed Dowling, writing in the November 30, 1968 issue of *The New Republic,* put the estimates for televised political advertising into a more realistic perspective when he noted, "According to one informed estimate, Nixon spent $10.5 million on TV this fall; Humphrey, $9 million; and the grand total for all political spending is put at $67.5 million."

Harry S. Ashmore supports Dowling's estimate of television expenditures by the national candidates in 1968:

For the relatively brief period of the general election campaign Richard Nixon mounted the most expensive effort in history—one that ran well over twenty million dollars, with more than half of it going directly into television and most of the remainder devoted to co-ordinated management and sales techniques geared to the TV campaign. During the eight weeks preceeding the election, the Washington Post calculated, Mr. Nixon's candidacy involved a dollar outlay far exceeding that for the leading commercial TV offering, Chevrolet, which spent only thirty million dollars during all of 1967. Mr. Nixon's agency even signed him on (along with Coca-Cola, Schlitz, Goodyear, Ford, Texaco, Pan American, and Reynolds Metals) as a sponsor of the broadcasts of the Olympic Games from Mexico City.

With the last minute surge of contributions that followed his spectacular rise in the public opinion polls Hubert Humphrey pushed his television spending up into the Nixon range. George Wallace came in for an officially recorded campaign expenditure of 4.7 million.[42]

On September 3, 1969, the Federal Communications Commission issued its final report on radio-television expenditures during the 1968 general elections. As usual, the data related reported expenditures for air time alone. Also, the figures are confusing due to the fact that different bases are used for their various computations.

If we take into account all the money that was reported to have been spent to purchase both television and radio time on behalf of all gubernatorial, senatorial, and Presidential races during the entire year of 1968 (including the primaries) we arrive at a grand total of $58,900,000. This is up $24,300,000 from the 1964 grand total of $34,600,000. The expenditures for television air time alone during the general election of 1968 on behalf of all gubernatorial, senatorial, and Presidential candidates equalled $27,087,027 as compared with the total of $17,496,405 that was reported in 1964 and the $6,635,946 total in 1956. Here, Republicans are reported to have spent $15,182,298 for television air time on behalf of all their gubernatorial, senatorial, and Presidential candidates; Democrats, $10,423,517; and the American Independent Party, $1,481,212.

Now if we look at the total amount of money spent for both radio and television air time for the major Presidential tickets alone we see that the Republicans spent $12,129,082; the Democrats, $5,965,474; and the American Independent Party, $1,697,765.

To many and, very importantly, to those in the advertising-campaign management world, the outcome of the 1968 national election was simply a matter of which advertising giant outspent the other. *Advertising Age,* a major trade paper in the advertising business, noted on February 20, 1969:

How did Richard Nixon win the Presidency? Partly, at least, because he outspent the competition in advertising. The extent to which that was true was again pointed up today with the Television Bureau of Advertising's release of 1968's biggest clients in network tv. Nestled among the top 100, in 79th place, between Schlitz Brewing Co. and Monsanto is United Citizens for Nixon-Agnew with an estimated net time and talent budget of $3,922,600. In addition, $175,000 was reported by the Nixon for President Committee.

Hubert Humphrey, the Democratic runnerup, was in 109th place, bracketed between Sperry Rand Corp. and Standard Oil Co. of New Jersey. His budget: $2,826,000.

Third party hopeful George Wallace didn't even make the first 200. He ranked 227th with an appropriation of $701,600. New York's Governor Nelson Rockefeller never reached the Presidential starting gate in the campaign, but he was third in terms of network TV dollars spent. An outlay of $852,800 placed him No. 210 in the ranking.

Spending for other politicos in network TV: Citizens for (Sen. Eugene) McCarthy, $141,000; Citizens for (Gov. Ronald) Reagan, $45,000.

Small wonder, then, that, as Robert MacNeil points out, "Broadcasters are quite happy with the trend. Short spots keep the politicians happy, do not annoy audiences by interrupting their entertainment, and make money."[43]

Whether or not televised political commercials actually affect the voter directly in terms of altering his choices is open to question—a question to which serious researchers have yet to address themselves.

Political television advertising has certainly demeaned the Presidential campaign so that only remnants of dignity are visible any longer. Under these circumstances candidates become dehumanized and are considered to be "products" suitable for clever "packaging" and "merchandizing."[44] Carroll Newton, long-time Republican campaign strategist, has put forth the basic formula for marketing the Presidential candidate: (1) through testing and research develop various appealing aspects of the "product"; (2) determine through motivation and attitude research what voters like and dislike about it; and (3) develop mass communications strategies and tactics which emphasize what is liked, and either change or play down what is reacted to unfavorably.[45]

There is no quarrel that such tactics may indeed be suitable for the marketing of the numerous commodities and services that are considered to be vital to the economy of the United States. After all, there is very little consequence (other than to the advertisers) if we reach for the shiny red package rather than the equally shiny green one at the local supermarket.

But what happens when contenders for the highest office in the land are handled similarly? Are not our sensitivities regarding the significance of that office dulled by such exposure? Are not our expectations of the qualities a man needs to fill that office properly distorted and truncated? Is not our reaction to exposure to thousands upon thousands of paid political commercials and other fare similarly contrived one that leaves us with the impression that we are being fully and realistically informed when in essence we are not at all being made truly knowledgeable about the persons, issues, and events that literally have the potentiality of destroying us?

Writing in the *TV Guide* of October 22, 1966, Arthur Schlesinger Jr. sounded this ominous warning:

This development can only have the worst possible effect in degrading the level and character of our political discourse. If it continues, the result will be the vulgarization of issues, the exaltation of the immediately ingratiating personality and, in general, an orgy of electronic demagoguery. You cannot merchandise candidates like soap and hope to preserve a rational democracy.

Mr. Schlesinger is not alone in recognizing the hazards that are posed by the contemporary trend in political advertising. Advertising men themselves are becoming alarmed. Addressing the Chicago Advertising Club on October 29, 1968, Don Nathanson, president of North Advertising Agency (which was involved in Adlai Stevenson's Presidential trials) appealed to his colleagues in advertising to "join in working diligently to make sure that evil men do not rise to power on the power of a broadcast . . . We need," he added, "advertising agencies of high moral purpose who will shun becoming accomplices of a man with evil intent."

Again, it must be pointed out that it is not our purpose to develop a conspiratorial theory of political communications here. It is profoundly difficult, if not entirely impossible, to put the blame for this state of affairs at the feet of any specific individuals, groups, or institutions. In contemporary politics it is sufficient to note that the television medium has indeed displaced the message, and that, as a consequence, we have entered into a new, bewildering, and perhaps even threatening phase of politics.

Today's television fare is made up of heavy doses of entertainment intertwined with smaller doses of news and advertising. In tune with the demands of TV's realistic entertainment demands, political campaigning is becoming more and more "entertaining" as the years go by. In all aspects of the contemporary national campaign can be found a definite "show biz" flavor. Candidates make brief "personal appearances" as guest stars on popular entertainment programs; news coverage of their activities are heavily flavored with entertainment values; and, when possible, candidates perform as feature stars of their own shows. This turn of events has, for one thing, "made drama critics out of political writers," according to Harry S. Ashmore.

On the critical night before Election Day, 1968, the voters of America were given the opportunity of viewing either the Humphrey-Muskie spectacular on the ABC network or the Nixon special (Spiro T. Agnew, the controversial Republican vice-presidential contender, was conspicuously absent from the proceedings) on the NBC network.

The Humphrey-Muskie show was considerably more earthy than was the restrained and more "dignified" (in other words, dull) Nixon opus. More than forty show-business celebrities encircled the beaming Democratic candidates—among whom were such notables as Buddy Hackett, Johnny Carson, Paul Newman, Bill Cosby, and Nancy Sinatra. Both Democratic candidates exchanged meaningless pleasantries and gags with the show people in a last desperate appeal to the American electorate. In contrast, the Nixon special placed heavy emphasis on wholesomeness, and, instead of the usual show business accoutrements that signify big-time television variety entertainment, Mr. Nixon was surrounded by attractive girl-next-door type young ladies (including the two Nixon daughters). Questions that were phoned in from viewers were delicately relayed to the candidate by an admiring, reverent, and equally wholesome former football coach.

All candidates featured on the two televised marathons on Election Eve were attempting to project the imagery of "regular guys"—likeable, oriented to youth, and men of humor. Nixon's appeal was directed to the sedate middle majority whom he had labelled as having been "forgotten." Humphrey and Muskie were making a blatantly apparent pitch to the McCarthy hold-outs and to the Wallace defectors with their down-to-earth, "contemporary" orientation. To the discerning observer, both shows resembled exercises in the theatre of the absurd.

Rather than gaining specific information in depth regarding the candidates' policies and plans directly from the candidates during the few remaining hours prior to Election Day, American voters were offered a heavy tray of entertainment-laden goodies —all looking attractive and sugary, filled with what advertising men refer to as "appetite appeal" and "beauty footage"—but received very little in the way of real nourishment. Once again, it is highly unlikely that much direct influence upon the voters occurred that evening. There is very little doubt, however, that the traditional, libertarian democratic process which rests upon the public's need for meaningful enlightenment rather than upon diverting amusement was not enhanced in any manner on Election Eve, 1968.

Robert Lewis Shayon's pertinent though melancholy observations serve as a serious admonition to us all:

The comic and the candidate mixing fun and issues in a sort of Hellzapoppin, symbolized the leading edge of the love affair between TV and politics that steadily grows hotter every four years. Where are we heading?

. . . Certainly we have not yet attained the apogee of the show biz-politics orbit. Some people worry about demagogues with huge budgets and Madison Avenue savvy winning Presidential power in the future. The worriers suggest voluntary advertising agency-network-party guidelines for a more honest pattern of TV campaigning. But as TV pulls the candidates nearer to voters, the candidates tend to draw back from close scrutiny, and to place symbols of themselves between the voters and the real men. The sad prospect is more manipulation and less restraint.[46]

Unless the current trend is checked, we can expect more and more that the new politics will exploit the voters' penchants for seeking pleasure rather than "work" from their communications environment. By providing ever-increasing amusement and ever-decreasing information, the "game of politics" as it has come to be played in the United States today may become a deadly one.

This state of affairs poses an awesome ethical question for American democracy. We know that the voter need not be appealed to cognitively; and we know he does not behave in a purely cognitive, rational manner as far as politics go. In fact, there is considerable evidence that indicates that noncognitive, emotional appeals serve far more effectively in predisposing voters to a particular partisan posture. Given this knowledge, do candidates, campaign managers, party workers, and media executives use the nonrational techniques of mass persuasion that are readily available for the benefit mostly of the candidates, or do they pursue the less effective, but seemingly more responsible course of appealing to the voter in his role as Homo sapiens?

The "new politics" has developed out of the near total disregard for man's need to know, and has oriented itself to man's need to experience, albeit vicariously, via his color television receiver. Marshall McLuhan suggests that the process whereby cognitive responses to political communications are displaced by experiential reactions as stimulated by television spells the doom of democracy as we know it. He says,

The day of political democracy as we know it today is finished. Let me stress again that individual freedom itself will not be submerged in the new tribal society, but it will certainly assume different and more complex dimensions. The ballot box, for example, is the product of literate Western culture—a hot box in a cool world.

. . . Voting in the traditional sense is through as we leave the age of political parties, political issues and political goals and enter an age where the collective tribal image and the iconic image of the tribal chieftain is the overriding political reality.[47]

Mass Communications and the Game of Politics

All too often in our discussions of the effects of mass communications, the image of man to which we address ourselves is one that defines him as exclusively cognitive. We generally tend to ignore the other side of the image coin—that man is capable of emotional behavior as well as thinking behavior. Thus, "learning," as such, is not the only experience that man derives from being exposed to communications. As L. A. Dexter and D. M. White put it, in *People, Society and Mass Communications*, "a good many people listen to great orators, preachers, and teachers

—not to be instructed but to be entertained, 'thrilled,' amused, or comforted." We might add "politicians" to their list.

We have already indicated that the classical Jeffersonian image of the voter—the voter who is capable of making purely rational judgments based upon the (factual) political information he seeks out and receives—is simply a quaint hyperbole in light of present social-science evidence. For the great mass of the electorate, politics, as viewed by professional politicians, is of peripheral interest.

For most men life is a dull, uninteresting affair that lacks glitter and excitement. Moreover, life is fraught with frustrations, disappointments, and anxieties. The fare that the ordinary citizen seeks out and finds in the mass media relieves the tedium of daily life, and, through complex processes of identification, fantasy, wish-fulfillment, catharsis, and the like, man derives pleasure from the media.

Much of what we see and hear in the mass media is designed to help us to ward off past anxieties and to cope with future causes of pain. The child achieves this relief through play and games. The adult accomplishes it by the fantasies that are generated within him through exposure to drama and fiction.

Not only do games and fantasies per se provide us with simple pleasures and amusement, they also serve as socializing processes whereby we "learn" a great deal about both ourselves and the society in which we live. In this manner, the mass media provide us with incidental learning. The media, Klapper indicates, very often afford audiences an entertaining "school of life."

When we are engaged in fantasy induced by the content of mass media we are aware that we are engaged in fantasies just as we are aware of dreaming when we dream. Through the process of "distancing" we are able both to participate in our fantasies and to be witness to the fact that we are so engaged. Simultaneously, we can be both participant and spectator in our own fantasies. In itself this can be a most pleasurable experience. The mass media are replete with fare that invites participant-spectatorship. This is particularly true of the television medium in its audience-involving presentations of sports events, dramas, and political events.

It has already been seen that television is not only the nation's major entertainment source, but that it also serves as its major source of general news and national political information. It is quite plausible that the dynamics by which we derive pleasure from entertainment fare are similar to the manner in which we respond to political fare.

The massive audiences attracted by television presentations of legislative hearings, nominating conventions, electioneering speeches, "Great Debates," and Election Day vote tallies cannot be understood as being simply demonstrations of the public's need for political information. As Campbell has asserted, there still exists a substantial proportion of the population that remains politically uninvolved.[48]

If there is one significant principle underlying the dynamics of mass communications it is that those persons most likely to seek information are already the best informed. Thus we find that people who follow election campaigns most closely on television are precisely the same ones who read the most about them in newspapers, books, and magazines.

It is among those at the other end of the scale, the quarter or third of the population that is generally uninvolved and un-informed, that television might have hoped to have its greatest impact. But this group, alas, is very incurious about politics; its demand for mere information is exceedingly modest. Its members can apparently be induced to watch an occasional "spectacu-lar," such as a nominating convention or a debate, but, for the most part, their detachment from political matters remains un-disturbed.

It is clear that much of the political stuff to which the ordinary citizen is exposed by television every day is more entertaining than it is "educational," in the formal sense. Whatever political "learning" may occur as a consequence of exposure takes place incidentally and haphazardly. Politics on television afford voters a sense of participation in the dramatic political events of their time without the work that is involved in understanding the se-rious abstractions involved.

In developing his "play" theory of mass communications, Wil-liam Stephenson elaborates on Szasz's pertinent communication-pleasure postulate. For Stephenson communication-pleasure is a direct consequence of personal experience with nonserious, non-work communications situations.

> . . . Communication-pleasure calls for no action; communication-unpleasure is a command for action.
> . . . Communication-pleasure is enjoyment, contentment, serenity, delight, such as is characteristic of entertainment, art, drama, conversation, sociability, and the like. In attendance upon it is a certain enhancement of self-existence.[49]

It is clear that sitting in on a televised Senate hearing, a nominating convention, an Election Night vote tally, or a run-of-the-mill Presidential press conference falls short of witnessing "a command for action." Yet the clash of forces and counterforces in the continuing battle to either achieve or maintain political power is "drama" of the highest order. Because few calls to specific actions are explicit in these spectacles and the voter remains a participant-spectator (via television), no psychological work is required. As a consequence, the experiences derived are pleasurable in themselves.

The mass media, then, allow the electorate to play vicariously at the game of politics. From the television experience in particular many voters derive a simulated sense of actual participation in the political process even though real participation is not literally possible. Not only is communication-pleasure derived from direct experience with political fare in the mass media, but it also extends beyond the mass media situation into the realm of interpersonal communications. Playing at the game of politics requires some awareness of "what is going on" and of who the "bad guys" and "good guys" are. Thus the mass media provide us with many of the symbolic components that go into our daily informal conversations, interpersonal exchanges, and gossip.

On this point Stephenson concludes:

> In politics few really know what they are doing, yet all speak knowingly. They have learned to use a vocabulary of politics, a language of charades and cliches to use in disputation . . . In every instance, the "argotese" is without real meaning, involving little adequate understanding of anything. But in its terms one can dispute and argue as well as the next person. Politics is carried on, as far as

voters are concerned in a context of relative ignorance and prejudice as on a stage outside reality—it is a play, so as to make political conversation possible.

. . . political language is indeed very largely play; it keeps people talking with little reference to reality as a scientist would understand it.[50]

TELEVISION AND THE NEW POLITICS

The cover of the November 1968 issue of *Psychology Today* depicts a political candidate standing on the rear observation platform of an old-fashioned whistle-stop train. He is confronted with a serious dilemma of the times. On his right an eager mother lifts a baby for him to kiss. To his left, a television camera is held up to him. No conflict. The politician leans over to plant a buss upon the video camera.

This image highlights the orientation of value-priorites of candidates working in the new politics: Get on television if you want to win. The illustration suggests that television's job is simply that of garnering votes during campaigns. The old hypodermic-needle concept of the influence of mass communications is still at work. What is difficult to realize is that had the hypodermic power of television been anywhere close to its alleged potency, Richard Nixon—who, as a candidate for the Presidency in 1968, spent more money for television exposure than any previous Presidential candidate—should have won the election by a far greater plurality than his 43.3 percent (which, incidentally, was just some four percentage points above the popular-vote percentage that obliterated the candidacy of Barry Goldwater in modern America's greatest Presidential defeat).

Regardless of whether television does or does not cause voters to switch their votes during campaigns, it has spawned four major changes in traditional American politics:

1. It has altered the processes of nominating candidates at party conventions.

2. It has altered campaigning.

3. It has altered traditional party structures and functions.

4. It has helped to encourage the questioning of the traditional ways of choosing and electing candidates, and, as a consequence, will aid in ushering in the new politics of the future.

Sophocles opined, "None loves the messenger who brings bad news." In its coverage of the Democratic nominating convention in 1968, television indeed appeared to bear bad news. It spoke to the electorate, who voiced amazement and shock at what they witnessed on their television screens, and, even more importantly, it spelled near-tragedy to many professional politicians, whose very political lives were put into jeopardy by television's incisive scrutiny into one of America's most cherished political institutions.

As will be recalled, not only were viewers at home treated to the simultaneous swirl of events that engulfed the Democratic gathering in Chicago, but delegates to the convention, confined in the security-tight Chicago Amphitheatre, were made painfully aware of the impact-laden occurrences that were taking place outside by the television recording of the clashes that involved the Chicago police, the Illinois National Guard, and the anti-Vietnam war and anti-Humphrey demonstrators at Chicago's Conrad Hilton Hotel.

As they were actually taking place, these events, because of the presence of television, affected both the viewing public and the delegates to the convention. Thus they served as immediate inputs into the convention itself. Recall, as one case in point, Senator Ribicoff's direct address to Mayor Daley in which he referred to the "Gestapo tactics" of the Chicago police, and the Mayor's fist-shaking response.

Reactions to the Chicago Democratic convention by the professional politicians were swift and predictable. Because they did not particularly like what they and the voters saw on the television screen, and probably because they wished to divert public attention from suddenly apparent major flaws in the political process, they immediately sought out television as their prime scapegoat. As a result, television itself became an important issue in the 1968 Presidential election. A newspaper article headlined "Dirksen Calls TV's Convention Coverage Outrageous: Urges Ban on Cameras," and by-lined by the late Minority Leader of the United States Senate, Everett McKinley Dirksen, is illustrative. Wrote Senator Dirksen:

The Miami Beach convention moved us to penetrating thought about TV reporting. The Chicago convention crystallized it. From Miami Beach, the TV people told the nation how boring it all was. From Chicago they pulled the switch and helped make it interesting indeed—and tragic and nauseating.

A television person has no more right to force his tricks and his opinions from the floor of a convention than a newspaperman has a right to print his editorials right there on the convention floor.

The television coverage of the two recent conventions is an outrage against the democratic process. . . .[51]

The trade publication *Broadcasting* noted the following on page 44 of its September 9, 1968, issue:

Political Washington last week returned from convention combat and members of both parties turned to a common foe—the news media. In the inevitable post-mortems, controversy raged about the role of media and especially network television in its coverage of the battle of Chicago. During the week most of the slings and arrows levelled at broadcasters were oratorical, but more substantial moves were in the works.

Focus of the anti-media (and pro-law-and-order) uproar was the Congress which devoted a good part of its first day back in session to denunciations of coverage of the Democratic national convention and surrounding disorders.

Out of these congressional discussions grew the 1969 Senate Communications Subcommittee hearings that were held in February and March of that year under the chairmanship of Senator Pastore. The Senate subcommittee took advantage of the situation that arose in Chicago to launch into a broad-based, far-afield "investigation" of television's "responsibilities" in areas relating to self-regulation on matters of both violence and sex in its entertainment fare! The 1969 hearings shed very little light on what had been a primary issue in 1968—network coverage of national nominating conventions. The motivations of Congress in selecting out the television medium as a prime target for its wrath were placed under serious suspicion, as indicated in this remark attributed to Senator Russell B. Long: "We won't actually do anything to you (the media), you understand; we just want your consciences to hurt a little."[52]

As one consequence of the 1968 television coverage of both the Republican and Democratic conventions, and particularly the latter, an awesome spectre threatened to show itself on the American political scene—direct governmental intervention in the news-gathering and reporting processes. Jack Gould, the respected *New York Times* Television Editor, noted:

> . . . under one guise or another government is showing an inclination to intrude in the specifics of reportage, to reach a judgment on what is right or wrong to put on the screen, to assert itself with respect to program content. Private TV may have its faults, but they are insignificant in comparison with the possibility of government sitting in the editor's chair in television. For substantiation of such a consequence there is one place to look: French television under De Gaulle.[53]

It is most unlikely that future nominating conventions will resemble those of the past, at least as the electorate will be able to witness them via television. Ever since the late President Eisenhower launched his bitter attack upon the news media at the 1964 Republican convention and stated his subsequent recommendations for changes in convention procedures there has been a growing demand for modifications in this particular institution.

It is quite conceivable that conventions of the future will be considerably more subtly "managed" than heretofore, that they will be considerably shorter in duration, and even that television may be barred from conventions or so subject to control that it will refuse to cover these events. If the public is denied entree into the convention process either by the manipulation of the conventions themselves or by the barring of television from such meetings as they actually occur, it is similarly quite conceivable that the nominating convention as we have known it will no longer exist in the age of the new politics.

Immediately following the 1968 nominating conventions, Senator Gaylord Nelson called for drastic changes in the convention nominating process, observing in an Associated Press release on September 2, 1968, that ". . . a majority of the American public, regardless of party, is fed up with our quadriennal political party conventions." Nelson suggested that a new federal commission be established to come up with reforms in the nominating procedures for the Presidency. As of this writing his call has gone unheeded, despite the observation of Harry S. Ashmore that "[it] has taken a cycle of three national elections to prove the point, but there seems to be little doubt now that the communications revolution has reduced political conventions to essential irrelevancies."[54]

The impact of television on Presidential campaigning has been discussed at length in this chapter. A footnote to how dead the old-style, east coast to west coast, whistle-stop approach really is is the fact that Richard Nixon travelled some 51,000 miles by jet aircraft in contrast to a mere 375 miles by whistle-stop train across Ohio in the 62 days of his 1968 formal campaign effort. It is quite probable that even the jet airplane will be displaced by television in the future. The Gallup Poll of November 23, 1968, reported that nearly half (44 percent) of the Americans sampled would not care if the entire campaigns were conducted by radio and television only. Right now one of the prime reasons that Presidential candidates go scooting about the country is simply to provide footage for both local and national television newscasts—footage whose only differentiating quality is the physical locale serving as a backdrop for the predictably unenlightening "speech" that makes no news.

Three aspects of the influence of television upon Presidential campaigning are worth reiterating in a somewhat different light. These aspects are related to the issues raised by the overwhelming commercialization of Presidential campaigning via television, to the problems that are raised by the high costs of commercial televised campaigning, and to the issue of precampaigning campaigning in the effort to attain a high degree of television exposure.

As has been indicated, the 1968 campaign was primarily oriented toward image-making. Thus communications in all three political camps were oriented toward the creation of affects—emotional responses to consciously fabricated mood stimuli. Little emphasis was placed on the cognitive or rational processes that are involved in serious decision-making of consequence.

Thus even the tepid attempt to introduce some semblance of rationality into the campaign by affording a temporary suspension of Section 315 of the Communications Act, which would have allowed for direct debates among the major candidates, fell in ignoble defeat in Congress. The understandable reluctance of candidate Nixon to engage in direct debates plus the irresponsibility of Congress' reluctance to afford voters even this small token to rational political decision-making have caused much concern among citizens, scholars, and responsible politicians alike regarding television's responsibilities in the political process. In an interview with the *Chicago Daily News* several days prior to the 1968 Election, former FCC Chairman Newton Minnow observed ". . . the tragedy of the 1968 campaign on TV and radio is that what we are getting is each candidate's own appeal (paid political broadcasts) without confrontation to draw a comparison."

In a letter to Dr. Frank Stanton, President of the Columbia Broadcasting System, dated October 25, 1968, Thomas Hoving, Chairman of the National Citizens Committee for Broadcasting, wrote, "There is nothing to prevent a more thorough job of covering the campaign except the financial interests of the networks." Hoving continued, noting that candidates, "are being seen primarily in paid political announcements—commercials—where they are shown to their best advantage. With the great majority of electioneering being done this way, the institution of free elections in this nation is being reduced to the level of selling soap suds and dog food."

The apparent lack of responsibility in the 1968 Presidential campaign cannot be placed solely upon the commercial broadcasters. Currently there are more than 175 so-called educational television stations on the air throughout the United States. They make up what the Carnegie Corporation euphemistically designates as "public broadcasting" in America. These "educational" stations operate under the same FCC regulations that govern commercial broadcasters, with one important exception—a good portion of their financing is derived in one way or another directly from public taxes.

Preliminary findings from a study being conducted by Harold

Mendelsohn and Melvyn Muchnik of the University of Denver's Communication Arts Center indicate that the "public broadcasting" sector did very little indeed to enlighten the voting public regarding the issues and the candidates in the 1968 election campaigns. Certainly there is no evidence from this study to indicate that public broadcasters suffered enough pangs of responsibility to make any significant attempt to fill the apparent gaps in informing the public, gaps which were left open by the nation's commercial broadcasters during the 1968 campaigns. Hobbled by politically cautious school boards, state legislatures, and university trustees who represent the majority of public television's licensees, station managers in the nation's "educational TV" enterprise generally stayed clear of political "controversy" in 1968, either hiding nervously behind the "fairness" and "equal time" doctrines that have managed to cover many sins of the commercial broadcasters or behind the rationalization of not "competing" with their commercial counterparts. If the record of commercial broadcasting's role in the 1968 election campaigns is suspect, the record of public broadcasting in that critical political year was nothing less than shameful.

If any semblance of rationality is to be recaptured in the nation's electioneering process, television-communications reforms are urgently needed. It is obvious that a major overhauling of the FCC's regulatory role in political broadcasting is necessary. Coupled with this necessity is the need for controls requiring balances between the amount of paid time that bona fide candidates will be allowed and the amount of free time that will be made available to legitimate candidates on commercial broadcasting outlets. Perhaps the most drastic reform proposal yet put forth comes from the pen of Harry S. Ashmore who recommends that either through congressional legislation or by FCC regulation, commercial broadcasters simply be prohibited from accepting paid political advertising, since such advertising cannot be considered to be truly in the public interest.

The proper use of television for direct political campaigning would require that the station play no role beyond that of common carrier, and would provide that the actual conduct of political broadcasts be arranged and supervised by an appropriate public agency. This implies no restriction on news coverage and commentary; on the contrary, it should free the broadcasters of some of the more inhibiting effects of the FCC's so-called fairness doctrine. The only objection the station owners could bring to such a requirement would be that it might cost them some money and cause them some inconvenience, and this is less than compelling in the case of an industry that derives phenomenal profits from government-granted monopolies on broadcast channels. Nor could the worn theoretical objections to any kind of interference with private enterprise be taken seriously in this instance; if any human activity can be properly classified as public it must be an election.[55]

Additional proposals for regulating commercial political broadcasting—at least during Presidential elections—have been forthcoming. In this regard, the Twentieth Century Fund's independent commission on campaign costs has suggested that "voter's time" programs be purchased by the federal government at half the usual broadcast-time charges (at an estimated cost of $265,-000 per thirty-minute program) and aired on all radio and television stations simultaneously at prime time. Under the proposal six half-hour broadcasts would be allotted to candidates of major parties. Minority-party candidates who managed to poll at least one-eighth of the popular votes in a preceding national election and who are on the ballot in seventy-five percent of the states would be allowed two thirty-minute programs. A bill introduced in the Senate in the fall of 1969 by Senators Philip Hart and James Pearson (S-2876) would require broadcasters to provide air time for senatorial and congressional candidates at approximately thirty percent of usual commercial rates. The bill proposes that these rates apply to a total of one hundred and twenty minutes of prime air time to be afforded senatorial candidates plus sixty minutes of prime air time to congressional hopefuls during the five weeks immediately preceding the date of election.

It appears clear that the role of public broadcasting in the political process must be carefully reappraised so that it no longer remains absolved from its true public responsibility. Until the time when changes are made, by whatever means, in the manner in which commercial broadcasters are allowed to handle political campaigning, the public broadcasting sector must indeed be made to serve truly in its self-proclaimed role as an "alternative" to commercial television.

One immediate step that can be taken is for the FCC to encourage public broadcasting channels to make massive amounts of time (time that ordinarily is devoted to such "educational" matters as the preparation of Quiche Lorraine, interviews with reformed dope addicts, discussions of the "real tragedy of James Fenimore Cooper," and serious debates on whether the community needs more meter maids or not) available to *all* bona fide political candidates throughout a given national election year. Failure to do this should result in reappraisals of public broadcasters' licenses in terms of the criterion of serving the public interest. It is altogether apparent that we need a new gutsy public broadcasting endeavor that addresses itself seriously to the serious aspects of politics in the nation. The public broadcasting sector has the further obligation of making its time, talent, and facilities available to all legitimate local and state candidates who presently cannot afford the high costs of commercial television. In an era where "involvement" and "relevance" are rallying cries for the development of a more rationally oriented new political system, the public broadcasting sector must play its educational role. Public broadcasting must be taken out of the hands of wall-hugging boards of directors that are dominated by professional educators and placed into the hands of the voting public in order that this medium can be used for the political enlightenment of that public.

For years now political observers have been sounding alarms regarding the monumentally escalating costs of political campaigning—costs that, for the most part, represent the utilization of television. Current estimates suggest that a congressional candidate in an average race in a populous area requires some $100,000 to make an effective run. In 1966 a minimum of $5 million was spent on Nelson Rockefeller's campaign for the governorship of New York with an estimated 75 percent of that sum going to the broadcast media. In 1968, American labor unions poured some $30 million into the Presidential campaigns, with industry matching and outmatching that sum in kind. The scandalous lack of publicly available, reliable figures on *actual* total expenditures by political candidates and their supporters makes accurate tallies of total expenditures nearly impossible to discern. What does remain apparent is that political campaigning in the age of television is tremendously costly—to put it mildly.

As things stand presently, without significant reforms in our present system political offices will remain reserved for either the very affluent or those who are willing to accept substantial financing from groups or individuals representing special interests. Contributors of large sums are not completely altruistic in their giving. They expect something in return, and more often than not they get it.

Federal curbing of excessive campaign spending is supported by more than two-thirds of the American public. On this score, a Gallup Poll reported in *The New York Times* on November 24, 1968, revealed that sixty-eight percent of its sample of Americans favored a "law which would put a limit on the total amount of money which can be spent for or by a candidate in his campaign for public office." Twenty-four percent expressed opposition to such a reform, and eight percent held no opinion on the matter.

Somehow changes in financing high-cost political campaigns will come about. Such changes have been needed for decades, and perhaps the demands of paid political broadcasting will serve as an impetus for developing them. Among the various proposals concerning the financing of political campaigns in the future one element is common—namely, the necessity for broadening the base of financing across all sectors of the electorate spectrum. Whether this comes about through income tax allowances for voluntary contributions to political parties, or through nominal dues to be paid for membership in the political parties (which can be deducted from income taxes), or from some other source, the increasing costs of political broadcasting will some day result in promoting more direct participation in the election process by larger numbers of ordinary voters.

If nominating conventions have turned into political "irrelevancies" as a consequence of television, campaigning itself may become similarly insignificant. Such a consequence is predictable if costs continue to spiral in near geometric progression; if campaigns degenerate into one steady stream of commercials, and voters simply become bored; if reforms are instituted regarding the amount of paid political broadcasts that are allowed; and if the quaint fiction that campaigns alone win elections is quietly phased out. If it has not actually become irrelevant, campaigning already has taken on an air of sheer ritualism. The real political game is being played more and more *between* formal campaigns rather than during them. The playing field is the television screen, and the name of the game is "exposure."

The new politician is a creature of the amount and kind of television exposure he manages to get well before any formal hat-in-the-ring tossing takes place. Without considerable television exposure there can be no "build-up," and without a proper "build-up" there can be no serious candidacy. "Exposure" and "build-up" via television are on-going political processes in our time. No sooner are the polling booths closed down on Election Day than the speculations regarding who the candidates will be "next time" begin to circulate. Will there be a Muskie-Kennedy ticket in 1972, or a Kennedy-Muskie slate? Will Nixon go with Agnew again, or is the dump-Agnew movement already in progress? Speculations regarding Wallace's role in the 1972 Presidential lists were resolved by Wallace's own announced intention to try once again, not more than sixty days after the inauguration of President Nixon. And so it goes. Every move of the President who was elected in 1968 will be dissected and analyzed to detect what impact it will have on his candidacy in 1972.

It is unlikely that we have heard the last of cries of "news management" and "credibility gaps." The contenders within the out-party will spend great amounts of effort and energy jockeying for television exposure, very much like packaged-goods manufacturers maneuvering for favorable shelf-space in the supermarkets. And throughout the quadrennial hiatus separating 1968 and 1972, the voter-viewers will be making assessments, judgments, evaluations, and even decisions well before the formal 1972 campaign is actually launched. (As early as February, 1969, the Gallup Poll was investigating public receptivity to Edward Kennedy as a Presidential prospect, and on May 4 it issued the results of a Nixon-Kennedy-Wallace "trial heat.")

Calls for reforms in the political process generally narrow

down to calls for controlling formal campaigns. The problems involved in precampaign campaigning are generally overlooked, even though by comparison they loom as monumental. Still, it remains a fact of political life that, abetted by the sheer presence of the television medium, the precampaign campaign is a formidable fixture in the new politics.

Although American political parties have been vested with a variety of functions by scholars, politicians, and voters—functions that include serving as a super-employment agency for use by winning candidates faced with the task of filling new jobs, recruiting and grooming suitable candidates, mediating between opposing political ideologies, providing information regarding the pulse of the electorate, and fund-raising for the candidates—the fact remains that, as Clinton Rossiter has put it, "The primary function of a political party in a democracy such as ours is to control and direct the struggle for power."[56]

Despite the fact that the American political-party system has developed and has been nurtured outside the parameters of the Constitution, the American political-party system up until 1932, when Franklin D. Roosevelt became a Presidential candidate, managed to be the dominant element in the nation's political structure. Developing refinements in political information-gathering and in the means of mass communications have been eroding that dominance ever since 1932. Prior to that year it was the political party that sought to create candidates in its own image. Since then, the ability to take the electorate's pulse directly through the use of political-opinion polls and the ability to communicate directly and dramatically with voters in their own homes without the mediation of the party allowed strong candidates to emerge on their own. From 1932 on, political parties, for the most part, have desperately been attempting to shape themselves in the images of their candidates. The struggle of political parties to "control and direct the struggle for power" has been slowly shifting away from the parties and towards the strongly individualistic candidate and his management teams. In recent years, the management teams, emerging in response to developments in public-opinion polling and in the means of mass communication through the electronic media, have not only applied their management skills to candidates, but they have applied them as well to the political parties which ostensibly are responsible for the candidate's nomination. The consequence of this application of management skills, has been the near disappearance of functioning political parties on the American scene. Witness this observation by Ashmore:

Whatever the intent of the founders and their successors in the places of power, it is quite evident that the political parties no longer perform the functions assigned to them. The protracted and chaotic Presidential nominating process still takes place through primaries and conventions that bear the traditional labels, but the candidates use them principally as a means of dramatizing individual appeals beamed directly at the public at large. As they barnstorm through the scattered primary states the contenders take along their own fund-raising, public-relations, and grass-roots organizing machinery, and they determine their stand on issues by consulting public opinion polls, not local party leaders.[57]

That potential and actual Presidential candidates can make substantial inroads into the electorate's vote-giving propensities without the support of the formal Republican and Democratic party structures has been more than peripherally demonstrated by the political efforts of John F. Kennedy (in his primary campaigns), Nelson Rockefeller, Robert F. Kennedy, Eugene McCarthy, and George Wallace. In each of these instances the candidate sought to shape his party's posture and orientation to what *his* beliefs were, and consequently was forced to operate outside the formal structure of either major party. In John Kennedy's case the attempt to sway the party was successful. For the rest it was not. Nevertheless, in this age of politics by polls and television it has become ever more evident that the days of the change-resistant, strong two-party structure of American politics have passed. The glowingly optimistic, romantic prognostications that political parties will continue doing business *status quo ante*, expressed by expert observers such as Clinton Rossiter, are made without adequate account taken of the impact that the innovations in electronic media have made on traditional party politics in this land.

As far as my own weak eyes can see into the future, the parties look like the parties of today [1960]—loose, supple, overlapping, decentralized, undisciplined, interest-directed, and principle-shunning enterprises in group diplomacy that are encircled and penetrated by a vigorous array of interest groups. They will be—in short, what they have always been—parties that aspire seriously to majority rule in a vast and motley democracy.[58]

The candidate of the winning party in 1968 did not win by virtue of a numerical majority mandate. The 1968 "Constitutional crisis" brought on by the Wallace challenge heralded as a serious possibility the emergence of a pluralistic party system. The successes achieved in the primaries by Eugene McCarthy in 1968 and his subsequent failure to win his party's nomination have touched off a rash of introspective exercises in the Democratic Party which virtually guarantee that that particular organization will *not* always be what it has been.

Exactly what the functions of the political party in the new politics will be are difficult to predict. The optimists say that nothing will change substantially. The old party structures will simply absorb the pressures for change and continue as of old. The pessimists predict the complete disappearance of political parties, and, as Marshall McLuhan has already declared, there will follow the emergence of all-powerful "tribal chieftains" who will come to power on their own via television and will rule by direct, computerized, daily plebiscites.

Observers of the moderate stripe see the functions of contemporary national political parties being reduced to simple fundraising and doorbell-ringing among the local grass roots unless constitutional reforms of the entire election process are quickly instituted. Generally, suggestions for reform concern themselves mainly with the standardization of procedures in the primaries, with opening up popular caucuses for the selection of delegates to nominating conventions, with making nominating conventions more responsive to minority points of view, with either modifying or eliminating the Electoral College system, and with controlling or eliminating private financing of political campaigns.

Again, no matter what happens, the national political parties of the future will no longer be the same as in the past. Television has made the voter's home the campaign amphitheater, and opinion surveys have made it his polling booth. From this perspective, he has little regard for or need of a political party, at least as we have known it, to show him how to release the lever on Election Day.

After two decades of experiential learning from political television there is evidence throughout the land that the electorate has not been particularly entranced by what it has been viewing. Cries for reforms of all sorts in the political process echo from living rooms throughout the republic. The sense of simulated involvement in the American political process that has been induced through exposure to televised politicking has begun to be translated into the reality of sentiment. More and more Americans appear to be expressing the view that if they are in fact participants in the political process, which before television was merely an abstraction to most, they want more *actual* participation than was afforded to them previously.

At this point, the urgency for broadening actual participation in the political process reflects itself in the support for reforms that are designed to correct some of the more obvious faults of the politics of old. Testimony to such support are the results of various public-opinion polls that have been conducted since the 1968 Presidential election. As examples, the Gallup Poll reported that the proportion of Americans who say they would support a black candidate for the Presidency rose from thirty-eight percent in 1958 to sixty-seven percent in February, 1969. Majorities also now endorse lowering the voting age to eighteen and favor the selection of Presidential candidates via a nationwide primary instead of a political-party nominating convention.

On the matter of direct reform in the election process itself, it has previously been reported that, in view of the problems that are raised by ever-mounting campaigning costs, nearly seven in ten Americans would look favorably upon some federal controls regarding the amounts of money spent in any given political campaign for office. Another method for cutting down the costs of Presidential campaigns was suggested by sixty percent of a national sample of adults who told Gallup Poll interviewers during the days immediately following the 1968 election that they would favor "shortening Presidential campaigns to five weeks" instead of the customary ten. Whether economy or boredom are the motivational forces behind this public suggestion, the electorate is expressing a degree of distaste with campaigns as they have been waged in our most recent televised past, a disenchantment that cannot be disregarded.

Perhaps the most startling of all public expressions regarding the current reformist mood of the nation's electorate comes from the findings of a November 23, 1968 Gallup Poll as reported in *The New York Times*. The *Times'* story begins with this lead:

> The Gallup Poll reported today that 81 per cent of the public favored basing the election of the President on the popular vote throughout the nation rather than the present system where a candidate can be elected President even though he runs behind in the primaries.
>
> This new post-election percentage represents a dramatic rise in the proportion in favor of such a change since a September (1968) survey. That survey showed 66 per cent in favor.
>
> The American public has approved reform of the Electoral College on 18 different occasions. Majorities in every survey—as long as 1948—have either favored abandonment of the present system or a radical change to make it reflect more accurately the sentiment registered at the polls.

It appears that the vicarious political participation by voters in the United States that has been induced by exposure to television has created a paradox. The greater the degree and intensity of vicarious participation that is induced by merely watching political events, the greater seems to be the cry for realistic participation in them. Whether this demand is real or whether it merely reflects a new set of political clichés is difficult to ascertain at this point. What can be noted with certainty is the fact that the communications revolution that television has induced in American society indeed has within it the makings of a new politics.

Thus, to understand the new politics we must first understand the new communications. If we persist in equating the effects of political television with simple vote changes we are overlooking the essence of this barely understood communications force—its total impact upon our total lives. We must begin to take seriously the warning of Marshall McLuhan:

> Today, in the electronic age of instantaneous communication, I believe that our survival, and at the very least our comfort and happiness is

predicated on understanding the nature of our new environment, because unlike previous environmental changes, the electronic media constitute a total and near instantaneous transformation of culture, values, and attitudes. This upheaval generates great pain and identity loss, which can be ameliorated only through a conscious awareness of its dynamics. If we understand the revolutionary transformations caused by new media, we can anticipate and control them; but if we continue in our self-induced subliminal trance, we will be their slaves.[59]

We must also take into account the synergistic effect of the broadcast-communications technology in combination with the survey method for information-gathering. Since the 1930s a radically new style of politics has been evolving as a direct consequence of the use of these techniques by some politicians, a style that came into full flower in the 1960s. Franklin D. Roosevelt pioneered the use of both broadcast communications and polls in American politics, and almost every Presidential candidate of the 1960s, successful or hopeful—including John F. Kennedy, Richard Nixon, Lyndon B. Johnson, Barry Goldwater, Hubert Humphrey, Robert F. Kennedy, Nelson Rockefeller and George Romney—has followed in his path.

As a direct result of the use of television and polls by these Presidential aspirants in the 1960s, the old-line party mechanism has become obsolescent and irrelevant. The past decade has witnessed the emergence of personal followings controlled and directed by technical specialists who report to the candidates themselves. To the extent that top echelon party functionaries have accommodated themselves to this development by becoming part of a candidate's entourage, they have been able to maintain their political viability. However, the process of institutional change creates tensions that will erupt into conflict unless and until new forms come into being that are adequate to control these tensions. In 1968 the old, expiring political forms had reached the point where they were no longer capable of containing conflicting political factions. In this light the "children's crusade" for Eugene McCarthy, the upheavals at the Democratic convention in Chicago, and the partial success of George Wallace's demagoguery are best understood as *symptoms* of political change rather than as the change itself.

The twin impacts of instantaneous communications and mass

playback via opinion polls were first to foster and then to intensify and underscore the impotency of the old politics. Whether the new institutional forms will prove adequate to the task of generating an orderly politics that maintains democratic values is still a moot question. The potential of television and polls for unprincipled manipulation and phoney participation, as we have seen, is ever-present. On the other hand, there is no intrinsic reason why the use of polls and television should lead to these negative consequences. The challenge is to create institutional controls that will inhibit such developments and foster genuine two-way communications between political leaders and citizens in accordance with democratic principles. That challenge remains to be met.

NOTES

1. William Stephenson, *The Play Theory of Mass Communications* (Chicago: University of Chicago Press, 1966), p. 106.

2. Ithiel de Sola Pool, "The Mass Media and Politics in the Modernization Process," in L. W. Pye, ed., *Communications and Political Development* (Princeton: Princeton University Press, 1963), p. 250.

3. A report in *The New York Times* on November 15, 1968, notes, "The smallest percentage of voting-age Americans in 12 years cast ballots in the 1968 election. An analysis of national totals shows the estimated total of 72 million people who voted Nov. 5 represents 60 percent of the 120 million Americans of voting age. Not since 1956, when 60.5 percent of the voting population turned out has the percentage been so small. . . . By comparison, the 70.6 million ballots cast in 1964 represented 62 percent, and the 68.8 million votes in 1960 . . . was a record 63.8 percent."
This report contrasts with the turnout rates reported in Table 1, Chapter 3 because the *Times*' percentage base includes all persons of voting age, including aliens and the institutional population.

4. Kurt Lewin in Dorwin Cartright, ed., *Field Theory in Social Science: Selected Theoretical Papers* (New York: Harper and Row, Publishers, 1951).

5. Jacques Ellul, *Propaganda: The Formation of Men's Attitudes* (New York: Alfred A. Knopf Co., 1964), pp. 18–19.

6. Ithiel de Sola Pool, "TV, a New Dimension in Politics," in E. Burdick and A. J. Brodbeck, eds., *American Voting Behavior* (Glencoe: Free Press, 1957), p. 241.

7. Henry Field, and Paul F. Lazarsfeld, *The People Look at Radio* (Chapel Hill: University of North Carolina Press, 1946).

8. Neville Miller, "Radio's Code of Self Regulation," *Public Opinion Quarterly* (Fall 1939), p. 683.

9. Angus Campbell, "Has Television Reshaped Politics?" in E. C. Dreyer and W. A. Rosenbaum, eds., *Political Opinion and Electoral Behavior* (Belmont, California: Wadsworth Publishing Co., Inc., 1966), p. 319.

10. M. L. DeFleur, *Theories of Mass Communication* (New York: David McKay Co., Inc., 1966), p. 66.

11. Harold D. Lasswell, "The Structure and Function of Communication in Society," in L. Bryson, ed., *The Communication of Ideas* (New York: Harper and Row, Publishers, 1948); Charles R. Wright, *Mass Communication* (New York: Random House, Inc., 1959); and Harold Mendelsohn, *Mass Entertainment* (New Haven: College and University Press, 1966).

12. Cited in L. Sussman, "FDR and the Whitehouse Mail," *Public Opinion Quarterly* (Spring 1956), p. 15.

13. Grace Tully, *FDR—My Boss* (New York: Charles Scribner's Sons, 1949), p. 88.

14. J. M. Burns, *Roosevelt: The Lion and the Fox* (New York: Harcourt, Brace, and Company, 1956), p. 118.

15. F. Freidel, *Franklin D. Roosevelt: The Triumph*, vol. 3 (Boston: Little, Brown & Company, Inc.), pp. 30–31.

16. F. L. Mott, "Newspapers in Presidential Campaigns," *Public Opinion Quarterly* (Fall 1944), pp. 348–367.
The opposition to Roosevelt by the nation's press persisted throughout FDR's administrations and campaigns. Mott points out that in the 1936 Presidential campaign, 63 percent of the nation's dailies and 58 percent of the weeklies opposed Roosevelt. During the 1940 campaign 74 percent of the daily newspapers in the United States and 63 percent of the weekly press opposed FDR.
E. Brandenburg, "FDR's International Speeches," *Speech Monographs* (August 1949), p. 39. Brandenburg notes that in the 1940 campaign 700 daily newspapers that supported Willkie had a combined circulation of 16,387,145 as against the total circulation of 5,332,905 for the 216 newspapers that endorsed Franklin Roosevelt.

17. E. J. Wrage, and B. Baskerville, *Contemporary Forum* (New York: Harper and Row, Publishers, 1962), p. 136.

18. *Ibid.*, p. 137.

19. Cited in Hadley Cantril, *Public Opinion: 1935–1946* (Princeton: Princeton University Press, 1951), p. 759.

20. Marshall McLuhan, *Understanding Media* (New York: McGraw-Hill Book Co., 1964), p. 299.

21. Harold Mendelsohn, "TV and Youth: A New Style for Politics," *The Nation* (June 6, 1966), p. 671.

22. B. Roper, "Emerging Profiles of Television and Other Mass Media," *Public Attitudes* (New York: Television-Information Office, April 5, 1967).

23. Fifty-five percent cited newspapers; twenty-eight percent cited radio.

24. Roper, *loc. cit.*, p. 9.

25. Campbell *loc. cit.*, p. 322.

26. McLuhan, *loc. cit.*, p. 299.

27. H. Brandon, "A Talk With the First Lady," *New York Times Magazine* (September 10, 1967), p. 160.

28. B. Rubin, *Political Television* (Belmont, California: Wadsworth Publishing Co. Inc., 1967).

29. R. Hill, "Political Uses of Broadcasting in the United States in the Context of Public Opinion and the Political Process, 1920–1960," unpublished doctoral dissertation (Evanston, Illinois: Northwestern University, 1964), p. 214.

30. D. W. Brogan, *Politics in America* (New York: Doubleday and Co., 1960), p. 211.

31. H. Hyman, and P. B. Sheatsley, "The Political Appeal of President Eisenhower," *Public Opinion Quarterly* (Winter 1953–54), p. 459.

32. Ithiel de Sola Pool, *loc. cit.*, in Burdick and Brodbeck, p. 248.

33. Douglas Cater, "The Cool Eye of John F. Kennedy," *The Reporter* (December 10, 1959), p. 27.

34. Rubin, *op. cit.*, p. 83.

35. Mendelsohn, *loc. cit.*, p. 671.

36. Theodore H. White, *The Making of the President 1964* (New York: Signet Books, 1966), p. 25.

37. *Ibid.*, p. 45.

38. Quoted in Robert MacNeil, *The People Machine: The Influence of Television on American Politics* (New York: Harper and Row, Publishers, 1968), p. 204.

39. *Ibid.*, p. xvii.

40. Revised edition (San Francisco: Chandler Publishing Co., 1968), p. 193.

41. The FCC revealed that some $700,000 was expended for the purchase of national network television time alone on behalf of the George Wallace candidacy, but the Commission's report did not break down this figure in terms of expenditures for network commercials. Under present circumstances relating to disclosure of campaign expenditures it is impossible to derive accurate tallies of actual costs for any candidate.

42. Harry S. Ashmore, "Electoral Reform: What Can Be Done When Everybody Loses?" *The Center Magazine* (Santa Barbara, California: a publication of The Center for the Study of Democratic Institutions, January, 1969), p. 6.

43. MacNeil, *op. cit.*, p. 195.

44. The speculation that candidates in the 1968 Presidential election were being "merchandised" has been given sound substance by Joe McGinniss in his well-documented book, *The Selling of the President 1968* (New York: Trident Press, 1969).

45. MacNeil, *loc. cit.*, p. 197.

46. Robert Lewis Shayon, "The Show-Biz-Politics Scene," *Saturday Review* (December 7, 1968), p. 61.

47. "Playboy Interview: Marshall McLuhan—Candid Conversation," *Playboy* (March 1969), pp. 71–72.

48. Campbell, *loc. cit.*, p. 323.

49. Stephenson, *op. cit.*, p. 57.

50. *Ibid.*

51. *Denver Post*, October 13, 1968.

52. *Broadcasting* (September 9, 1968), p. 44.

53. *The New York Times*, November 17, 1968.

54. Ashmore, *loc. cit.*, p. 4.

55. *Ibid.*, p. 8.

56. Clinton Rossiter, *Parties and Politics in America* (Ithaca, New York: Cornell University Press, 1960), p. 39.

57. Ashmore, *loc. cit.*, p. 4.

58. Rossiter, *op. cit.*, p. 164.

59. McLuhan, *loc cit.* (*Playboy*), p. 56.

Selected Bibliography

COMMUNICATIONS BEHAVIOR

Berelson, Bernard, and M. Janowitz. *Reader in Public Opinion and Communication*, 2nd ed. New York: The Free Press, 1966.

Berlo, David K. *The Process of Communication*. New York: Holt, Rinehart & Winston, Inc., 1960.

Dexter, Lewis A., and David M. White, eds. *People, Society, and Mass Communications*. Glencoe: Free Press, 1964.

Hovland, Carl, A. A. Lumsdaine, and F. D. Sheffield. *Experiments in Mass Communication*. Princeton: Princeton University Press, 1949.

Klapper, Joseph T. *The Effects of Mass Communication*. Glencoe: Free Press, 1960.

May, Mark A., and A. A. Lumsdaine. *Learning from Films*. New Haven: Yale University Press, 1958.

McLuhan, Marshall. *Understanding Media*. New York: McGraw-Hill Book Co., 1964.

Schramm, Wilbur, ed. *The Science of Human Communication*. New York: Basic Books, Inc., Publishers, 1963.

Steinberg, Charles S., ed. *Mass Media and Communication*. New York: Hastings House, Publishers, Inc., 1966.

POLITICAL BEHAVIOR

Berelson, Bernard R., Paul F. Lazarsfeld, and William N. McPhee. *Voting*. Chicago: University of Chicago Press, 1954.

Burdick, E., and A. J. Brodbeck. *American Voting Behavior*. Glencoe: Free Press, 1959.

Campbell, Angus, Gerald Gurin, and Warren E. Miller. *The Voter Decides*. Evanston: Row, Peterson and Company, 1954.

Campbell, Angus, Philip E. Converse, Warren E. Miller, and Donald E. Stokes. *The American Voter*. New York: John Wiley & Sons, Inc., 1960.

Dreyer, E. C., and W. A. Rosenbaum, eds. *Political Opinion and Electoral Behavior: Essays and Studies*. Belmont, Calif.: Wadsworth Publishing Co. Inc., 1966.

Lazarsfeld, Paul F., Bernard Berelson, and Hazel Gaudet. *The People's Choice*. 2nd ed., New York: Columbia University Press, 1948.

Lipset, Seymour M., Paul F. Lazarsfeld, Allen H. Barton, and Juan Linz. "The Psychology of Voting: An Analysis of Political Behavior." Chapter 30 in *Handbook of Social Psychology*, vol. II, Gardner

Lindzey, ed. Cambridge, Mass.: Addison-Wesley Publishing Co., Inc., 1954.

Lipset, Seymour M. *Political Man*. New York: Doubleday & Company, Inc., 1960.

Pool, Ithiel de Sola, Robert P. Ableson, and Samuel L. Popkin. *Candidates, Issues, and Strategies*. Cambridge, Mass.: The MIT Press, 1964.

TELEVISION AND POLITICS

Ashmore, Harry S. "What Happens When Everybody Loses?" *The Center Magazine*, a publication of the Center for the Study of Democratic Institutions. January, 1969.

Becker, Samuel L. "Presidential Power: The Influence of Broadcasting." *Quarterly Journal of Speech*, XLVII, 1961.

Blumler, J. G., and D. McQuail. *Television in Politics: Its Uses and Influences*. Chicago: University of Chicago Press, 1969.

Campbell, Angus, Gerald Gurin, and Warren E. Miller. "Television and the Elections." *Scientific American*, May, 1953.

Campbell, Angus. "Has Television Reshaped Politics?" *Columbia Journalism Review*, Fall, 1962.

Communications Subcommittee, Committee on Commerce, U.S. Hearings July 10–12, 1962. *Political Broadcasting*. Washington, D.C.: U.S. Government Printing Office, 1962.

Fuchs, Douglas. "Election Day Newscasts and Their Effects on Western Voter Turnout." *Journalism Quarterly*, XLII, Winter, 1965.

———. "Election Day Radio-Television." *Public Opinion Quarterly*, 30:2, Summer, 1966.

Glaser, William A. "Television and Voting Turnout." *Public Opinion Quarterly*, 29:1, Spring, 1965.

Hill, Ruane. *Political Uses of Broadcasting in the U.S.* Unpublished doctoral dissertation, Northwestern University, 1964.

Kelley, Stanley. "Campaign Debates: Some Facts and Issues." *Public Opinion Quarterly*, 26:3, Fall, 1962.

Kraus, Sidney, ed. *The Great Debates*. Bloomington: Indiana University Press, 1962.

Lang, Kurt, and Gladys E. Lang. "Television Personality and Politics." *Public Opinion Quarterly*, 21, Spring, 1957.

———. "The Mass Media and Voting." In Bernard Berelson and M. Janowitz, *Reader in Public Opinion and Communication*. Glencoe: Free Press, 1965.

———. *Voting and Nonvoting*. Waltham, Mass.: Blaisdell Publishing Company, 1968.

MacNeil, Robert. *The People Machine: The Influence of Television on American Politics*. New York: Harper and Row, Publishers, 1968.

Mendelsohn, Harold. "TV and Youth: A New Style for Politics." *The Nation*, June 6, 1966.
———. "Exposure to Election Broadcasts and Terminal Voting Decisions." *Public Opinion Quarterly*, 30:2, Summer, 1966.
Rose, Richard. *Interviewing Voters: A Study of Campaign Rationality.* New York: St. Martin's Press, Inc., 1967.
Rubin, Bernard. *Political Television.* Belmont, Calif.: Wadsworth Publishing Co. Inc., 1967.
Thomson, Charles A. H. *Television and Presidential Politics.* Washington, D. C.: Brookings Institution, 1956.
Treneman, J., and D. McQuail. *Television and the Political Image: A Study of the Impact of Television on the General Election of 1959.* London: Methuen & Co., Ltd., 1961.

PUBLIC OPINION POLLS

Bogart, Leo. "No Opinion, Don't Know, and No Answer." *Public Opinion Quarterly*, Fall, 1967.
Bruner, Jerome S. *Mandate from The People.* New York: Duell, Sloan & Pearce, 1944.
Cantril, Hadley. *Gauging Public Opinion.* Princeton: Princeton University Press, 1944.
———. *The Human Dimension: Experiences in Policy Research.* New Brunswick: Rutgers University Press, 1967.
Crossley, Archibald M., and Helen M. Crossley. "Polling in 1968." *Public Opinion Quarterly*, Spring, 1969.
Fenton, John M. *In Your Opinion.* Boston: Little, Brown & Co., 1960.
Gallup, George, and Saul Rae. *The Pulse of Democracy.* New York, Simon & Schuster, Inc., 1940.
Klapper, Joseph T. *Bandwagon: A Review of the Literature.* Office of Social Research, Columbia Broadcasting System, Inc., June 17, 1964 (mimeographed).
Meier, Norman C., and Harold W. Saunders, eds. *The Polls and Public Opinion.* New York: Henry Holt and Company, 1949.
Mosteller, Frederick, Herbert Hyman, Philip J. McCarthy, Eli S. Marks, and David B. Truman. *The Pre-Election Polls of 1948.* New York: Social Science Research Council. Bulletin 60, 1949.
Perry, Paul K. "Election Survey Procedures for the Gallup Poll." *Public Opinion Quarterly*, Fall, 1960.
———. "Gallup Poll Election Survey Experience 1950–1960." *Public Opinion Quarterly*, Summer, 1962.
———. "Election Survey Methods." *Gallup Political Index*, no. 7, December, 1965.
Robinson, Claude E. *Straw Votes.* New York: Columbia University Press, 1932.
Rogers, Lindsay. *The Pollsters.* New York: Alfred A. Knopf Co., 1949.

POLLS AND TELEVISION IN RECENT
POLITICAL CAMPAIGNS

Chester, Lewis, Godfrey Hodgson, and Bruce Page. *An American Melodrama: The Presidential Campaign of 1968.* New York: Viking Press, Inc., 1969.

McGinnis, Joe. *The Selling of the President 1968.* New York: Trident Press, 1969.

Nixon, Richard M. *Six Crises.* Garden City: Doubleday & Company, Inc., 1962.

Ogden, Daniel M., Jr., and Arthur L. Peterson. *Electing the President.* San Francisco: Chandler Publishing Company, 1968.

White, Theodore H. *The Making of the President 1960.* New York: Atheneum Publishers, 1961.

———. *The Making of the President 1964.* New York: Atheneum Publishers, 1965.

———. *The Making of the President 1968.* New York, Atheneum Publishers, 1969.

Index of Names

Index of Subjects

327